SPARKS

FROM

SHEFFIELD SMOKE:

A SERIES OF LOCAL AND OTHER

POEMS,

BY

FRANCIS BUCHANAN.

SHEFFIELD:
LEADER AND SONS, BANK STREET.
[COPYRIGHT.]

Sparks from Sheffield Smoke (1882). Courtesy of Sheffield's Local Studies and Archives.
Title page includes handwritten reference to W. Andrews and J. Dufty.
(See 'In The Deep, Deep Wood').

Quotations from Sparks from Sheffield Smoke.

FROM SHEFFIELD AS IT IS, 1882.

Strange time, thy evolution brings
With every year new offerings;
As thy ephemeral hours glide by
Their dust and ashes multiply.
Piles on the piles of other days
Rise up to feed their gaunt decays;
The worms above, the worms below
Are ever gnawing, as they grow,
Science and beauty,—dust to dust,—
Earth to its earth, crust to its crust;
What are thy greatnesses that be?
Motes floating to eternity.

FROM PARKWOOD HILL.

Upon the threshold step of toil
Thy beauty rests, and thro' the wile
Art dreaming in thy solitude,
Unconscious that one little road
Divides thee only from the roar
Which surges at thy outer door;
On thy bright face the critic eye
Nor stain nor blemish can descry
So near, but all unshrined still,
From smoky turmoil, Parkwood Hill.

FROM WHARNCLIFFE CRAGS.

Ah, need we roam to other lands,
From England and her rifted strands,
In quest of beauty, need we stray
To catch the beams of summer's day.
More gorgeous other climes may be,
But England hath no rivalry,
Tho' humble are her scented flowers,
More meet are they for heaven's bowers,
To birds of Ind gay plumes belong,
To ours are given the gift of song;
Sweet summer-time, sweet song, sweet flowers,
Ye are the angels of our hours,
Ye 'tice strange birds across the sea,
To mingle in your harmony.

Name
Address
No. of Copies

IN PREPARATION AND WILL BE PUBLISHED SHORTLY,

Sparks from Sheffield Smoke.

FIRST SERIES COMPLETE.

PRICE ONE SHILLING.

Crown 8vo, 100 Pages. By Post 1/2.

BY FRANCIS BUCHANAN.

In giving publicity to these poems, (the first series of which will treat of Sheffield's scenery principally,) the author feels a hesitancy, well knowing that the same ground has been traversed before both by Elliott and Montgomery, but as the ideas are dissimilar he hopes, at least, to gain the meed of originality.

At the suggestion of a number of friends, he is impelled to issue the first series as soon as possible, otherwise it was not his intention to publish this poems at all.

187, FOWLER STREET,
SHEFFIELD, MAY 1882.

"RAMBLER" in the *Sheffield Daily Telegraph*, Dec. 21st, 1881, writes:—

"Several poems have been sent to me during the last six weeks, with a request that my verdict should be given. Of all the productions sent to me, the only one which betrays any merit is entitled 'The Poet,' and is written by F. Buchanan. This is really clever, and is worthy of honorable mention."

Original promotional leaflet / order form relating to Francis Buchanan's book of poems, published in 1882.

For my mother Patricia, a great admirer of Francis' poetry

and

To the memory of Diana Dodds

The poems in this book appear as when originally published, and include misspellings, Old English and Scots Language

Cover designed by Think Tank Creative Design Ltd., Doncaster.
Photograph: The Smokey Industrial Lower Don Valley showing River Don Works, Mottershaw Photography. Image no. s11492 provided by Sheffield Libraries and Information.

CONTENTS

Preface		6
Prologue	'The Interview – A Poem'	9
1	Francis	16
2	Wincobank Hill	35
3	In The Deep, Deep Wood	56
4	To The Pimpernel	63
5	A Sheffield Character	81
6	Love	95
7	Sheffield Castle	106
8	Lines Written in Ecclesall Churchyard	115
9	King Frost	125
10	Sheffield's Scenery The Valley of the Don A.D. 1580 and A.D. 1882	132
11	Parkwood Hill and Lines Written in Shirecliffe Hall Lane	151
12	The Dying Poet	169
13	Faith	175
14	A Sheffield Worthy	179
15	Rotherham	195
16	Sheffield Manor	211
17	Wharncliffe	227
18	Haddon Hall	241

19	War Poems	264
20	Perthshire Poems	285
21	The Duftys of Sheffield	327

Epilogue	339
Selected Bibliography	342
Acknowledgements	346
Index	348

Published in the United Kingdom by Arc Publishing and Print 2024

Text Copyright © S. K. Buchanan 2024

All rights reserved. No portion of this book may be reproduced, stored in a retrieval system or transmitted at any time or by any means mechanical, electronic, photocopying, recording or otherwise, without the prior written permission of the publisher.

The right of S. K. Buchanan to be identified as the author of this work has been asserted by her in accordance with the Copyright, Designs and Patents Act 1988.

The information in this book is given in good faith and is believed to be correct at the time of publication. Neither the author or the publisher accepts any responsibility for errors or omissions.

All views and comments in this book are those of the author and should not be attributed to the publisher.

PREFACE

During the 1980s my cousin Maggie Pike, travelled from London to Sheffield in order to meet Mr Sidney Boswell – a kindly old gentleman who responded to her appeal in a local newspaper for information relating to the Buchanan family. Although Maggie hailed from Sydney, Australia we shared one set of great-great-grandparents, and her research had uncovered connections to Sheffield requiring further investigation. Indeed she hoped to learn more about a certain poet.

As it happened Mr Boswell was eager to impart some invaluable information. He held in his possession, an original copy of a volume of poetry composed by his late wife's paternal grandfather. His name was Francis Buchanan, and *Sparks from Sheffield Smoke: A Series of Local and Other Poems* was published in 1882. Sincerely delighted, whilst relieved to discover a genuine relative, Mr Boswell handed the delicate, timeworn little book of poems to Maggie, secure in the knowledge that a keepsake once cherished by his dear wife Nellie Buchanan, would remain with her family.

Oblivious to events, my vague awareness of an ancestral poet would not surface for almost twenty years, when my own research led me to Donald Buchanan, an ardent family historian residing in Tasmania. My newly discovered cousin willingly introduced me to Maggie by means of written correspondence, and disclosed a great deal of information – to include photographs of ancestors I never expected to see. Donald was simply thrilled to encounter another descendant of Francis and his wife Susannah. Maggie sadly died a year after we had become acquainted, and she left for me a wonderful collection of family history material. In amongst it was a delicate, timeworn little book of poems.

Regrettably, my new-found relatives central to this remarkable tale of unfolding events are no longer with us. They will not see the revival of Francis' poetry, which saddens me greatly. I feel certain they would have embraced it with a great sense of elation, and welcomed my exploration of the numerous settings and local characters at its heart. Donald was a descendant of Francis' son, Thomas Richard Buchanan and Maggie's predecessor was Thomas' brother, Charles Clyde Buchanan. Both settled in Australia and feature within the pages of this book.

Several years after Maggie's successful pursuit for information, with great delight I am able to resume the story. Another devoted family historian is particularly interested in my edition of Francis Buchanan's Sheffield volume of poems. As it happens Sidney Boswell was known to her as great-uncle Sid, who sadly departed this life some years ago. But how wonderful it is to share photographs, family history, and such memorable details with Caroline Hook. We are equally thrilled by our family connection, and knowledge of events that would almost certainly not have transpired without Mr Boswell's very kind gesture. And quite possibly, this book might never have happened.

S. K. Buchanan, 2022

Donald Buchanan

Maggie Pike

The marriage of Sidney Boswell and Nellie Buchanan, Sheffield, *1935*.

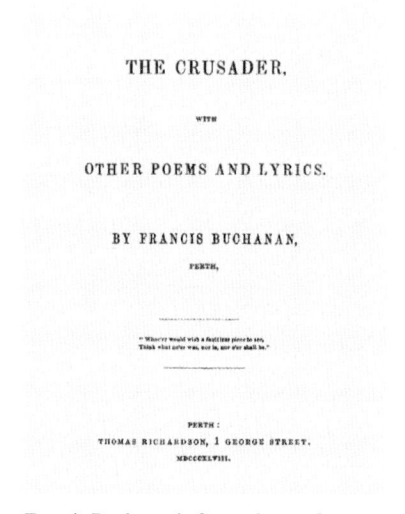

Francis Buchanan's first volume of poems and songs - published in Scotland in 1848.

PROLOGUE

'THE INTERVIEW – A POEM

The ev'ning mild had closed the sultry day
As o'er Tay's flowery banks I chanced to stray:
The southern wind play'd round me soft and cool,
And in the east the moon rose clear and full –
Athwart the landscape shone her mellow beam,
Nor cloud, nor filmy haze did intervene
To mar the silvery beauty of the scene.
Beneath the umbrage of a stately tree
I sat me down in deepest reverie;
Recumbent on a grassy knoll I lay,
And gazed, abstracted, on the noble Tay;
Nought there disturb'd the stillness of the hour;
Nature had yielded to the balmy power
Of drowsy Somnus – all was hush'd around,
Nor from the forest was there heard a sound
Save now and then the twitter of an owl,
Or, at long intervals, the deep-mouth'd howl
Of canine sentinel, which warn'd away
The prowling thief or stranger with his bay; –
'Twas such a night – congenial to my soul

The time and place, and o'er my senses stole
A listless stupor; drowsy I became,
Half sleeping, half awake, – confused my brain;
Methought I heard the notes of music sweet
Around me float, enticing me to sleep:
Anon they more distinct and softer grew,
When, all at once, to my astonished view,
A peerless maiden, robed in shining white,
Stood still before me in the broad moonlight;
'Twere vain for me to paint her noble form, –
Her lovely face that rivall'd blushing morn,
Her heaving breast that shamed the mountain snow;
Her flowing locks that vied the blackest sloe;
Her alabaster brow, stamp'd with command;
Her dark fring'd eyes, piercing, yet mild and bland:
She sylph-like stood, a paragon of grace
And majesty; nor time can e'er efface
The beatific image from my mind
Her faultless form and highborn looks combined.
"Mortal," she said, and held aloft her hand,
"I'm patroness of poesy in this land,
To teach the youthful bard's my pleasing care,
To fire his ardent soul, – his mind prepare:

I love to lead him where the ocean raves,
And beats the frowning coast with angry waves;
I love to look upon his kindling eye,
As lightnings gleam, and thunders roll on high;
I love to mark the youth's ecstatic glow,
As eagerly he gazes down below
From utmost verge of some dark, giddy rock,
Whose iron sides the winds and billows mock –
Or where the blooming wild flowers grace the dell;
Where warbling birds their loves and sorrows tell;
Where woods and groves, and purling streams are seen,
Where nature wears her lovliest garb of green,
I love to see him musing there alone,
His looks all beaming as he wanders on;
Or when the moonlight bathes the greenwood glade,
Where the huge oak tree lifts his branchy head,
I there delight to see him pensive lie
While light and fragrant breezes round him sigh;
Wrapt in the thoughts I in his mind inspire,
I make him long to strike his native lyre;
Or when the sun's last lingering ray is seen,
Tinging the western hills with yellow sheen,
I love to see him in the churchyard lone,

Bend o'er some half obliterated stone:
I love to see him weep o'er man's last bed,
"And hold high converse with the mighty dead;" –
'Tis there, while musing on his brief career,
I lead him, on wing'd Fancy, to a better sphere;
'Twas thus I watch'd and rear'd your country's boast,
And raised him far above the duller host,
I found him at the plough a rustic swain,
With simple manners, and an honest name,
Unpolished as the diamond in its mine,
Brought from its dark concealment but to shine.
I saw him, when his daily toil was o'er,
Seek with an eager step the sounding shore;
I saw him linger there with fond delight,
And listen to the ocean's gathering might;
I saw the admiration of his soul
In his wild eye, as listening to the roll
Of mighty thunders, he would gaze around
Upon a scene which would a common breast astound;
Or when he wandered by his favourite stream,
(The classic Doune,) beneath the silvery beam,
Absorbed in thought, I've seen the peasant bard
With glowing cheek walk o'er the velvet sward;

'Twas there he framed his bolts of keen satire,
Which drew down on his head the church's ire;
'Twas there he framed his sweet unrivall'd lays,
Which gain'd to him a world's lasting praise;
'Twas there I've seen the man put on the child,
And as a torrent unrestrain'd and wild
His tears gush forth, when Mary's loved name
Hung on his lips: then throbb'd his burning brain
Intensely, as he pondered on her fate –
Their former joys – now all was desolate;
What was the earth to him without that smile,
Whose radiance did his saddest hours beguile?
What was the earth to him without that form,
Which wont to cheer him as a summer's morn
All nature cheers, or as the early spring
Diffuses freshness, where, all withering,
The green reviving landscape lay before,
Ice-bound, but not subdued, by winter hoar?
What were they now to him, those lovely scenes,
Where oft he roam'd with her in waking dreams?
What were they now to him, the blackbird's song,
Or lark's carol, since she he lov'd was gone?
Thus oft exclaim'd he with a tearful eye,

His breast sear'd with intensest agony;
And on the dewy ground he'd kneel in prayer,
When none of mortal kind beheld him there;
Then would he rise again, and walk along,
Sooth'd by the pathos of his growing song;
Then would the Scottish bard, inspir'd by me,
Pour forth his soul in plaintive poesy!
Peace to his manes! – he was my favourite son;
Bold independence mark'd him for its own;
Though poor he scorn'd to play the sycophant:
Before he'd whine and fawn he died of want;
And Scotia calmly gazed upon his fate,
Nor stretch'd her arm to save ere 'twas too late!
She saw her fault when in the tomb he lay,
And shed her bitter tears o'er senseless clay;
She rais'd him stately monuments of stone,
And boasted then, and claim'd him as her own;
He whom she spurn'd when life within him flow'd,
Now prais'd and wail'd him when beneath the sod!
Ah! Scotland! Scotland! you may weep and moan,
But all your weeping never will atone:
Your name is sullied – on your shield's a stain!
Till time shall cease to be it shall remain."

The maiden paus'd, and with a flashing eye
She held again her graceful hand on high:
"Go, youth," she said, "ere summer's lost its bloom,
And gaze upon the poet's sacred tomb,
And ponder well his hard and brief career,
And wet the grave of genius with your tear,"
She said, and vanish'd from my wondering sight,
While music softly swell'd upon the night.'

Francis Buchanan
The Crusader with other Poems and Lyrics
Perth, Scotland (1848)

1

FRANCIS

Verse fondly composed in times of yore,

Prevails in your poems, which I read and adore;

Rhyme surged readily, skilfully, from your pen,

Transporting the reader to a coppice, a glen . . .

A hilltop, a river, an ancient hall,

Sights of Perthshire, Don Valley, you captured them all;

Your vivid depiction confirms you were there,

As with passion and vigour, you exploited your flair.

They say you're a lesser-known poet; why so?

If only we'd *met* – (unfeasible, I know);

And if only there were *more* poems to delight us,

You may well have wound up as *wealthy* as Plutus! *

Ah! But I know you! You're the poems I perceive,

(To write verse of your merit – one hopes to achieve);

Forgive me dear forebear, for mirroring your style,

How I envy your gift, and declare no denial.

Your spirit beside me, is guiding my pen,

Forming verse to be proud of time and again;

Poet, guru, and mentor of my utmost regard,

'Tis an *honour* to revive thy 'Sparks', fine Bard!

* Greek God of Wealth.

S. K. Buchanan   Sheffield, 2022

(An exceptionally proud great-great-granddaughter.)

A review of Francis' newly published Sheffield collection of poetry appeared under 'LITERARY NOTES' in the *Sheffield and Rotherham Independent* dated 21st September, 1882. It begins with the title, and name of author: 'SPARKS FROM SHEFFIELD SMOKE: A Series of Local and other Poems. By Francis Buchanan.' And the comments which follow are most complimentary from the outset: 'Mr Buchanan's little book contains some genuine poetry. It is like one of those mountain streams, whose wild, sweet music he so delights in. What critic could be hard upon a bard who thus modestly ushers his volume of songs to the world?' The review then presents a selection of lines from Francis' poetic preface, but what follows is the unabridged version:

'TO MY MUSE

Go, my Muse; go take thy flight,
Up to-day, or down to-night.
Plume thy pinions to the storm,
Some sunny ray may gild thy form.
If to gloom thou be consigned,
Thou must nathless be resign'd.

Go, my Muse; go face the blast,
Tho' it threaten to o'ercast:
Thou may'st be assured of this,
Some may praise, tho' many hiss;
So 'tis now as heretofore,
Talent may not always soar.

Go, my Muse; scholastic wit,
Thou hast gotten none of it;
If thou had'st thou might'st have been
Better than a random quean,
As thou art; now must thou be
Critic doom'd, or soaring free.

Go, my Muse; go on thy way,

Thou art honest as the day;
If thou'rt scorn'd – if worth thou lack'st,
Thou shalt then be trebly tax'd –
Outcast; yet thou'lt have a shrine,
Aye within this breast of mine.'

My forebear let it be known the decision was made, and his poems were to be published. Yet he was prepared for poor reviews . . . prepared to be scorned, which renders me perplexed, and saddened to realise he may have considered himself and his poetry not worthy. Fortunately (and unsurprisingly) it seems his misgivings were unfounded. 'Some may praise', Francis' preface supposed. Indeed the local press appraisal continues with a small selection of verse from 'A Sheffield Character' and 'Lines Written in Shirecliffe Hall Lane' – the latter drawing further worthy comment: '[. . .] Mr. Buchanan can see the romantic side even of a coke oven [. . .]

Coke oven, looming from afar,
Tier'd like a ship of war:
Glare of forge, with heat intense,
And Bessemer magnificence;
Cluster'd constellations fly,
Like bright meteors in the sky,
And science wears her fiery crown,
In honour of her favourite town.'

Further positive evaluation emerges concerning the poem about Sheffield's Wincobank Hill, and Parkwood Hill: 'Like a good painting, Mr. Buchanan's poems are full of atmospheric effect [. . .].' The columnist clearly recognised fineness, and his piece ends with an encouraging finale: 'People who love our old town and its beautiful environments will enjoy these artless, and at times, most musical poems.'

* * *

'THE atmosphere of Sheffield, one would think, could not be very favourable to the development of genius, yet she can long claim to having nursed men whose "Sparks" of genius have shot through the murky sky of "Sheffield Smoke," and cheered and comforted many lovers of poetry in far distant parts.'

Irvine and Fullarton Times, 24th October, 1884

The Scottish newspaper continues with '[. . .] readers can judge for themselves of the merits of "Sparks from Sheffield Smoke," by Francis Buchanan, (Sheffield: Leader & Sons, Bank Street.) It is a neat 8vo.* Volume, in paper cover, and contains a series of local and other poems that well repay perusal.' The article refers to a number of poets recognised for their achievements in Sheffield, such as Montgomery, the Irvine Poet, Elliott, the Corn Law Rhymer, and Joseph Dufty – all of whom are featured within the pages of this book. It seems Francis Buchanan is central to the piece, and an evaluation of his poetry is heartening. A number of personal points are forthright, poignant, and from my standpoint, favourably received. A selection of detail from the newspaper item would be more appropriately placed in the epilogue, which is where my readers will find it.

*8vo signifies the Latin word Octavo, meaning in eighth. It defines the format of a book and size of the leaves after folding a full sheet of paper a number of times.

The *Sheffield Independent* of 21st September, 1933 published an article of interest concerning a Sheffield poet. A *minor* Sheffield poet. It may come as no surprise to learn this is what partially inspired me to write a poem to Francis – given that my great-great-grandfather is the poet in question. A correspondent with the newspaper made enquiries about the 'forgotten poet' at the local library, where he discovered Francis' volume of poetry, but nothing about the author's life. Thus the write-up centres on *Sparks from Sheffield Smoke*, published and printed in 1882, and refers to several of its poems, including 'Sheffield Castle', 'Lines written in Shirecliffe Hall Lane', 'Rotherham', and 'Sheffield Manor'.

The local press story came about as a result of a letter from a reader who was reminded of a little book of poems published in the 'eighties', after reading another letter in the paper, with mention of the Rt. Hon A. J. Mundella, who happened to be one of the subscribers to Francis's volume. If indeed you are following this . . . the second correspondent felt sympathy for Francis, claiming to have once been acquainted with his grandson, who revealed the poet's struggles and disappointments. The grandson, and details of Francis' troubles are not identified, though his dislike of employment as a draper is widely documented. He also dearly missed Perth, and further indications arise later in this book. It is worth noting the author behind the letter which generated the story about Francis (over fifty years after his book of poems was published), made it known the work of this 'minor poet' was rather engaging. The letter almost suggests Francis deserved more recognition, (to which I am in full agreement) and samples of his accomplishments were enclosed. Incidentally, in case you had not noticed, the twentieth-century correspondence submitted by a local reader was published in newsprint on 21st September – as was the review of 1882.

In 1888 an anthology of poetry with the title *Yorkshire Poets Past and Present* was published in Bradford and London. This charming collection, fervently edited by Charles Frederick Forshaw would serve as a useful reference book concerning Yorkshire poetry, according to the *Bradford Daily Telegraph* of the time. It was expected to be both useful and popular, and indeed it is. The volume defines its editor as a Doctor of Dental Surgery, author of *Wanderings of Imagery* and other works, President of the West Riding Literary Club and Honorary Representative of the Society of Science, Literature and Art of London. Clearly an industrious man, in 1882 Dr Forshaw founded The Bradford Dental Hospital of Westgate, and gradually gained a worthy reputation. He somehow found time for another interest very dear to him . . . poetry, and would occasionally compose his own verse – though compiling and editing works of recognised wordsmiths seemed to take precedence.

In amongst Forshaw's selected Yorkshire poets, is my great-great-grandfather, and as I browsed through the index of volume one, his name leapt from the page. Then something else caught my attention. Francis could be found a little further down the list from the following: 'BRONTË, ANNE, BRONTË, CHARLOTTE, BRONTË, EMILY J'. This was indisputable proof of my ancestor appearing in print virtually alongside the Brontë sisters! Alphabetical arrangement of surnames is immaterial, since fundamentally their biographies and poems were published within the pages of the same book. The piece relating to BUCHANAN, FRANCIS is not only very informative, but serves as the perfect introduction for my readers:

It begins by referring to his first collection of poems and songs: *The Crusader, with other Poems and Lyrics* (1848) Perth, followed by his Sheffield volume of 1882. In Forshaw's words: '[Francis Buchanan] is a native of Perth (Scotland), where he was born in March, 1825. At an early age he evinced a love of the muse, always happy in the solitude of the wood and glen – embracing every opportunity of conversing with nature and even, frequently playing truant to attain that pleasure.' The short biography informs us that Francis was educated at Kinnoull School, '[. . .] and to his great dislike was afterwards apprenticed to a draper. He ran away at the age of 13 to become a sailor but was ignominiously brought back to the drudgery of the counter, which occupation he has continued until recent years.' Following numerous changes and locations, '[…] he married and settled in Sheffield, where he still remains. He was elected Bard to the Worshipful Brotherhood of Royal Arch Freemasons of Perth and has been honoured by having a sketch of his career, and examples of his poetry [in various anthologies].' Francis also contributed to local, Scottish, and even Australian newspapers. There is mention of him in other anthologies, and in Catherine Reilly's *Late Victorian Poetry*

1880-1899 – An annotated bibliography, J. Edward Vickers' *A Popular History of Sheffield,* and a nineteenth-century publication entitled *Recreations of an Antiquary in Perthshire History and Genealogy* by Robert Scott Fittis. And there were more, which will be revealed throughout this book.

Kinnoull offers incredible views over the River Tay, and woodland walks through trees of pine and beech. The setting, with its splendid surroundings has been savoured by many for years immeasurable. Samuel Lewis was writing about Kinnoull during the mid-nineteenth century, and his book *A Topographical Dictionary of Scotland* describes this parish in the county of Perthshire – with its name probably of Gaelic origin – as a rural district and an area of woodland with plantations, as well as arable, meadow and pasture land. Lewis explains that 'The surface is diversified with woodland hills of pleasing aspect, of which the hill of Kinnoull, rising from the bank of the Tay [. . .] is justly celebrated for the romantic beauty of its scenery.' This is where Francis Buchanan was born. It is where he grew up, and spent innumerable hours absorbing the beauty of nature. It is what inspired him to compose his first lines of poetry.

The parish of Kinnoull is a district of Scotland's city of Perth in the council district of Perth and Kinross, Perthshire, and is known not only for its lush woodland and exploratory walks, but its hill and folly. The tower on the edge of Kinnoull Hill, known as the Hill Tower, was built for Lord Gray of Kinfauns in 1829. He was inspired by castles in Germany's Rhine Valley, and his tower is known as a folly, as it was built solely for decoration. It stands teetering on the edge of the hill, overlooking the spectacular River Tay. Though it appears isolated, the tower is actually set between walls, arches and battlements, which can be enjoyed by walkers who head toward the summit. Kinnoull Hill was clearly very dear to Francis, and naturally, it features in his poetry, as does the River Tay. Today the charming peak and rocky cliffs attract large numbers of visitors, and I imagine those exploring it during the 1830s may have occasionally stumbled upon a curious child, happily observing his surroundings. They may have stumbled upon a budding poet, entirely unaware of course that 'Kinnoull Cliff' (see Perthshire Poems) would one day emerge from his pen. The once plentiful boats and small ships on the River Tay between Kinnoull and Perth, was almost certainly what inspired my forebear to flee his home with the intention of becoming a sailor.

Francis' father, James Buchanan was born in Callander, Perthshire and he married Catherine Ewan of Kinfauns. The couple settled in Bridgend in the parish of Kinnoull, where James established himself as a joiner and cabinet maker. Francis was born, on 23rd March, 1825, by which time his parents had experienced the joy of a new arrival, and the sorrow of loss in equal measure. Their children Margaret, John, Jean and Ann entered this world, only to depart too soon. Only their first-born son James, daughter Catherine, and youngest child Francis would survive beyond infancy. James relocated to Edinburgh, where he married Jane Innes Allan, and prospered as a High Court Solicitor. Of their two daughters Catherine Jane (known as Kate) and Mary, only Kate was to survive beyond childhood, and did not marry. Francis' sister Catherine unfortunately suffered from ill health, and spent much of her life in need of care.

Francis' first volume of poems and songs was published by Thomas Richardson of George Street, Perth in 1848, when the author was 23 years of age. Much of it concerns his profound attachment to Kinnoull's glorious scenery – a selection of which, I consider to be exceptional. One such poem has served as a most fitting prologue for this book, and I can only speculate at my forebear's response! The opening page of Francis' book greets the reader with

>'Whoe'er would wish a faultless piece to see,
>
>Think what ne'er was, nor is, nor e'er shall be'

and it is dedicated 'TO JAMES VAUGHAN ALLEN, ESQ., OF INCHMARTINE. THIS SMALL VOLUME OF POEMS AND LYRICS IS, BY PERMISSION, VERY REPECTFULLY INSCRIBED BY HIS SINCERE AND OBLIGED SERVANT, THE AUTHOR.'

Inchmartine is an ancient parish of Perthshire, close to Errol and is where the listed building, Inchmartine House proudly stands. During the mid-nineteenth century it was occupied by James Vaughan Allen, and whether or not my great-great-grandfather was personally acquainted with the gentleman remains to be seen. Francis compiled a heartfelt preface to his work:

'In submitting to the public eye the following productions in a collective form, the author feels a diffidence; and with but slight hopes he tenders the firstlings of his muse to the world, aware that he may incur its censure by obtruding himself on it in such a character.

These Poems (if they have the slightest pretensions to such a name) were written with a view to beguile a leisure hour or two, after the toil and business of the day had been gone through, and for the most part at an early age. They no doubt bear the internal stamp of a boyish mind – this it is perhaps unnecessary to tell – but though the consideration "cannot excite the voice of praise, it may at least arrest the arm of censure." The die is cast, and the fate of these effusions lies in the hazard of the throw. Should they be meritorious enough to pass the iron-sheathed gate of criticism, so much the better; on the contrary, should they incur the displeasure "of gods, and men, and columns," and the author be deemed a presumptuous intruder, and he, along with his productions, be thrust without mercy down the profound abyss of obscurity: should he be

"Laugh'd into Lethe by some quaint review,"

then he shall submit without a murmer [sic] to his lot, and endeavour to sooth his misfortune (as he wanders through the interminable forest of weeds "that grows on Lethe's brink") by humming to himself some *auld Scottish sang*. It is probable that the author "may have dared much and done little," for in the words of Cowper "it is one thing to write what may please our friends, who, because they are such, are apt to be biassed [sic] in our favour, and another to write to please everybody, because they who have no connection, or even knowledge of the author, will be sure to find fault if they can."

To a few of the author's own age, the contents of this volume may afford amusement; and he trusts, that those of more mature years, (if they are inclined to give them a reading,) will at least find them harmless. Far be it from him to enter the lists with genuine bards. They may derive fame by their labours, while he, as a rash interloper, may sink into oblivion. Without repining, he resigns the hope of immortality, and will content himself by gazing from the base of Parnassus on those laurel crowned sons of genius who have deservedly attained its summit.'

Francis' poetry occasionally refers to writers, poets and Greek Mythology. In the preface of his first volume of poems, 'Laugh'd into Lethe by some quaint review' is a quote from 'Hints from Horace' by Lord Byron – Horace being a Roman poet. Lethe was the spirit of oblivion and forgetfulness, and a river in the underworld (ruled by Hades), which made humans forgetful. If Shakespeare's 'Hamlet' does not take revenge on Claudius, he will be duller than a weed that grows on Lethe's brink', and brink denotes river bank – originally 'wharf' in Shakespeare's play. Also in Greek mythology, the Muses presided over science and the arts, and lived on a mountain named Parnassus.

Francis' poem 'School Days' speaks of happy times and fond memories: 'Oh! what a pleasant thing it is / On boyhood's scene's to gaze! / How loups the heart when thinkin' on / Our early, happy days.' In contrast, there are some rather heart-rending lines. Part of the old Kinnoull School still stands – making it clear for one to appreciate how close it is to the graveyard. Close enough for a schoolboy to wander in that direction, and be drawn towards it:

> 'Noo let me turn adoon yon grove
> O' auld an' stately trees,
> Wha's gnarl'd trunks, in search o'nests,
> We spield wi' supple knees:
> It takes me to the auld kirk yard,
> Whar rest my kindred's banes;
> And weel I like to look upon
> The humble moss-grown stones.
>
> The aisle, auld fashioned, standeth there;
> The sun's departin' beam
> Glints through the lofty winnocks bright,
> Same as in days lang gane;
> Ah' there's the nook whar strangers sleep:
> Here rest unkent remains :
> Unwept they lie – nae stanes to mark –
> Nae tribute to their names!'
>
> Francis Buchanan

Kinnoull's old burial ground is indeed where my forebear's siblings were laid to rest, and how moving it is to learn from his poem, that Francis visited their grave as a child. The headstone was erected in 1819 by his parents, James and Catherine in memory of their children. When Catherine died in 1855, and James in 1860, both were interred beside their beloved infants. In the above poem, the 'aisle' refers to the Kinnoull Aisle – an ancient monument and burial site of the Kinnoull family, and what remains of the medieval parish church. 'winnocks' is a Scottish term meaning windows, and 'unkent', also Scottish, means unknown, not recognised.

In 1849 the following Literary Notice was published on page 64 of *Macphail's Edinburgh Ecclesiastical Journal and Literary Review (Volume VII)*: 'The Crusader, with other Poems and Lyrics. By FRANCIS BUCHANAN Perth: Thomas Richardson. This is a volume of verses on a variety of subjects. How much precious time and abilities which might have turned to the advantage of the versifier or his friends, do we find wasted by persons like Mr. Buchanan in the production of useless and stupid books like this.' With the intention of overlooking this dismal review, I promptly moved on. However, after some consideration, and further scrutiny of the author's concise, and somewhat punitive criticism, I was overcome by the need to defend Francis' legacy. You may think me biased, but I feel sure his talent was appreciated by the mid-nineteenth-century reader, just as it is today. On reflection, the comments seem to relate to the number of poems and their subjects, rather than his ability to compose verse. It seems the critique believed Francis could have been more productive . . . utilised his time more effectively. In answer to this, I must declare with certainty that his early work (not to mention my present-day adaptation) would be all the poorer if deprived of splendid verse such as 'The Interview – A Poem' (himself being the promising poet and interviewee), the intended pleasure trip to the Bell Rock, and the remarkable tale of the captured crusader . . . need I go on?

Not far from the River Tay, and barely escaping the shadows of Kinnoull Hill stands an imposing Victorian house with a deep-rooted history. Bowerswell House is besieged with tales of love and romance, speculation and scandal. In the midst of it all are three people, destined to meet. The *Dundee Courier and Advertiser* of 30th July, 1946 reported that Bowerswell house was to be sold, following the death of its owner and occupant, Mr Melville Gray. It sparked interest, because Mr Gray had reached his 99th year, and as a result of his connection to Euphemia Chalmers Gray – otherwise known as Effie Gray – who was in fact his sister. She was also the legendary woman who married the art critic, philosopher, philanthropist and writer, John Ruskin. And following the annulment of her marriage, one of the founders of the Pre-Raphaelite brotherhood, the celebrated painter John Everett Millais was to become her second husband.

1848 saw the publication of Francis' first volume of poems, and it was also the year Miss Gray and Mr Ruskin were married at her family home, Bowerswell House. Previously owned by the Ruskin family, the house was purchased and rebuilt by the Grays during the nineteenth century. Though Francis Buchanan and Effie Gray were born in Kinnoull, Perth only three years apart, it is rather unlikely the two ever crossed paths. Their backgrounds were markedly dissimilar. Miss Gray attended an English boarding school for girls, far from Perthshire, and in later years when she and Millais resided in Kinnoull for a time, Francis had settled elsewhere. Bowerswell House, referred to by some as a mansion house, may have been visible in the landscape from his beloved hill: 'Far as mine eye can reach the verdant plain / Displays its gorgeous beauty, rich, serene. / There rears a noble mansion, here again / A clump of lowly cottages is seen, / With woods, green fields, and rivers interspersed between.'

Ruskin and Millais were drawn to the same woman, and both were drawn to Perth and the River Tay. The nineteenth-century author Francis Hindes Groome was editor of the *Ordnance Gazetteer of Scotland: A Survey of Scottish Topography, Statistical, Biographical and Historical.* It describes Bridgend as a suburb of Perth situated by the river Tay, in the parish of Kinnoull, and home to the paternal aunt of Ruskin, who '[. . .] had [. . .] a garden full of gooseberry bushes, sloping down to the Tay, with a door opening to the water, which ran past it clear brown over the pebbles 3 or 4 feet deep; an infinite thing for a child to look down into.' As Ruskin delighted at the marvels of his aunt's plot of land and the River Tay . . . quite possibly an inconspicuous, youthful poet was roaming along its banks nearby.

As revealed by various anthologies of poetry, Francis (grudgingly) became a draper's apprentice as an adolescent. The 1841 census confirms this, whilst revealing he continued to reside in the village of Bridgend, Kinnoull, with his parents, and sister. Shortly after the publication of his first volume of poems, my great-great-grandfather journeyed towards further employment opportunities in England. He evidently settled in Sheffield, but not before experiencing a number of other locations. According to the census of 1851, Heaton Norris near Stockport provided him with a home and employment at this time. Now aged 26, Francis assumed the duties of an assistant to a silk mercer and general draper in Heaton Lane, working alongside a number of staff and servants from far and wide.

In December 1852 Francis married Susannah Lloyd in Manchester. My great-great-grandmother hailed from Oswestry in Shropshire, which is where the couple's first child, James

Lloyd Buchanan was born in 1854. One can only assume Francis met Susannah in Manchester, where she did in fact reside during the early 1850s, employed as a household cook. Her brother Charles Edward Clarke Lloyd was one of the founders of a well-known nineteenth-century wholesale jewellers, based in Manchester. He worked in partnership with Charles Payne and Francis Amiel to form Lloyd, Payne and Amiel, a supplier of imported fancy goods. The company's merchandise, such as silver and pewter tea services, and watches and clocks remains popular, if not rather collectable today.

Birth records of Francis and Susannah's children make it possible to follow the family's trail to an extent. During the 1850s Francis Ewan Buchanan was born In Oldham, Lancashire, and another two sons, David Lloyd Buchanan and Charles Clyde Buchanan, in Hulme, Manchester. The first child to be born in Sheffield was their only daughter, Catherine Ann in 1860, followed by a further son named Tom in 1863, but he sadly died before his first birthday. Thomas Richard Buchanan was born in 1864, and Henry in 1866. Another child not to survive infancy was William Buchanan, in 1868. The family inhabited numerous abodes in the Pitsmoor area of Sheffield, and in 1881 can be located at 187 Fowler Street (today known as Fife Street). This was home to Francis (now a draper rather, than a draper's assistant) when his second volume of poems was published in 1882. In fact by the late 1870s Francis was managing his own business as a draper and hosier, at 40 Spital Hill. According to the census of 1891, now a retired draper aged 66, he and Susannah were living with their son David

Lloyd Buchanan, a draper's manager who was quite possibly, taking care of his father's business.

A grandson and great-grandson of Francis and Susannah managed the Hallamshire Vinegar Company Limited. The well-known business occupied the old Neepsend United Methodist Chapel on Farfield Road in Sheffield, and operated for many years. Francis and Susannah's son Henry was drawn towards the ballroom and became an accomplished dancer and MC (Master of ceremonies), attending dances throughout Britain. He married Kate Sissons, who grew up at the Gaiety Palace Inn and Music Hall, which once stood on West Bar in Sheffield. Two of their sons were also ballroom dancers, and in Rotherham the 'Dancing Buchanans' were a household name.

For Francis and other members of his family life could be challenging, and readers will learn of the difficult choices they faced as time progressed.

2

'WINCOBANK HILL

HERE, by this well-worn rustic stile,
Let me the evening hour beguile,
If thou would'st view aright the scene,
Thou must select a Summer e'en,
Just as the sun is dipping low,
When blue mist shadows creep below,
While high above, the sloping green
Is painted in a golden sheen,
And all the valley trills with song,
As weary rustics trudge along,
Happy in their humble sphere,
The labour done – the cottage near.
There is a calmness in the air,
There is a beauty in the view,
That weans the mind from worldly care,
And lifts the soul in raptures new.
There is a parting glory there,
As the great shield-like sun goes down,
A glow that brightens dull despair,

And blanches out the wrinkled frown;
There is a choristry of sound,
Yon amber-halo'd hills rejoice,
These amphitheatred woods around,
And the small streamlet's tinkling voice.
The humming bee returning home,
Gives thanks for sweetness cull'd to-day,
In yonder garden sees her dome,
And buzzes o'er the fragrant way.
There is a sanctity that chides
The wavering and doubting mind,
A Presence which rebukes our prides,
And bids us look above our kind.
The lark carols the evening sky,
And o'er the hill the moon appears;
The corncraik, with its curious cry,
Clamours its croaking in the ears
Of the green rustling corn;
And spinking, thrush, and blackbird too,
Join nature's universal lay
(The parting song of love's adieu)
Ere evening shuts the gates of day,
And Cynthia* shows her horn.

This great cathedral-church of God,
Domed with the lattic'd arch of heaven,
And paved with green and flowery sod,
To thee, O Man, was surely given.
Employ thy mind to rule thy will,
Take lessons from instinctive ways,
The God who made the lark to trill
Is also He whom angels praise.
Come, let me higher still ascend;
As yellow rays with shadows blend,
Yon azure field is scaled with gold,
And cirrus clouds curl up the sky,
From western gate to zenith high,
And sinks the sun his majesty,
As evening's purple wings infold.
Far o'er the plain the quiet scene
Is moonbeam'd with a modest light;
The hills throw shadows down between
The silvern and the golden sheen;
Day lends his lustre to the night.
I love the twi-light's solemn hour –
Religious hour of blissful rest,
Ere night resumes her starry power

O'er the dimm'd glories of the West.

I love the calmness that pervades

As fluttering creatures seek the nest –

Deep in the woodland's darkling shades,

Where brooklets babble them to rest.

Hark, to the modulated lays!

Where dew-drops gem the lawn beneath,

A nightingale sings to the rays

Of moonlight, flick'ring thro' the sprays,

Between the hawthorn's scented wreath.

See yonder ruin in the wood!

Around its walls the woodbines cling,

A time mark in the solitude,

Left there alone to rot and brood,

Old tottering and neglected thing.

What secret charm delays me here?

Why do I linger on this hill,

When yon grey hamlet is so still,

And the dead Day sleeps on his bier

What charm compels me to remain?

I cannot leave this witching place,

So lone, yet with so sweet a face,

A fairness like an angel's grace,

That would a mortal's soul enchain.
What charm compels me to remain?
I cannot leave this spell-bound scene;
Those moonlit woods and valleys green,
Yon river that glides on between,
Like serpent thro' the plain.
What charm compels me to remain
Upon this old embattled ground,
Where Roman legions rais'd the mound,
And scarp'd the ditch with slope around.
Long ere the Saxon and the Dane
Fought for supremacy of reign?
Upon this far commanding height,
That overlooks the vale below,
My fancy takes a backward light,
And in the stillness of the night
She hears the clashing of the fight;
Grim foe repelling foe.
She hears the skin-clothed warrior there
Yell his defiance on the air;
She hears his soul-despairing prayer
Wing'd to his country's gods.
There stood Rome's fierce centurions,

The conquerors of Franks and Huns,
The masters of the Gaul.
With sword and shield and javelin,
They hurl'd down in the crashing din –
Hurl'd down in mutilated death,
As oak is split by lightning's scathe,
Down from the mound and wall.
That skill-less host of noble foes,
Which swept and howl'd like storm that blows;
Like wave that follows wave, it rose,
But as against a rock.
It launch'd its fury-spending power
Against the fosse, the wall and tower,
That grim and darker seem'd to lour,
Above the battle's shock.
The Zulus in their savage might,
Dared England, conscious of their right;
They fought like demons in the fight,
As savage heroes fell.
The lance and whizzing assegai.
But whetted hunger for the fray,
But check'd the handful on its way;
And tens charged thousands in array,

> And stunn'd the savage yell.
>
> So was it with old British men,
>
> They fought for mountain, wood and fen;
>
> Death had no coward terrors then,
>
> They fought for liberty.
>
> But Roman power and Roman skill
>
> Triumphed o'er the heroic will;
>
> Rome conquer'd, tho' she could not kill,
>
> The yearning to be free.
>
> * The Moon'
>
> Francis Buchanan

Those familiar with Sheffield's Wincobank Hill, its ancient woodland and remarkable history, will no doubt be aware of the Iron Age Hillfort and Roman Ridge that it proudly presents. This much loved prehistoric and archaeological expanse is treasured by ramblers. They welcome the vast open space, the abundant nature . . . the incredible panoramic views of the Don Valley and beyond.

I suspect little has changed since my great-great-grandfather followed the pathways, as he mounted the hill. The outlook however, is somewhat altered. Nowadays keen wanderers will not be greeted with scenes enjoyed by Francis during the second half of the nineteenth century. That is not to say the outlook from Wincobank Hill fails to impress today's expectant hiker, indeed the twenty-first century aspect is rather magnificent. The route trails the sights and suburbs of South Yorkshire, encompassing Sheffield City Centre. The scene before Francis (though just as far-reaching) was less inhabited – offering fewer homes and sites of industrial development. It was undoubtedly more rural, more exposed, and lush foliage was plentiful. There exists some debate concerning the significance of the hill – its past, its purpose and practicality at different times throughout the centuries.

But certainly on the peak of the hill is an Iron Age Hillfort. The listed monument covers an area of two and a half acres, with a single rampart and a surrounding ditch and bank. Its location on the hilltop commands a position of prominence overlooking the lower Don Valley area of Sheffield, beyond age-old woodland crowded with revered trees of oak, beech and birch. A Roman Ridge forms part of the hill's hike and runs for ten miles in South Yorkshire, from Sheffield to Mexborough. Some believe the important earthwork may have been built by the Roman Empire as a defence structure. Whatever its purpose, my imaginative ancestor clearly enjoyed the enchantments of the hill, and I believe his connection with the site equalled that of today's group of volunteers known as 'Friends of Wincobank Hill'. They are committed to promoting this unique and natural scene of beauty, whilst preserving its heritage, woodland and wildlife. Members proclaim the importance of the ancient site, and occasionally organise meetings and nature walks, as well as educational, fun-filled endeavours. They campaign for the preservation of Wincobank Hill, which they continually aim to protect from destructive actions and development, thus ensuring it can be enjoyed by all. I feel certain that my great-great-grandfather would (if it were only possible) willingly offer his loyal support.

Wincobank Hill undoubtedly never failed to entrance the explorer, the nature enthusiast, artist, and poet in bygone times. I suspect little has changed. And of course not forgetting the passionate historian. The twentieth-century Sheffield librarian and archivist Mary Walton, produced a wonderful book entitled *SHEFFIELD Its Story and its Achievements*. This beautifully written, comprehensive work provides an informative and enjoyable account of the history of Sheffield. I was thrilled to obtain permission from Sheffield Newspapers / JPI Media to quote from pages 253/4 of the edition published in 1968. Indeed her enchanting words describe how the people of Sheffield

'[. . .] have always taken more pride in the splendid surroundings of their city than in their own achievements. But there is a strong link between the two. He who would understand Sheffield should climb Wincobank Hill on a Sunday afternoon. There the wind blows as strongly and freshly as when the Brigantes watched from their fort. In the valley beneath, with only stray wisps of smoke to mark the ceaseless care with which the furnaces are tendered while the great city rests, lie the mighty works of man; and tier upon tier, all around the horizon rise the hills that cradled the infant community, that gave water, fuel and mineral resources to promote its sturdy growth. In that age-long partnership between man and nature is the secret of Sheffield.'

In his poem 'Wincobank Hill', my forebear rests by an old rustic stile in anticipation of a glorious scene of beauty, as he reveals that only on a summer evening can one fully appreciate the sight . . . just as the sun goes down. One can hear the weary workmen trudging homeward once their work is done, and the calmness in the air, complemented by such a splendid view is greatly uplifting. The woodland grows darker as a nightingale sings, and spellbound . . . Francis finds himself unable to leave the moonlit sight. His mind, now drifting into the past becomes occupied with visions of battling warriors amidst sounds of clashing swords and shields. And he realises that if such battles took place, all was observed by Wincobank Hill. The reader might hear the rushing water, the harmonious wildlife . . . the horrors of ancient battle. Francis was undoubtedly aware that the secluded spot on Wincobank Hill was not exclusively his to delight in. There were others, certainly.

I must share with you an extraordinary tale concerning an unassuming Sheffield resident named John Nixon, and his nineteenth-century poem. In 1926 a journalist with the *Sheffield Daily Telegraph* discovered upon his desk, correspondence from a reader with a story to subsequently be published on the 18th of December. It reveals that a local man named Mr Cooper had brought home from his trip to Australia, an old book he had purchased there. On opening the book a leaflet fell from its pages, which happened to be a poem written by John Nixon of Wincobank, Sheffield. It was entitled 'Wincobank Hill'! Selected lines appear in the newspaper along with a request for information about the author and a school mentioned in the poem, which provided shelter for children during winter evenings. Initially doubtful that a copy of the entire poem would ever be traced, I was thrilled to learn that it was stored in a collection of archival material at a Sheffield University library. Furthermore, I was granted permission to publish – for which I am most grateful. What follows is my selection of stanzas from this lengthy, though quite wonderful poem:

'WINCOBANK HILL

On Nature's vast Grandeurs we look with delight,
The scene all around is a beautiful sight,
The flowers with fragrance the air they do fill; –
These are the productions of Wincobank Hill.

It once was so barren, that nothing would grow,
But whins, broom, and bracking, upon its fine brow;
But now Cultivation has raised it, till
They grow corn, fruit and flowers, on Wincobank Hill.

Some centuries ago, amongst men of high rank,
This hill it was noted; they erected a camp;
Pursued till the blood through their veins it did thrill,
They fled here for refuge, to Wincobank Hill.

On the east, when the Romans did come to besiege,
They marched up their troops to the top of the ridge;
It was called Roman Ridge, – it retains its name still,
And this is connected with Wincobank Hill.

How lovely, delightful, transporting it looks, –
All around we see forests, and meadows; and brooks
Where sweet purling waters down the valleys do rill;
These, these! are the beauties of Wincobank Hill.

And spring is approaching, it looks more sublime,
When all that is lovely is regaining its prime;
The showers so copious, and gently distil,
Refreshing the beauties of Wincobank Hill.

Then summer comes on, and the sweet month of June,
With its lovely attractions puts all things in tune;
If the Artist should try, he would fail in his skill,
To pencil the beauties of Wincobank Hill.

As Autumn advances, its gay smiling morn
Bedecks all the fields and the meadows with corn;
What the fruit trees did promise in Spring, they fulfil,
And crown the rich harvest on Wincobank Hill.

When the north wind is raging, and Winter's keen blast,
With its strong icy fetters, around us is cast;
When all Nature looks cheerless with Winter's cold chill,

There is something attracting on Wincobank Hill.

Oh yes! there's a School, where we meet with delight,
To spend the dark hours of a cold winter's night;
We are sheltered from tempest and every ill,
And this is a blessing on Wincobank Hill.

No noise nor confusion, through its district is heard,
But the sweet pretty notes of the warbling bird;
The schoolboys with echoes the air they do fill;
This is all that molests us, on Wincobank Hill.

Then, who would not wish on this hill to reside,
Where Nature shines forth in its noblest of pride?
Our Hearts unto Him should with gratitude fill,
Who gives us these blessings, on Wincobank Hill.

JOHN NIXON, WINCOBANK   *April,* 1849
W. FORD, PRINTER, YORK STREET, SHEFFIELD'

The author was clearly captivated by the beauty all around. Come sunshine, rain or windstorm, the hill never loses its charm and appeal. And like Francis, Nixon alludes to the Roman Troops and Ridge in his poem. There was a huge response to the newspaper's request for information. Indeed Mr Nixon was known to many, and very attached to the village of High Wincobank. He was a great temperance advocate who liked to recite his lyrics from platforms, and became known as the 'Wincobank Poet'. A letter from Mr W.T. Gent informed readers that he had persuaded Mr Nixon to have some of his verse printed. Thus in all likelihood, you and I would have been denied the pleasure of reading his tribute to Wincobank Hill if Mr Gent had not intervened. And if Mr Cooper had simply walked on by the bookshop in Australia, this book would most certainly be the poorer for it.

William Thompson Gent's career began at the age of eleven as an apprentice to a pawnbroker, with 'wages' consisting of food and clothing. He eventually became the proprietor of a large furnishing concern in Sheffield, which sold furniture of every description (even pianos) and specified that it did not stock 'cheap trashy goods'. The well-known popular figure was elected as Liberal member for Brightside with Sheffield City Council, and served as a Councillor from 1896 to 1905. He was very concerned for the welfare of the needy, and for the environment. Indeed he remembered Brightside prior to industry, as an area of beautiful scenery with countless trees. He would later become the managing director of Attercliffe's Adelphi Theatre.

And what of the school at Wincobank Hill? The *Sheffield Daily Telegraph* went on to reveal some interesting historical facts. At the time of the newspaper's publication, the school was known as the High Wincobank Undenominational Church. It had served as a school where boys would meet during winter evenings, and was later inaugurated by the Read family of

Wincobank Hall. The Hall was demolished in 1925 after falling into disrepair, and was replaced with social housing known as the Flower Estate.

Francis Buchanan may have met Robert Eadon Leader, printer, publisher, and proprietor of the *Sheffield Independent*. Indeed Leader and Sons of 18 and 20 Bank Street, published *Sparks from Sheffield Smoke* in 1882. Decades later Mr R. E. Leader – now in his 82nd year and old enough to remember the Wincobank of former years – wrote an article about its past for the *Sheffield Daily Telegraph*. Published in 1921, it reveals that Wincobank Hall was in a state of desolation, and 'Though not in itself a thing of beauty, it was beautiful for situation, and surely "grieving, if aught inanimate e'er grieves,"' He recalls the echoes of the once embracing woods, and offers a detailed history of the Hall and its inhabitants throughout the centuries. For the purpose of this book, I would like to explore the events of 1816, which Leader describes as '[. . .] a new chapter in the history of Wincobank.' The hall fell into the hands of Joseph Read of Attercliffe, who was concerned with silver and gold refinery. For himself, his wife and five children, this fine abode at High Wincobank (then a quiet, rural hamlet) no doubt proved to be a comfortable family residence. Mr Read purchased land at the rear of the property which reached as far as woodland, and the pathway to the Hillfort. He greatly enhanced the plot of land with orchards, meadows and beautiful gardens . . . beyond which stood Wincobank Hill.

The Read family worshipped at the Zion Chapel in Attercliffe, and when it was rebuilt in 1802 Joseph provided funding. Wincobank required its own place of worship and in later years, once the Reads had relocated there, arrangements were put in place to provide one. In the absence of a suitable structure, a Sunday school was established in the family laundry, together with a chapel in the hall's coach house. Despite the incongruous arrangements, the residents of Upper Wincobank were happy to attend. Much later the school became a chapel, and in fact the Grade II listed building known as Upper Wincobank Chapel still exists.

It did not end there. Mr Read's wife and eldest daughters established the Sheffield Anti-Slavery Society, and as a result of this and other campaigns, the family and the small Sheffield community rapidly gained global recognition. But by 1835, following the financial ruin of Joseph Read, the estate of Wincobank Hall was on sale. He sadly died impoverished, and his daughter Mary Anne Read married William Rawson of Nottingham. When *he* died his widow inherited his family's legacy, and subsequently the hall at Wincobank was to provide the Read family with a home once again. Mary Anne and her sister Emily opened a private school for young ladies at the hall, and later a day school for local children. Mary Anne Rawson died in 1887, and was laid to rest in the family vault at the Zion Chapel's graveyard. **Today a** voluntary group known as Friends of Zion Graveyard, have raised funds and purchased the disused burial ground. The group aims to preserve it as a heritage site for the benefit of future generations, and is working towards a comprehensive Habitat Management Plan. Volunteers concerned with the graveyard's environment undertake tasks such as gardening, which also benefits wildlife. An Oral History Project aims to collect memories from people who lived in the community, and a list of graves may be viewed on the group's website: ziongraveyard.chessck.co.uk

Relatives may wish to contact the group, and volunteers are always welcome.

During the Read family's early years at Wincobank Hall, a governess named Dinah Ball was employed to educate the children. She liked to compose verse, and was clearly inspired by the nearby woods known as Winco Wood. This is also held in a collection of archival material at a Sheffield University library, and I am once again grateful for permission to publish. Thanks must go to my brother Nick, who helped me decipher the age-old hand written lines, enabling a greater part of it to be printed:

'Winco Wood

Where distant far my feet shall stray,
And thine still haunt at close of day
These shades, where every wing is blest,
And songsters trill themselves to rest;
Where the least Blackbird seems to speak,
And night's hoarse beetle fans thy cheek,
And not a zephyr moves the tree,
Say, will a whisper talk of me?
And when the thicket's break unveils
That Paradise of woody dales,
And summits touched with evening's beam

And purple shades that downward stream;
Where distant crags their forms unfold,
Or seem to melt in floods of gold,
When God himself almost you see,
Then breathe a secret prayer for me.

Here have I heard His voice at even
When this green wood seemed joining Heaven,
Its deep shade tending to inspire
More sacred awe than twilight choir;
His voice, who chose the evening hour
When first his Temple was a Bower;
And when waged my fervent plea
I thought, may Mary turn, on thee.

If that sweet, hastened, hallowing beam
Around my wakeful conch should gleam,
And joys, long past, but ever dear,
Shall prompt the unavailing tear,
I'll hide that grief and view the ray,
Still shining on till opening day,
And in its changeless beauty see
Friendship, and Constancy, and thee.

And when I pass a mossy dell
Where summer's buds profusely swell,
Or where the pale Fern still is green,
Though Winters land has scathed the scene,
Where the bright herb seems ever new,
Screened from the blast, and steeped in dew,
Then my admonished thought shall flee
To end life happiness with thee.

D. Ball

18th July, 1821'

Another poem by Miss Ball displays strong sentiments concerning slavery. It appears in Mary Anne Rawson's collection of contributions of prose and verse, *The Bow in the Cloud or the Negro's Memorial*, published in 1834. Here are the opening lines:

'HOPE

Written after first hearing of the formation of *Ladies'* Anti-Slavery Associations.

> SLAVERY! silent hopeless anguish
> British souls have felt they care:
> Yet their firmest efforts languish –
> Into all the slave's despair.
>
> Is there hope? – The thought were glory,
> Piercing through a darksome cave:
> Statesman, poets, tell thy story,
> Yet is found no hand to save.'
>
> D. Ball.

The celebrated Scottish bard James Montgomery (1771-1854) also contributed to Mary Anne Rawson's published collection. He settled in Sheffield, supported the anti-slavery campaign, and was in fact acquainted with Mrs Rawson. Montgomery also engaged in calls for the abolition of children being forced to sweep chimneys, and produced the skilfully written, heart-rending 'The Climbing Boy's Soliloquies'.

My forebear was familiar with at least some of Montgomery's work, evidence of which will emerge within the pages of this book. Though Francis indisputably yearned for Kinnoull Hill and the River Tay (see 'Perthshire Poems'), he seemed resigned to his situation, and purposely uncovered comparable retreats with gratifying scenery. Wincobank Hill was just one of his chosen refuges, though I sense it was a very much *favoured* spot. Far from the bustle of daily activities, he characteristically absorbed his surroundings, and was delighted to realise that they too provided the perfect setting for a poem.

3

'IN THE DEEP, DEEP WOOD

I KNOW a nook in the deep green wood,
Of old Nature's own creating,
Where Echo mocks in the solitude
The songs that the birds are making –
In the solitude of the deep, deep wood,
When the forest heads are shaking.

In this lonely place, away from care,
Where the wild rose has its dwelling,
Where the timid deer and gamesome hare
Their loves and their fears are telling –
In the solitude of the deep, deep wood,
Where the crystal streams are welling.

'Tis sweet to muse in the noontide hour,
When the silent ray is streaming
Thro' the leafy roof of the scented bower,
As the nodding oaks are dreaming,

In the solitude of the deep, deep wood,
   Where the hyacinths are gleaming.

'Tis a holy place, this pathless dell,
   Where the choral-birds are singing –
Where the woodbines cling to the rocky cell,
   And the flowers their sweets are flinging;
In the solitude of the deep, deep wood,
   Where the glades with joy are ringing.

In the twilight time of declining day,
   When the faint-puls'd breeze is sighing,
The golden clouds and the evening grey
   Spin a robe for the god who is dying;
And the solitude of the deep, deep wood
   Sings low where the shades are lying.

'Tis sweet to be in the silence there,
   As the mellow'd light is blending
With the ether arc of the dark blue air,
   When the star-lamps their rays are lending

> To the solitude of the deep, deep wood,
> As the dew to the flow'rs is descending.'
>
> Francis Buchanan

Francis' poem 'In the Deep, Deep Wood' is simply bursting with detail concerning woodland activity – albeit calm, and unhurried. It is a poem I enjoy reading often, and on each occasion I am drawn further into the tranquil isolation he describes, whilst becoming more and more aware of the all-pervading detail. Indeed each time I delve into this delightful, enigmatic refuge, I find there are further enchantments waiting to be discovered. In just six verses, Francis shares with the reader a great diversity of phenomena. His secreted 'nook' is in fact *bustling* – yet all is serene. It is what he describes as a lonely place, but only in the most agreeable sense, for this precious retreat is far from the hubbub of life. Absorb his words only to find yourself drawn into another world. Remain within its boundaries, and hear the sweet sound of a flowing stream, which becomes increasingly harmonious as birdsong enhances its tune. Admire the curious wildlife, the abundant flowers and trees, and take in all around you, regardless of the hour, for other than subtle changes to the light . . . little alters here.

The poem is fairly typical of my great-great-grandfather's style, but what is noticeable in this instance is his use of rhythm. It flows with tempo, and the way it skilfully rhymes becomes all the more perceptible when the lines are read aloud. I wonder if Francis was especially fond of this poem. It is, after all set within surroundings he cherished, and he perhaps spontaneously grasped his pen in order to convey his adoration by way of eloquent verse. The theme of this poem is dear to me also, which in addition to my overall fondness of Francis' poetry, gives ground for my connection with his words.

Unsurprisingly this poem was selected for publication in the original edition of *Sparks from Sheffield Smoke*, but it also appeared in more than one newspaper. My desire to learn when the verse was written was fulfilled, when I unearthed Francis' charming lines within the pages of the *Sheffield Independent* dated 22nd July, 1880 – two years prior to the publication of his book. On this occasion the poem appeared with an unfamiliar, but fitting title: 'The Retreat', (the original heading no doubt) and I was none other than thrilled to see that it is dated 19th July, 1880 and the author is named.

Thus it seems that unless it was an old poem he resurrected, these lines were written during my predecessor's time in Sheffield, but questions loom to the surface. Indeed precisely *where* did my forebear compose them, and what inspired him? Sheffield and the rolling countryside of Derbyshire boast much woodland, which was no doubt richer and more plentiful in 1880. I like to think this is where Francis discovered his retreat – though it may in fact be a celebration of the ubiquitous hidden woodlands: secret hideaways accessible only to the privileged few. It is certainly possible, but I cannot ignore the niggling notion which presents in my mind scenes of Kinnoull, in Perth. I believe this place was to take precedence throughout Francis' life, as he sought out spots that mirrored it. Necessity would lead him far from Perth, but he engaged with new surroundings – spending infinite hours in the mysterious woods . . . of which he never tired.

Two years after Francis' Sheffield volume of poetry was circulated, the poem in question appeared on two separate occasions during October, 1884, in the *Androssan and Saltcoates Herald* – a newspaper established on the North Ayrshire Coast of South-western Scotland. It covers an area far from Francis' homeland, but in actual fact, his poems did occasionally appear in various Scottish newspapers. In 1885 the same newspaper announced in the 10th July edition, a newly published book of poetry entitled *Modern Yorkshire Poets*, by William Andrews. This compilation I am very familiar with, and do in fact own a copy. It comprises poems and brief biographical details concerning Andrews' choice of relatively local poets, and I can proudly inform you that Francis Buchanan is one of them.

The author of numerous articles and books – not only relating to poets and their published work, but the history of townships and their churches – Andrews was born in Kirkby Woodhouse, Nottinghamshire, but relocated to Hull during the 1870s. He was appointed librarian at the Hull Subscription Library and was one of the founders of the Hull Literary Club, where he became Secretary. Passionate about books, verse, and literature, he regularly composed poetry, and relished the task of compiling the work of worthy poets. These books offer samples of their poetry and details of other life achievements. In the preface to *Modern Yorkshire Poets*, Andrews acknowledges that his anthology is not the first of its kind and pays homage to other works, such as *The Poets of Yorkshire*, which was commenced by William Cartwright Newsam, and completed after his death (as an offering to his widow) by John Holland, of Sheffield – who orchestrated its publication in 1845. Also *The*

Poets and Poetry of Yorkshire by William Grainge, published in Wakefield in 1868, and *A Garland of Poetry; by Yorkshire Authors, or relating to Yorkshire*, assembled and published by Abraham Holroyd in 1873. In *Modern Yorkshire Poets* Andrews expresses that he trusts his work will be regarded as a complementary supplement to those mentioned, rather than an attempt to supersede them. From time to time I have found it necessary to refer to one of the numerous and popular nineteenth-century anthologies of Yorkshire poets. Indeed Andrews' collection also focuses on John Hall – a successful businessman and gifted poet – whom my readers will become acquainted with on reading 'A Sheffield Worthy'.

In the short biography concerning Francis Buchanan, Andrews tells the familiar tale of his desire to become a sailor, which resulted in a failed attempt to escape an impending draper's apprenticeship. And he reveals Francis' deep love of poetry and occasional indulgence in composition, amidst work commitments that would dampen his fervour. As a consequence, he largely refrained from creating verse – until that is, an accident that was to fundamentally incapacitate him from occupational duties, meant his dedication to all things lyrical was restored. Andrews reveals that *Sparks from Sheffield Smoke* would result in the sale of 800 copies, and his biographical piece relating to my forebear is complemented by 'In the Deep, Deep Wood'.

My precious, fragile little book of Francis' poems parted with its title page long ago. However, the copy which appears in this book was obtained from Sheffield's Local Studies and Archives, who kindly allowed me to publish it. In the event, I noticed it bore a few hand-written words: 'W. Andrews Esq.

With J. Dufty's compliments'. I was able to identity both parties immediately, and was rather astounded: William Andrews, author of *Modern Yorkshire Poets* (1885) and Joseph Dufty – one of Andrews' selected poets. In truth either one could have written it, but it was more likely to have been Dufty – a person I recognise as a gifted poet, and dear friend of Francis Buchanan. My readers will learn more about their sincere friendship in the final pages of this book, and become acquainted with Joseph, and particular members of his family.

Perhaps an image of this *particular page* was destined to find its way into my rekindled edition of *Sparks from Sheffield Smoke*. Moreover, Francis' inclusion in Andrews' anthology could conceivably be a consequence of Joseph Dufty's role in ensuring Hull-based William Andrews was equipped with a copy of the nineteenth-century edition. Nonetheless, tempting as it is to ruminate, we must now depart the enchanted solitude of the deep, deep, wood and proceed towards the open fields and meadows. Here we may stumble upon an unsuspecting pretty little wildflower. We may stumble upon the charming pimpernel.

4

'TO THE PIMPERNEL *

'MIDST meadows green and growing corn
    Thy scarlet leaves the fields adorn.
The dews have gone to seek the sun;
    Long has the lark his song begun;
    And all thy kindred flow'rs are up,
    But yet thou openest not thy cup.
Thou bashful, blushing, tender thing,
    Art shy to show thy blossoming?
Dost know that by the clock 'tis seven,
Yet thou'st not seen the morning heaven?
Rouse thee, and open wide thine eyes;
    No rain to-day will thee surprise.
The shepherd knows what thou infers,
    Thou cheapest of barometers -
When thy close petals tell the rain,
    Will glad the thirsty hill and plain;
Thou draws't thy hood, and in thy cell
Thou cares't not if it comes pell-mell.

All thro' the summer's verd'rous prime
Thou hast a merry, pleasant time;
For thee the warblers flit and sing,
The forest echoes laugh and ring;
And on thy scarlet-petal'd breast
The wand'ring bee still loves to rest.
All thro' the greening May and June
Thou listens to the cushat's croon;
When other flowers droop and die,
Thou dares the fierceness of July;
And in brown August thou art seen,
A beauty speck 'midst withering,
Till autumn winds thy frame pervade,
Then thou art with the russet laid.

* This pretty wilding is known as "The Poor Man's Weather-glass," the flowers opening at about seven in the morning, and closing about three in the afternoon; and also "The Shepherd's Barometer," closing on the approach of rain.'

Francis Buchanan

This is quite simply, a lovely little poem from the pen of Francis. Clearly engaged with this particular wildflower, he tenderly treats it with respect, using gentle words, which serve to elucidate its daily life and routine – the significant role of the pimpernel. The reader's mind is instantly drawn to this pretty and diminutive bloom, and one almost feels the need to cherish it.

Francis occasionally uses symbols and footnotes in his poetry, which I find quite touching. This highly descriptive and edifying poem pays homage to the pimpernel, but nonetheless, provides further detail by way of annotation. My great-great-grandfather went to the trouble of ensuring his readers were presented with all the facts – particularly concerning the all-important weather! The pimpernel is indeed known as 'The Poor Man's Weather Glass' because of its knack of predicting the onset of rain, by closing its sensitive petals due to a darkening sky or increased humidity. Habits such as this not only serve to protect its inner flower from showers, but make it a dependable friend to those in need of a weather forecast. Since time immemorial, people have relied on tendencies of the sun, the sky and its clouds – and even nature and wildlife – to predict weather events. Most certainly there was a time when mariners, farmers, and shepherds thought nothing of living by informal folklore known as weather lore, and aphorisms relating to the weather became commonplace: 'Pimpernel, pimpernel, tell me true. Whether the weather be fine or no. No heart can think, no tongue can tell. The virtues of the pimpernel.'

Anagallis arvensis is its true name in floral terms, which does initially seem a rather portentous description of this 'pretty arable weed' – a weed however, with a dutiful role, and it seems this is precisely what its name alludes to. Whilst Anagallis is derived from Greek terms referring to the flower repeatedly opening and closing in response to weather conditions, arvensis is the Latin adjective meaning 'in the fields'. Notice Francis' reference to the flower's scarlet appearance – a sight which adorned the cornfields around him. The pimpernel generally produces a red flower in Britain, but other colours are visible, and it is thought the sunnier the climate the more likely the flower will flourish with petals of the blue variety, which is perhaps why Southern Spain is festooned with them. Firmly rooted on British soil, Francis undoubtedly encountered the red pimpernel frequently, as his woodland walks steered him towards open fields and country rambles.

The red flower is prevalent throughout England and Wales, whilst confined mainly to coastal areas of Scotland, and I do wonder whether Francis was aware of the existence of other colours. Though clearly conversant with the red or 'scarlet' petals, I'm certain that for Francis, this little flower would not have revived echoes of the fictional tale *The Scarlet Pimpernel*, for he would never be acquainted with it. Indeed the flower became linked with the story from the time it was written in 1905, when the Hungarian-born British author, Baroness Emmuska Orczy published her novel following the success of the stage play that was co-written with her husband. This narrative penned by the successful playwright and novelist, was centred upon the main character Sir Percival Blakeney – the British aristocrat who heroically rescued French innocent victims from the impending lethal guillotine amid the French

Revolution. And following his swashbuckling events, Sir Percy routinely left as his trade-mark a card depicting a scarlet pimpernel. Hence the familiarity of the phrase 'the elusive pimpernel' commonly in use today. Blakeney would sign the mocking notes that were left for the revolutionaries, as he outwitted them. There are a number of theories relating to the author's choice of flower. It is known as the symbol of assignation, which can mean arrangements at a time and place. And concerning *The Scarlet Pimpernel*, has been interpreted by some as the prisoners condemned to death, and by others as the sensitive flower's knack of projecting wet weather. Or perhaps the Baroness was captivated by its somewhat endearing name, which she fully anticipated would prove widely popular and well-remembered – a probability which unquestionably came to pass. Or did she simply admire the shape and colour of the flower, which was deemed striking and memorable – the perfect monogram of a brave protagonist.

Whatever the reason, this unassuming little flower has become known as one of the most famous characters in English literature. But who essentially muses over the pimpernel? Francis most certainly did, yet sadly his endearing verse had fallen into the depths of time, only to be forgotten. A situation I hope to resolve with the revival of his profound words. For they surely deserve appreciation.

From dahlias to daffodils and lilies to lavender, poetic verse on the subject of flowers and herbs has oozed from the visionary bard for centuries. The pimpernel, described by Baroness Orczy as 'a humble wayside flower' is no exception. And as Francis roamed the woods, the forests and fields, all the time articulating what he saw . . . in a far-off place across an ocean, the pimpernel had caught the eye of Celia Thaxter. Those unfamiliar with the nineteenth-century American poet and author of short stories, must allow me to introduce her.

This exceptional woman was (and most definitely *is*) recognised not only for her literary success, but her passion for flowers, island life, the sea, and its coastal shorelines. Born Celia Laighton in Portsmouth, New Hampshire in 1835, much of her childhood was spent on the Isles of Shoals – a group of small islands off the coast of New Hampshire. Her father, Joseph took on the role of lighthouse keeper on one of the isles, known as White Island. Celia is best known for her incredibly delightful book *An Island Garden*, published in 1894, which today is as popular as ever. The illustrated journal gives a detailed description of the charming garden she created on another island belonging to the Isles of Shoals. Hog Island, which Celia's father renamed Appledore, became the family home for many years and Joseph was to build a successful hotel there, named The Appledore . . . but that's another story.

Both garden and book were a result of Celia's deep love of flowers, which she described as dear friends and inspirers, offering comfort and cheer. She was persuaded to produce a book so that others could learn from her horticultural success. During her relatively short life (she died in 1894, the year her garden book was published) much of her poetry appeared in print, which included poems for children. But for the purpose of this book, what I am drawn to is a poem written in 1882. As the publication of *Sparks from Sheffield Smoke* was in progress, what emanated from the pen of Celia Thaxter was a poem entitled 'The Pimpernel'.

Known as a European herb, the 'wildflower' that is the American pimpernel produces mainly red flowers, but occasionally white – and they are often to be found at roadsides or in rock crevices at the seashore. This was likely inspiration for Celia, who on mailing the poem to a cousin, informed him of how the flower grew profusely on the Isles of Shoals and never failed to warn of stormy weather. The poem is also a reflection of the many who perished in stormy weather, in the Atlantic Ocean that she looked out upon. Her poem, which is quite beautiful and overflowing with atmosphere, lures the reader to the seashore, who then shares the thoughts and bears the emotions of the fretful woman central to it. Though it proffers sentiment and romance, fundamental to the poem is a wise and colourful flower; and its forewarning concerning the approach of a storm is imperative to the outcome of the lovers' reunion. Thaxter's unabridged poem tells the story:

'The Pimpernel

SHE walks beside the silent shore,
The tide is high, the breeze is still;
No ripple breaks the ocean floor,
The sunshine sleeps upon the hill.

The turf is warm beneath her feet,
Bordering the beach of stone and shell,
And thick about her path the sweet

Red blossoms of the pimpernel.

"Oh, sleep not yet, my flower!" she cries,
"Nor prophesy of storm to come;
Tell me that under steadfast skies
Fair winds shall bring my lover home."

She stoops to gather flower and shell,
She sits, and, smiling, studies each;
She hears the full tide rise and swell,
And whisper softly on the beach.

Waking, she dreams a golden dream,
Remembering with what still delight,
To watch the sunset's fading gleam,
Here by the waves they stood last night.

She leans on that encircling arm,
Divinely strong with power to draw
Her nature, as the moon doth charm
The swaying sea with heavenly law.

All lost in bliss the moments glide;

She feels his whisper, his caress;
The murmur of the mustering tide
Brings her no presage of distress.

What breaks her dream? She lifts her eyes
Reluctant to destroy the spell;
The color from her bright cheek dies, –
Close folded is the pimpernel.

With rapid glance she scans the sky;
Rises a sudden wind, and grows,
And charged with storm the cloud-heaps lie.
Well may the scarlet blossoms close!

A touch, and bliss is turned to bale!
Life only keeps the sense of pain;
The world holds naught save one white sail
Flying before the wind and rain.

Broken upon the wheel of fear
She wears the storm-vexed hour away;
And now in gold and fire draws near
The sunset of her troubled day.

But to her sky is yet denied
The sun that lights the world for her;
She sweeps the rose-flushed ocean wide
With eager eyes that quick tears blur;

And lonely, lonely all the space
Stretches, with never sign of sail,
And sadder grows her wistful face,
And all the sunset splendors fail.

And cold and pale, in still despair,
With heavier grief than tongue can tell,
She sinks, – upon her lips a prayer,
Her cheek against the pimpernel.

Bright blossoms wet with showery tears
On her shut eyes their droplets shed.
Only the wakened waves she hears,
That, singing, drown his rapid tread.

'Sweet, I am here!' Joy's gates swing wide,
And heaven is theirs, and all is well,

And left beside the ebbing tide,

Forgotten, is the pimpernel.'

Celia Thaxter

Dr Edward Jenner would have expected to be dutifully remembered, if not celebrated. For he was the ingenious physician behind the pioneering smallpox vaccination that saved countless lives. But for his name to evoke lines of a poem (well . . . *poems* in actual fact) he may not have foreseen. His life began in Berkeley, Gloucestershire in the year 1749, and his career in medicine commenced when apprenticed to a surgeon as a fresh-faced, zealous youth. Dr Jenner wasted no time in ascertaining his worth and by his early twenties found himself well established as a practitioner and surgeon, whilst engaging with experimental research concerning cowpox and smallpox. He himself had been inoculated for smallpox as a schoolboy; but it was to affect his general health and he resolved to discover a more agreeable alternative. Mindful of the fact that milkmaids who contracted and suffered the mild effects of cowpox did not become infected with smallpox, Dr Jenner injected a young boy with cowpox. His efforts aimed at creating immunity against smallpox, proved successful and led to the revolutionary discovery of a protective vaccine.

He then concerned himself with informing the world of this discovery and was posthumously greatly honoured for doing so. His research into smallpox was chronicled, and during the latter part of the eighteenth century it was published. But as far as I know his poetry was not. However the poem I would like to draw your attention to is very well known, and has appeared in numerous British newspapers throughout the years. Those familiar with Jenner's poems may be expecting to cast their eyes over 'Address to a Robin'. That being the case . . . I am sorry to disappoint! For as charming and justly popular the aforementioned may be, my choice lies with his unique creation relating to the weather – expected rainfall in actual fact. Originally given the title '40 Signs of Rain', different variations of the poem have sporadically emerged – one being 'SIGNS OF RAIN, Forty reasons for not accepting the invitation of a friend to make an excursion with him'. Indeed it is widely believed this is precisely what he did – as the weather was looking doubtful, and the planned excursion would have to be cancelled. His imaginative notions resulted in a possibly hurried, yet fastidious and idiosyncratic rhyming verse, which in all probability he scribbled down in holograph form. And I can't help thinking that he must have been smiling as the lines emerged before him! The poem offers forty signs of impending rain, from age-old weather prophecies to the behavioural patterns of wildlife. And it may come as no surprise to learn that Edward Jenner did not overlook the wise and dependable pimpernel:

'40 Signs of Rain

The hollow winds begin to blow,

The clouds look black, the glass is low;

The soot falls down, the spaniels sleep,

The spiders from their cobwebs peep.

Last night the sun went pale to bed,

The moon in halos hid her head;

The boding shepherd heaves a sigh,

For see, a rainbow spans the sky.

The walls are damp, the ditches smell,

Closed is the pink-eyed pimpernel.

Hark! how the chairs and tables crack,

Old Betty's joints are on the rack;

Loud quack the ducks, the peacock's cry;

The distant hills are looking nigh.

How restless are the snorting swine,

The busy flies disturb the kine,

Low o'er the grass the swallow wings;

The cricket, too, how sharp he sings;

Puss on the hearth, with velvet paws,

Sits, wiping o'er her whiskered jaws.

Through the clear stream the fishes rise,

And nimbly catch the incautious flies;

The glow-worms, numerous and bright,

Illum'd the dewy dell last night.

At dusk the squalid toad was seen

Hopping and crawling o'er the green;

The whirling wind the dust obeys,

And in the rapid eddy plays;

The frog has changed his yellow vest,

And in a russet coat is drest.

Though June, the air is cold and still;

The mellow blackbird's voice is shrill.

My dog so altered in his taste,

Quits mutton bones, on grass to feast;

And see, yon rooks, how odd their flight,

They imitate the gliding kite,

And seem precipitate to fall -

As if they felt the piercing ball.

'Twill surely rain, I see with sorrow;

Our jaunt must be put off to-morrow.'

Edward Jenner

As previously mentioned, what was to become known in later years as 'the elusive pimpernel' (thanks to Baroness Orczy), did by no means elude the attention of many a distinguished bard, including the English poet Alfred Lord Tennyson (1809-1892). For several years during the second half of the nineteenth century, he was to embrace the esteemed accolade of Poet Laureate of Great Britain and Ireland. One of Tennyson's well-known poems (of which there are many) is the intensely powerful 'Maud: A Monodrama' – an explosion of emotions, from anger, bitterness and frustration . . . to passion and desire, which all the while tells a tale. Not short of controversy and grave reviews on its publication in 1855, it is both lengthy and compelling. And what is regarded as Part II of the monodrama (often played out in song) is set within a moonlit garden, and begins with the words 'Come Into The Garden Maud', where in amongst the beautiful florae and amid matters now more serene, is the pimpernel. Oblivious to unfolding events the little flower, besieged by darkness, has in all probability closed its petals . . . and is enchantingly described by Tennyson as *dozing.*

Another great poet to be seduced by the pimpernel – its delicate beauty and enthralling ability to reliably forecast rain – was John Clare (1793-1864). Fondly known as the Northamptonshire Peasant Poet, Clare dearly loved rural landscape and as a farm labourer, avidly observed the intricacies of nature. With comparisons not only to my ancestor's poetry, but that of several versifiers outlined in this book – all of whom lure the reader to a world beset with natural surroundings – much of Clare's poetry offers astonishing description. His lengthy verse entitled 'The Shepherd's Calendar' romantically describes all that surrounds him, and embraces the familiar actions of the pimpernel and its significance to the shepherd. Arranged as a calendar, which describes in detail nineteenth-century farm duties, the author alludes to the vibrant, petite prognosticator under the month of May:

> '[. .] And scarlet-starry points of flowers
>
> Pimpernel, dreading nights and showers

> Oft call'd "the Shepherd's Weather glass,"
> That sleeps till suns have dried the grass,
> Then wakes, and spreads its creeping bloom
> Till clouds or threatening shadows come –
> Then close it shuts to sleep again:
> Which weeders see, and talk of rain [. . .].'
>
> John Clare

Mr Clare was uneducated, but his misfortune did not prevent songs and poems – often regarded as works of genius – filling his mind. He became somewhat unexpectedly, yet justly renowned and in the preface to his book comprising 'The Shepherd's Calendar', he discloses feelings of gratitude:

'I have met with a success that I never dare have hoped to realize, before I met it [. . .] I leave the following Poems to speak for themselves – my hopes of success are as warm as ever.' He addresses his readers further with touching trepidations, which might be construed as heart-rending – considering the man's clearly fruitful gift: 'I hope my low station in life will not be set off as a foil against my verses, and I am sure I do not wish to bring it forward as an excuse for any imperfections that may be found in them.' Later Clare became stricken with ill health and died in an asylum. Perhaps his unease and frustration was partially instigated by the transformation of his beloved landscape due to the 'enclosures'. This practise would have undoubtedly affected both his lifestyle and identity, ultimately contributing to his decline, whilst regrettably silencing his pen forever.

Thomas Hood, the English poet, author and humourist penned numerous lines of verse during his lifetime between the years 1799 and 1845, including a delightful poem about (indeed *for*) children, given the title 'Bed-Time'. He was the son of a bookseller and publisher, and his poems were always very popular. One of Hood's most admired poems is 'I Remember, I Remember'. First published in 1844, this delightful verse recalls the author's childhood years with precise detail and wistful language. 'Bed-Time' (equally charming) tells of how all is sleeping as the day ends . . . even the pimpernel: 'Shut up for the night is the pimpernel red; / It's time little people were going to bed!'

Rosamund Marriott Watson was born in London in 1860, and during her rather brief life that was to end in 1911, loved to write about nature, gardens, their flowers and the seasons. Yet reference to the pimpernel in her poem entitled 'Vespertilia' is by no means associated with the little flower's habit of projecting an imminent rain shower – rather she is enamoured with its colour, and principally the distinctive redness. In this mysterious poem the woman, likened to the female bat (hence the title) experiences love, loss and regret. It is a melancholy tale, which not only speaks of the woman's sadness, but uses convincing and imaginative description concerning her appearance. Indeed the redness of her mouth is more colourful and intense than that of the pimpernel.

This chapter has proved to be something of a remarkable journey, and has presented an enchanting glimpse into the past.

Romantic visionaries and their poetic marvels rose to the surface, and I have learned a great deal about this delicate little flower. Scarlet in colour or otherwise, it should on no occasion be taken for granted. I hope my readers will join me as I henceforth look on it only with fondness and respect, as I remember those who chose to take up their pens and pay tribute to the pimpernel, before chronicling their accomplishments . . . for readers and potential versifiers alike.

5

'A SHEFFIELD CHARACTER

"UPSY DAISY'S" his name,
Do I know him? – the same;
He sells leather laces,
And *gives* his grimaces,
That youth with the vitreous eye;
A simpleton? Well you *jest* try,
I reckon he's *fly*.

Can he give out your bills?
Aye, and puff too your pills
With a bland-looking stare,
Like a sheep or a hare;
That youth with the crystalline eye,
With the hat that is boxy and high;
I guess he *is* spry.

Drunk, did you observe?
It's only a swerve –
A see-sawy nerv-

Ously, fidgety way;
He's a fool did you say?
Mebbe-like, with a downy-
Ish, sort of a browny-
Ish, glare from his sensitive eye,
That youth who is now plodding by;
Mistaken? you try.

Can he shout? Hear the "Grecian,"
"*Ev'ning Star,* third e-di-tion;"
Like a musical sphere,
He stuns on the ear,
That youth with the innocent eye,
Lacka*daisical,* soft-looking eye,
Bewitchingly sly.

Has a murderous stick!
It is only to flick
The rears of small boys
Who mimic his voice;
Who wink at his stoic-like eye,
That youth with the ancient-like pry
With the clerico-coat, passing by;

> Half knowing – half shy.
>
> "Upsy Daisy's" his name,
> And imply would the same
> Of a modestish charm,
> Which the same is no harm;
> That youth with piscatory eye,
> With the deep – basso tubulous cry;
> Romancing? not I.'
>
> Francis Buchanan

What initially struck me about this rhyming verse was of course, the name of the 'Sheffield Character'. . . Upsy Daisy! It became clear that Francis knew the entity with the quirky name, thus I worked on the assumption that Upsy Daisy was in fact, an authentic character. Many will be familiar with this endearing, old-fashioned term, widely used as an everyday expression – particularly as reassurance if a child has stumbled, or is being lifted by a parent. It is also commonly used when a person has dropped something, tripped, or made a mistake. Why would someone be labelled with such an alias? One instantly conjures an image of a somewhat inept fellow – perhaps presenting with a drinking habit and its subsequent effects. But as I was about to discover – nothing could be further from the truth.

Undoubtedly, great numbers of local residents were familiar with Upsy Daisy when Francis' poem of the same appellation emerged. The poem reveals that Francis believes the character is generally thought to be cleverer than some would believe. He is pulling the wool over our eyes . . . he's *fly*. The lyrics capture the reader, who yearns to learn more about the chap 'with a bland-looking stare', yet his transparent, indeed *crystalline* eye and high, boxy hat convince Francis he is spry. He *is*, despite first impressions, a rather lively character, with a jaunty personality. Upsy Daisy keeps this hidden from view, and is in all likelihood, well aware of how people regard him . . . how they judge him. Although he appears a little fidgety and slightly nervous, Upsy Daisy is ready for anything, and Francis feels he is no fool . . . in some respects he is fooling us! According to my forebear's poem, this character is suitably equipped with a loud voice – advantageous of course to a street vendor, who it would seem, sold newspapers at one time. Poets universally quote from Greek Mythology and here Francis' poem compares Upsy Daisy to the Grecian, *Stentor* – a herald of the Greek forces, known for his very loud, booming voice during the Trojan War.

The poem depicts the character's innocent, lazy eye, as 'bewitchingly sly'. Could he be a little crafty? It would not be the least bit surprising, considering this character is challenged by boys, probably on a daily basis. The reader is somewhat reassured to learn that Upsy Daisy has armed himself with a stick, which despite its 'murderous' appearance, is actually rather harmless. A target and a source of amusement is Sheffield's street character, Upsy Daisy and in Francis' poem even a cleric – though curious and vaguely aware of the fellow's misfortunes – is reluctant to intervene and passes by.

In the final verse one envisages Upsy Daisy observing the streets, constantly aware of people and his surroundings, as if searching for resources to get him through the day. Described throughout this poem as a 'youth', one assumes he is relatively young, though certainly more mature than the small boys he endures. Francis essentially tells the story of this character's daily predicament through his eyes – the eyes of Upsy Daisy that is – insomuch as they reveal his relentless ill-treatment, as well as his accomplished methods of survival. How Upsy Daisy was perceived (poetically or otherwise) raises questions concerning his state of physical and mental health, in the midst of a nineteenth-century Britain largely unaware of a vast array of conditions recognised today. Upsy Daisy's life is by no means easy. He simply wants to make a living, but what an ordeal he faces. His tormenters think they know him . . . but *do they?* Upsy Daisy's his name . . . and he's more astute than you think!

So moved was I by this fellow's battle for survival, that my quest to discover a bygone vendor of leather laces with a bona-fide name was now all but imperative. Henceforth my search began . . . and I was not disappointed. Astonishingly, photographs of the little chap are held at Sheffield's Local Studies and Archives, appearing on the website 'Picture Sheffield'. Furthermore, a most enlightening piece entitled 'Some Sheffield Characters' appeared in the *Sheffield Weekly Telegraph*, dated 8th January, 1887. The author, named 'Jotter' explains that there are certain characters in most towns who become very familiar to the general public, and 'As we go to and fro we meet characters who become so familiar to our eyes that we should miss them if they were not in their accustomed places when we passed'. He goes on to say there were many such characters in Sheffield, and he would be writing about half a dozen of them, starting with 'that highly respectable personage 'Upsy Daisy'.' I confess that such a courteous portrayal of him filled me with a sense of relief. Perhaps life was not so bad for this ill-fated chap after all. I learned that he could be seen about town any day of the week and this short man (scarcely five feet high) never really altered year after year. Often positioned on Pinstone Street in the morning, Upsy Daisy was a very familiar sight and *sound*. Seemingly a melodious sales pitch customarily emanated from him: '[. . .] as he goes along the streets you hear him crying:-

Long leather laces, a penny a pair

The more you grease them the better they'll wear

The more you pull them the sooner they tear

Long leather laces, a penny a pair.'

Whilst my forebear's poem acknowledges the hawking of leather laces, according to the newspaper article, it seems he also sold other items – be it a black-lead brush or an Aud Moor's Almanack, and at some time had worked as a Bell Hawker. We hear from 'Jotter' that Upsy Daisy '[. . .] is one of those honest chaps whose whole life is one long struggle for an existence. Many a time he told me he had been out a whole wet day, and had only taken [. . .] 9d., and perhaps a bad cold into the bargain.' Oh dear . . . life did not bode well for him. One learns that Upsy Daisy, 'a staunch teetotaller' never entered public houses to sell his wares, and liked to attend temperance meetings during the evening, and church or chapel on Sunday. Having only recently taken up the habit of smoking tobacco (which would turn out to be an unwise decision) Upsy Daisy had formerly taken the view that if God had meant for us to smoke, he would have put chimneys on top of our heads!

The 'interview' provides a wealth of information, but I longed to know more about his somewhat ridiculous, if not amusing name. And *what* – if indeed he had one – was his *real* name? Thanks to the piece in the newspaper *and* 'Picture Sheffield', all will be revealed – but why 'Upsy Daisy'? He himself volunteered the reason behind his name to the interviewer, as he recounted the tale of how it began with 'a kind action' when he went to pick up a child who had fallen on the road, as he simultaneously (and no doubt jovially) uttered the words 'Upsy Daisy', '[. . .] an' its stuck to mi all mi life.' The newspaper item ends with 'His real name is Herbert Moss, but he is much better known as 'Upsy Daisy'. So there we have it. Dear Upsy Daisy did indeed possess a more respectable name, and I wonder how many people were aware of it. Now selling laces amongst other things, (it was once newspapers, as Francis insinuated, but Herbert Moss was to lose that job by allowing his customers to accumulate credit that was never settled) and not deterred by his persecutors, Upsy Daisy earnestly endeavoured to win customers by using inventive rhyming lyrics. With some of my questions answered, I was now on the trail of Herbert Moss.

It will never be known exactly when Upsy Daisy was 'born', but Herbert Moss entered the world on 3rd February, 1847 at

Porter Street in Sheffield. His father William Moss was employed as a pen blade forger, and his mother was Ann Moss, née Jones. The couple were married on 22nd March, 1847 at the Sheffield Cathedral Church of St Peter and St Paul. The marriage took place over six weeks after the birth of Herbert. According to census records, it seems Herbert resided with his paternal grandparents, John and Elizabeth Moss as an infant, but in later years with his *maternal* grandfather, Thomas Jones. By 1871, now aged 24 years, Herbert was lodging with a family and described as a Newsroom Clerk.

I wasn't prepared for the amount of press coverage (albeit local) relating to Upsy Daisy. He was in fact something of a celebrity, and was even cited in a review of the 'Popular Men Vote' in the *Sheffield Evening Telegraph* of 14th February, 1888. It was down to members of the public to nominate Sheffield menfolk and from thousands of votes, twelve front-runners would be selected. According to the Telegraph 'Quite a number of voters have conceived the notion of blending the sublime with the ridiculous, and have seriously placed the names of the distinguished personalities selected side by side with those of the town Characters. "Upsy Daisy" seems to have not a few admirers [. . .].' But alas Sheffield Characters were ultimately excluded, and Upsy Daisy was denied the chance of a taste of good publicity – not to mention a £1 cash prize!

During earlier stretches of time, life for Daisy proved to be as eventful as it was problematic, but it seems that some were troubled by his state of affairs. On 17th April, 1868 the *Sheffield and Rotherham Independent* published a letter from a reader who wished to express concern for the welfare of Upsy Daisy.

Given the title 'A WORD FOR DAISY', it delivers a strong message:

'Through your column I wish to call the attention and make an appeal to the peaceable inhabitants of this town to protect from molestation the person of a poor but honest and hard-working youth. His name is Herbert Moss, but the rude and vulgar have given him the cognomen of "Ups-I-daisy". He is a peripatetic newsvendor. This poor fellow is beset on all hands by mobs of lads, he cannot pursue his avocation without being mocked and jeered and oftentimes molested, violent hands being laid upon him; and no longer since than to-day a mob of these unruly lads set upon him in Occupation road and beat him most unmercifully. Owing to his poverty, he cannot afford the cost of summonses for his numerous tormentors; and thinking this would be the best way of making his case known, he asked me to write this short statement of his grievance. If you can spare a corner for its insertion you will oblige.'

How encouraging to learn that at least one compassionate individual was prepared to express dismay, and raise awareness concerning Upsy Daisy's distressing treatment. Yet despite this heartfelt plea, it appears the bullying continued for poor Herbert, although three years later there was – depending on a person's viewpoint – *some* progress. A report in the *Sheffield Independent* of 15th June, 1871 proclaims: 'BAILIFF CHARGED WITH ASSAULTING "DAISY".' The defendant named George Laver, a bailiff of Sheffield was charged with assaulting Herbert Moss, a newsagent of Scotland Street. Sheffield Town Hall heard 'The complainant is popularly known as "Daisy", and [. . .] is often subjected to the most cruel insults by thoughtless boys and equally thoughtless "men", as he pursues his calling in the streets.' On this occasion he was 'bonneted' three times by Mr Laver, who crushed Upsy Daisy's hat down over his face. 'Daisy' followed him and asked how his destroyed hat would be recompensed, only to be struck once more, verbally abused, and told he would not be believed if he took his complaint to the Town Hall. But there were witnesses – who did indeed bear testimony to the honesty of Upsy Daisy, claiming that his treatment was shameful. Furthermore, 'The Chief Constable remarked that he saw the complainant in the streets almost every day, and he was as decent a man as ever lived.' The case was also reported by the *Sheffield Daily Telegraph* of 15th June, 1871 and we are informed the defendant was already in custody on a charge of stealing lard, and appeared in the dock to answer the charges of assault. Herbert was most unfortunate to encounter this individual, who it appears, was frequently questioned, charged and imprisoned for a range of crimes – earning him a place on the 'Habitual Criminals Register'. On this occasion he attacked Upsy Daisy and was '[. . .] ordered to enter into his own recognisances in £10, and find one surety in £5 to keep the peace for six months.'

Throughout the years members of the public who remembered Upsy Daisy would share their recollections by way of letters, to be published in the local press. Not surprisingly, they referred to his rhyming melodies, but also described him as always wearing a top hat adorned with pins protruding upwards. No doubt an ingenious plan to deter those with the intention of 'bonneting' him! For Herbert Moss – Upsy Daisy – call him what you will, life was a challenge. And faced with such gruelling days at work as a hawker, he surely must have dreamt of better things. Which is probably why he would regularly insert notices in local newspapers seeking alternative employment – like this one which appeared in the *Sheffield Independent* on 4th February, 1876: 'HERBERT MOSS, better known as 'Upsy Daisy' who knows the town well, would like to meet with a Situation as a Porter [. . .].' And another from the *Sheffield Daily Telegraph*, 27th June, 1888: 'UPSY DAISY (Proper name Herbert Moss) desires situation as Light Porter, Bill Distributor, or light employment [. . .].' Sadly, his efforts were likely to have been futile and undoubtedly cost more than his meagre 'budget' permitted. Were things ever to improve for him? As well as a means of escape from perpetual bullying, other employment may have provided shelter from the wet and murky streets.

As the evidence suggests, some residents of Sheffield did express concern for the way life was treating Daisy, and one or two were prompted to put pen to paper. It was time for a local pastor to step in . . . but not for the reasons you might expect. On 26th July, 1883 a genuine letter of appeal from A.S.O. Birch and addressed to the editor, appeared in the *Sheffield Daily Telegraph*:

'[. . .] "Upsy Daisy" is a well-known Sheffield Character, and I should be obliged if you would allow me, through your paper, to make an appeal on his behalf. He suffers from bronchitis, and I am trying to get sufficient money to send him to the sea-side for a fortnight. Many tradesmen and others I am sure would be glad to assist me, and the more so, when they know that Herbert Moss is a member and a very regular attender of one of the congregations of this town. I shall be glad to call for, or acknowledge any amount which may be offered.'

In response to this, in the 31st July edition of the *Sheffield Independent* there emerged an editorial explaining that 'It is proposed to place "Upsy Daisy" in a convalescent home at Southport for a few weeks, and £5 or £6 will be required for this philanthropic purpose. Mr Birch has already received £2. 5s. as a result of his appeal, and it is to be hoped that he will soon obtain the remainder of the sum necessary.'

The mysterious A.S.O. Birch – full name Armer Silver Oliver Birch – was the man behind this benevolent plan. As Superintendent of the Workmen's Mission, he was intensely aware of the toils of working men, and immersed himself in improving their welfare. Upsy Daisy was in poor health and all things considered, this wretched little man would surely benefit from some kind-hearted intervention. Regarded as a deeply compassionate man, Mr Birch was a Missionary and Social Worker, and no-one was ever turned away from the Workmen's Mission Hall. Pastor Birch was born in Rotherham in 1847 (the very same year as Herbert Moss) and educated at the Wesleyan Day School in Chesterfield. He later moved to Sheffield and became an accountant's clerk, but knowing there was Christian work to be done, turned his attention to social problems amongst the poor. He was particularly concerned to hear that the majority of men in Sheffield did not attend a place of worship – mainly because their clothes were not fit for church or chapel – and hastily organised a meeting to address this. Subsequently, a place of worship was established at the Grand Circus on Tudor Street (now Tudor Square and home to the Lyceum Theatre). Picture the scene . . . indeed this somewhat curious setting attracted hundreds, if not thousands of local citizens who, adorned in their work clothes, would quite happily sing in praise amidst the sound of roaring lions, braying donkeys and numerous other animals! When passing by this particular spot, you may henceforth find yourself powerless to resist envisioning such a spectacle! And believe it or not, the incongruous arrangement proved so popular that further sites were introduced to manage the growing numbers. Pastor Birch became known as the founder of the Workmen's Mission in Trippet Lane, which was utilised as headquarters and named Birch Hall or the Birch Hall Institution. An incisive man of business, the pastor launched his own accountancy and estate agent firm. He married Letitia Flower (what a *beautiful* name) and devoted his life to helping the poor, leaving behind a legacy few could equal. Incidentally, when Pastor Birch was born his given name was Armer Oliver Birch and considering his surname, the inclusion of 'Silver' was perhaps inspired by the silver birch tree and may have become an endearing nickname. Of course all of this is speculation, but I think it right and proper to proclaim that Pastor Birch was a kind man, who devoted his life to making the lives of others more bearable. And he was kind to Upsy Daisy. I know what you are thinking . . . did poor Daisy ever make it to the seaside? The truth is I can't provide an answer, and regrettably we may never know. Nonetheless, it is somewhat heartening to *imagine* that he did.

Though sadly, it seems rather immaterial. Upsy Daisy finally succumbed to his troublesome bronchitis on 26th April, 1890, and his age at death was registered as 42 years. He was however, born in February, 1847 and was in fact 43. At some point abandoning the streets of Sheffield (almost certainly due to his failing health), he died at the Union Workhouse. Jotter's portrayal of Daisy was precise, and though the little fellow tried in vain to improve the life bestowed upon him, fate would inevitably intervene. He made the news once more when the people of Sheffield learned from a broadcast in the *Sheffield Daily Telegraph* dated 1st May, 1890 that 'Upsy Daisy' was dead. He was referred to as 'the butt of the boys' and a figure of fun – whose real name, Herbert Moss '[. . .] was almost lost in his *Sobriquet* [. . .].' He was remembered as '[. . .] an example to all men in self-reliance, honesty, and sobriety [. . .]', who led a blameless life. Worthy yet fruitless words perhaps, for at the very end Herbert (and Upsy Daisy) were buried at the Sheffield General Cemetery in a 'public grave' with a number of other underprivileged individuals. There is no headstone, no memorial inscription . . . nothing to remind us this vulnerable yet diligent, unfortunate little soul ever was.

That is all I can tell you about Upsy Daisy, and dreams of a happier ending to his story are sadly wasted. All we can do is remember him in the commendable way he deserves. And if you ever find yourself on Pinstone Street in Sheffield – or perhaps Lady's Bridge – spare a thought for 'Daisy'. *I* will, for certain.

6

'LOVE

WHAT is Love? a thing of earth?
Tell me where it got its birth, –
Where its dulcet notes first sprung –
Where its pristine music rung?

Did it in high heaven appear?
Was't by angels wafted here?
Was it unto mankind given
As a sweet foretaste of heaven?

Did it dwell with him alone
Who created flesh and bone, –
Ere the universe was framed,
Ere the seraphim were named?

None can tell from whence it came –
Where was kindled first its flame;
'Twas, it is, and e'er will be
Mated with eternity.

'Tis a fount that ne'er shall dry;

'Tis a flower that blooms on high;

'Tis the glory of the sky,

Love will live when Death shall die.'

Francis Buchanan

Another of my favourites, Francis' poem entitled 'LOVE' is brimming with questions from the outset. My great-great-grandfather – in my undeniably, biased opinion – possessed irrefutable faith in the sentiment. Thus his rhyming verse accepts love's veracity, probing only for enlightenment concerning its foundations: where were love's mellow, soothing notes first sprung, where did the tune of love primarily ring out? The poem asks: from heaven was it wafted this way by angels? Did it reside with God, where mankind and the world we live in were created alongside a sequence of angels named the seraphim? Francis' lines acknowledge that in reality, no-one can authenticate love's origins . . . though its flame will burn for eternity. Love is likened to a fountain that will never dry, and a flower that reaches the sky.

Inevitably, I would never become acquainted with my poetic forebear. Information concerning his life and poetry was gleaned from limited inherited material, accessible genealogical records, public archives, details provided by other descendants of Francis, biographical detail published in anthologies of poetry, and of course his poems. Thanks to distant cousins, I consider myself extremely fortunate to have at my disposal, copies of two of Francis' letters. Considerably more than antiquated forms of communication – the letters provide a glimpse of his life, his character . . . his thoughts and sincerity. Whilst his poetry instils me with pride, and creates sentiments of awe and appreciation, his letters reveal heartfelt faith in love. Correspondence such as this – written at a time when the throne was occupied by Queen Victoria – are priceless to a family historian.

Letter-writing was somewhat commonplace within families during the nineteenth century. Indeed our ancestors were faced with little choice, as means of communication were limited. For some however, I believe it was not regarded as a routine duty to be abhorred – far from it. Sending and receiving letters involved sharing news and sentiments, whilst enquiring about health and prosperity, and for many was an essential part of life – particularly if loved ones no longer resided close by. In reality, the availability of suitable work frequently determined a person's place of residence.

Genealogists are often overcome with emotion on discovering letters written by their ancestors. They are a joy to behold . . . from the paper they are written on, to the ink flowing from the fountain pen, from the archaic language used, to the inimitable handwriting and the stories unveiled. Confirming or discovering locations and addresses, additional aunts, uncles, cousins, or friends of both author and recipient only enhances such enchantment. If like me, you were born at the wrong time, you will appreciate the value attached to a musty old letter – to be devoured with the knowledge that it was touched by kin of long ago. Sadly, as the twenty-first century unfolds and handwritten communication wanes, rich findings such as this will gradually diminish. Indeed they will become a thing of the past, in more ways than one.

Francis Buchanan was a poet, hence somewhat predictably he created deep and meaningful letters. Of course his wife Susannah was perhaps the chief recipient – particularly during the early days of their relationship. Naturally, I feel inclined to believe my great-great-grandmother was showered with poetic lines filled with love and romance. Alas I have no proof of this, but thanks to family member I do have in my possession, a copy of a letter written by Francis to his beloved Susannah in 1852, only months before they were married.

On reading the letter written one Friday afternoon in July, it becomes clear that Francis was troubled and concerned, as Susannah seemed unhappy – possibly because he may be going away. If this was the case he would, without hesitation cancel his plans, but time nor distance would alter the deep and sincere affection he felt towards her. His departure (if indeed it came to pass) was to be to their mutual advantage, and he would remain devoted to her and her alone. He declared his affection would withstand the vicissitudes of time and speaks of her beloved company, and the happiness it would bring to be with her always. Francis sincerely hoped he had done nothing to hurt her feelings, which was far from his intention and revealed his plans to now go for a walk in the country alone, hoping to return later in better spirits. The letter closes with further terms of endearment. He quite simply adored her.

You must forgive my decision to offer merely a synopsis of this precious correspondence between my great-great-grandparents.

Regardless of time elapsed, for me it feels like a betrayal of privacy. Such open and intense words of true love and affection, intended for the young woman Francis would spend the rest of his life with should, I think, remain close to their hearts.

What follows is a more comprehensive reproduction of a letter written by Francis decades later, and is intended for one of his sons:

> '187 Fowler Street,
>
> Sheffield
>
> 2nd January 1885

My Dear Clyde

It gave me great pleasure to read about your welfare and I sincerely hope that it may henceforth steadily progress [and wish you] every happiness in the married state and mother and I send loving wishes to our new daughter [. . .].

You would receive [. . .] 'Sparks from Sheffield Smoke' which I sent [. . .] some month or two ago. Now if you could sell a couple of hundred copies amongst your friends that would be £10 towards our [voyage]. I have still a thousand copies on hand [and] I am wishful to come to you and your adopted country if I can see the way thoroughly clear [. . .] try and sell [. . .] a lot of Books and that in itself will mitigate matters.

Sheffield is considerably altered since you left it [. . .] so much so that you would not know some parts of it [. . .] old streets turned into handsome new ones and great extensions of buildings on every side.

Your mother and I conclude in wishing you Dear Boy and your kindly looking wife all the blessings that Heaven can shower upon you both and earnestly hoping we may meet on this earth once more.

We remain your ever affectionate

Father and Mother

F. and S. Buchanan.'

Clyde (full name Charles Clyde) Buchanan settled in New South Wales, Australia with his wife – who was not only well received by Clyde's parents, but recognised as their 'daughter'. In the letter to his son, Francis referred to his own volume of poems, *Sparks from Sheffield Smoke*. How intriguing (if not slightly concerning) I found it to learn of Francis and Susannah's plans to join Clyde (if indeed a reasonable amount of books could be sold in Australia) and effectively bring about such considerable upheaval. My book reveals how Francis, injured in an accident, was forced to retire from work. This is probably what he was alluding to in declaring '[. . .] you know our circumstances are very much altered [. . .] since you left us which makes a great difference in the financial department. If I was sure of a light employment suitable to my years when I get to Australia, I would not hesitate.' Francis clearly hoped significant book sales would assist with plans for himself and his wife to travel overseas. I wonder what became of those books selected for transportation to the other side of the world. Perhaps the few to survive are balanced on top of a pile of dusty old volumes, in a quaint little book shop. A romanticised fantasy maybe . . . yet truly an unrealistic fantasy?

The letter contains references to Sheffield and how it had significantly altered since Clyde's parting. Such thought-provoking comments prompt the reader to consider my ancestors' likely response to the Sheffield of today. The letter closes with genuine terms of affection, though with traces of sadness, for it is likely parents and child did not meet again. Francis and Susannah did indeed leave Sheffield for pastures new, but their alternative choice of destination was located far from Australia. On May 15th, 1895 – ten years after the aforementioned letter to Clyde – they boarded a ship named *Southwark* at Liverpool, which was bound for Philadelphia. Another son of my great-great-grandparents, Thomas Richard Buchanan, did however join Clyde in Australia and the brothers enjoyed prosperous lives. Offspring in their multitudes remain there to this day (see preface).

Jan Buchanan is the granddaughter of Thomas Richard Buchanan, and has very kindly allowed me to publish a very profound poem composed by Francis. It is addressed to his son Thomas Richard, whom he refers to as Tom, and was probably written during the 1880s:

'TO "TOM" IN AUSTRALIA

Ah! I am happy when I walk
The dreamy woods,
And listen to sweet Nature's talk,
In solitudes;
'Tis then, when scanning heaven's blue,
My soul is wafted out to you;
The mystic voices of the trees
Lull me with anthem melodies –
Reflective moods.

I hear the Master whispering
"Have faith in me;"
Seraphic blendings softly sing
In melody.
"Oh, doubting heart, oh, doubting ear,
Cast off thy doubts – be of good cheer" –
And in the evening's holy calm
The angels carry up my psalm –
A psalm for thee.

The summer's green-emblazon'd field
Is fraught with flowers –

Earth's star-bespangled host anneal'd
By fervent hours;
Each golden floweret shining there
Hath its Originator's care
Heaven's tear-beads temper flower and weed,
Love's holy benison, indeed! –
God's special showers.

Love's unpolluted holiness
I send to thee –
Ethereal kiss, a sweet impress
Of purity;
And oh! though thou art far away,
A spirit-cherub seems to say,
"Thy prayers are heard, God's will is done,
He watches o'er thy distant son
Beyond the sea."

Sheffield   Francis Buchanan'

Catherine Ann Buchanan, the only daughter of Francis and Susannah was born in Sheffield in 1860. She married a son of the family next door to their Sheffield home at Fowler Street, in 1884. His name was George Hare, and with sights set on a new life offering employment opportunities, the newlyweds set sail for the United States of America, eventually settling in Tennessee. Indeed Nashville was to be their home, and as it transpired, the home of my great-great-grandparents. Following their voyage of 1895, the Perthshire poet and his wife would spend the final years of their lives with Catherine, her husband George, and their only son John. The Hares later relocated to Memphis, and remained in contact with relatives in Sheffield. Thereby hangs a tale . . . and in fact, a potential sequel.

Francis Buchanan

Susannah Lloyd

Charles Clyde Buchanan

Thomas Richard Buchanan

The birthplace of Francis Buchanan
Bridgend, Kinnoull Parish, Perth, Scotland

Kinnoull Hill from
the River Tay, Perth

7

'SHEFFIELD CASTLE

I.

I CANNOT hail thee, tho' thou liv'st in story, –
Thy turrets and foundations all are gone,
And nought is left to indicate thy glory
But old tradition and the beam of song.

II.

Spectre of time! where are thy relics resting?
Where are thy battlements and lordly hall?
Nor vestige here, nor stone with noble crest in,
Nor remnant of a buttress or a wall.

III.

No effigy supreme, however broken,
No tottering gable in the sunlit glow,
No grey remembrance that would be a token
To mark us back to ages long ago.

IV.

Heard'st thou of any villainly and plotting

Within thy walls? perchance 'twas all a dream;

But as thou art, and all the others rotting,

Thou might'st impart the inkling of a gleam.

V.

No doubt thou look'd quite brave when thou existed,

And frown'd defiance to the hills around;

If thou the commonwealth had not resisted,

Thou might'st have still been standing on the ground.

VI.

Thou might'st have now been looking, grim and hoary,

Down on these busy thoroughfares below;

A mould'ring moral to the ancient story

That castles, men, and all, are dust – you know.

VII.

Ah! thou would'st startle now in sheer amazement,

If thou could'st only have one transient gleam,

'Twould make thee shake from bartisan to basement,

And fancy all this hubbub was a dream.

VIII.

The whirligigs of time and men and manners
Have very nearly sent us all ajee;
Grim science now evolves his steamy banners,
And on thy dust he crests his chivalry.

IX.

'Tis like a pantomimic transformation –
The Sheffield of thy days – the Sheffield now,
Thy hamlet-town has grown a little nation,
And Time wreaths chaplets still upon its brow.'

Francis Buchanan

The castle was destroyed. In the midst of the English Civil War it was ordered by Parliament in 1646, that the castle be completely demolished. It stood proudly on a site that was probably occupied previously by a wooden house with a thatched roof of straw, known as an Anglo-Saxon longhouse. And following the Norman Conquest, a slightly more resilient Motte and Bailey Castle made of wood, earth and possibly stone.

The stone built citadel of 1270 – though grand and powerful – was mercilessly reduced to rubble. Some of the residual stone was used to partially create new buildings, but the castle was gone. Profoundly aware of Sheffield's great loss, my forebear essentially created a poem intended *for* the absent castle. His words are indeed addressed to it. The reader is likely to be moved by his poignant, atmospheric, woeful lines, and join Francis in tribute to an ancient fortress gone long ago. The verse quite simply speaks for itself, and needless commentary from his great-great-granddaughter may detract from his proficiency! In short, I believe this poem is truly magnificent. Sheffield lost its castle many moons ago . . . and during relatively recent times, my ancestor's neglected poetry was almost lost too.

Robert Eadon Leader's *Reminiscences of Old Sheffield, Its Streets and Its People* includes a cast of 'characters' – or Dramatis Personae – who verbally share details of their knowledge and experience of Sheffield. And the named contributors (both ancient and 'modern' citizens) are joined by an Antiquarian. I uncovered a most interesting piece concerning Sheffield Castle, which comprises brief details of a guided tour of the site by one such individual, Mr F. Twiss: 'Passing on to Waingate we stand on classic ground, but it is a little foreign to the tenor of our usual conversation to go so far back as to try to conjure up an imaginary picture of what the old Castle used to be. The materials for such a picture are very scanty, and all that remains to us above ground is the name.'

It is followed by an extract from *Sheffield Castle and Manor Lodge in 1582* – a paper by John Daniel Leader (brother of the above-mentioned author), which was read before the Sheffield Architecture and Archaeological Society:

' "We know that the Castle stood on rather more than four acres of land, in the angle formed by the confluence of the Sheaf and Don, that it was fairly built of stone and very spacious, and stood around an inward court and an outward court. Antiquarians may show a stone in their museums that once formed part of its fabric [. . .]. But the castle itself is nowhere to be seen. Its site is defiled with killing shambles; its court-yards, barns, stables, and servants' rooms, its state apartments and its great dining hall, have given place to shops and works, public-houses, cottages, and stables. Sheffield Castle, once so massive and strong, has become a tradition and nothing more." '

During the twentieth century a number of exploratory digs took place on and around the former site of Sheffield Castle. They uncovered various artefacts, and evidence of the structure and its surroundings. An excavation is currently underway, with anticipations of unveiling more of the castle's ruins. The project involves various interested parties, whose objectives are to establish levels of preservation from both the thirteenth-century castle, and industrial development which occurred much later. Any remains of the thirteenth century castle were (catastrophically, some might say) completely demolished during the seventeenth and eighteenth centuries. Nineteenth-century steelworks and a market hall emerged, and later the twentieth-century Castle Market. The excavations have always been largely concerned with market sites, and their historical importance.

Like other voluntary groups referred to in this book, Friends of Sheffield Castle makes its interest and objectives known, and warmly welcomes new members. The group aims to protect and promote the archaeological site and the castle's history, and in doing so works alongside a number of local, regional and national organisations. Certain members of the group have formed a management committee, which offers a variety of valuable skills. Organised events including exhibitions, fairs, festivals, and meetings encourage members of the public to become involved. The group is in fact a charity, and Sir Tony Robinson has agreed to become a patron. Further information relating to the group of 'Friends' and membership, the castle's history, and the twenty-first century excavation can be found by visiting the website at friendsofsheffieldcastle.org.uk

It seems Francis was not alone in expressing sentiments of regret and wonder concerning Sheffield's lost castle. During the nineteenth century Edward Major lived and worked in Sheffield for a number of years. He was a hairdresser, and when I stumbled upon one of his newspaper advertisements, sharing it with my readers was to prove irresistible. For this (being a precise reproduction) is what appeared in the *Sheffield Daily Telegraph* of 21st March, 1859:

'ANCIENT AND MODERN SHEFFIELD:

CASTLE-HILL AND CASTLE-COURT.

In looking around is there more famous ground –

Where historical facts of past ages abound

To tell of Old Sheffield? – the chief to be found
Is CASTLE-HILL.
Where stood the old Lord of Hallamshire Hall?
Where did Cardinal Wolsey's dire sickness befal?
And Mary of Scotland's confinement appal?
On CASTLE-HILL.
Where lived the first Patrons of Cutlery skill –
The Lords of the Soil – of the Wheel – of the Mill –
Where the Rich and (at times) the Poor had their fill?
On CASTLE-HILL.
But how changed are the scenes since the Castle has gone!
And COMMERCE has reared a great shrine of its own –
The centre of which, all admit – everyone –
Is CASTLE-COURT.
MAJOR'S CENTRAL SALOON is the gem of the day –
There *Nature* and *Art* are combined to display
How *Pleasure* in *Business* carries the sway
In CASTLE-COURT.
There Music and Painting and Sculpture are found,
To arrest the attention of Patrons profound,
While the Hairdresser's skill and judgement redound
To CASTLE-COURT.
If in Cutting or Curling, Perfuming Shampooing,

> In first Style of Art you want your Hair doing,
>
> For Fashion and Comfort – where everyone's going –
>
> Is CASTLE-COURT.
>
> MAJOR'S CENTRAL SALOON,
>
> CASTLE-COURT, SHEFFIELD.'

The 'saloon' situated on 'Castle-Court' was cleverly promoted by means of rhyming verse incorporating local history, and mention of the lost castle. Like Francis' poem, Major's words bewail its loss, and point out that the site is considerably altered. There is mention of 'Mary of Scotland's confinement' in Major's verse, and of course on the website relating to Friends of Sheffield Castle. For further information please see my chapter entitled Sheffield Manor, which includes my Scottish forebear's poem, and details of a local author's book about the queen's imprisonment. The 'creative' hairdresser succeeded in producing a rather impressive rhyme cum advertisement! The unusual newspaper announcement possibly brought about prosperity, for the premises were newly refurbished and began to provide bathing facilities. During that time (the early 1860s) Edward Major and his wife Elizabeth resided at Parkwood Springs (see poem and chapter entitled 'Parkwood Hill').

Almost one hundred years ago – 9th August, 1924 to be precise – local residents' recollections of Castle-Court during the nineteenth century were published in the *Sheffield Daily Telegraph*. Edward Major was remembered as a popular barber, and the enterprising fellow (who was incidentally, born in

Doncaster) liked to display a large painting of Conisbrough Castle in his Tonsorium. Francis Buchanan, though relatively new to Sheffield, may quite possibly have called in for a spruce up. And the ensuing exchange concerning the remarkable painting (and perhaps other interesting works of art, as Major's rhyme suggests) undoubtedly led to a wholehearted discussion relating to another castle. A castle long lost.

8

'LINES WRITTEN IN ECCLESALL CHURCHYARD,

January, 1881

Stern Winter, hail! I love thy darkling days,
Thy boisterous turbulence, and angry glooms;
And while I listen to thy mournful lays,
Amidst the loneness of these sacred tombs,
I fancy, as thy song tunes thro' the aisle,
With its long cadenc'd wail and shrilly tone,
That down beneath that lettered floor, the while,
The dead are listening to thy gusty moan.
Yon ridgy upland's coverlet of snow
Is dancing to the music of the wind,
While swirling drifts are sweeping down below,
And swathing up the doorway of the hind.
The trees are jewelled o'er with glittering white,
Like fretted coral from the Indian sea;
And in the valley, and upon the height,
Thy beauty dazzles with its purity.
Ah! it is gladsome, in the bracing morn,

> To breast the hill and face thy icy breeze;
> Thy angry gusts laugh those to mocking scorn
> Who watch their freaks in idleness and ease.
> I would be free, as thou art, Winter, free,
> Prince dominant, o'er every plain and hill;
> Thy sister Summer smiles more joyously,
> But thou dost rule in majesty of will.'
>
> Francis Buchanan

With the poem beside me as I write, during the chilly month of January more than a century later, the garden outside is coated in frost and an assortment of ravenous birds are eagerly squabbling over their dependable feeders. And in my mind's eye there becomes visible an image of my great-great-grandfather in the churchyard. He is calm and contented, perhaps with writing materials to hand as he absorbs the ambiance, and is possibly seated on a fence, or a wall . . . a step, a tombstone. The idyllic background which serves as the title of this atmospheric and somewhat theatrical poem is the burial ground of Ecclesall's ancient place of worship, known as All Saints. The Grade II listed building of the eighteenth, nineteenth and twentieth centuries combined, began life considerably earlier, as a humble medieval chapel. Imbued with history, the site was to undergo numerous changes involving demolition, restoration and enhancement, resulting in what the Sheffield of today has become accustomed to.

Despite inevitable changes through the years, I find it by no means challenging to envisage Francis' surroundings as he composed his verse, for I have been there. I have seen the churchyard's beckoning entrance, the aged loyal trees, the tombstones and monuments – unremittingly shielded by the fine-looking church. Mystery surrounds only Francis' precise choice of location, and as my curiosity prevails, I cannot help but wonder which corner of the churchyard played host to a writer's compulsion. But as I walked in his footsteps, simply knowing he had been there would suffice.

Such an entrancing experience does raise goose bumps, but is not solely responsible for bringing me closer to my forefather . . . for I need only recite his poetry. Francis and I have much in common – whether it be the freedom of vast open spaces, complemented by fresh air and rural scenery, enigmatic woodland, or splendid views. But only on becoming acquainted with 'Lines Written in Ecclesall Churchyard' did I learn that he too relished 'the bracing morn' as he faced the icy breeze of winter. I feel sure he would gaze at clouds, rejoice at the sight of a spectacular sunrise, and muse philosophically, as by twilight the sun set. Our mutual adoration (no other word for it) of literature is especially important to me. At times I too have dabbled with poetry, and love to write – a flair most likely inherited, for which I am justly indebted, though for him, the gift of creating the written word in poetic form was undoubtedly essential to his soul.

My desire for further information relating to the history of All Saints led me to Margaret Naylor – a member of the church, who researches the history of both church and churchyard. What is more, as chairman of Ecclesall Local History Society her extensive knowledge of the area is invaluable. Margaret, clearly interested in my project, presented me with an informative booklet – *ALL SAINTS, ECCLESALL, A BRIEF HISTORY AND GUIDE.* Written by her some years ago, it contains a wealth of historical information, which explains the origins, growth and development of this house of worship, as well as the significance of memorials, woodcarvings and tablets in and around it.

I learned how it all began with The Manor Chapel of the early thirteenth century, when no village of Ecclesall existed – it simply being one of the sub-manors created out of the great manor of Hallam. Margaret explains how it was the duty of the lord of the manor to provide churches and common land, and regular attendance at the parish church in Sheffield (now the Cathedral) was not possible due to the distance between the hamlets. Thus a chapel of ease was built by Ralph de Ecclesall during the thirteenth century, which was actually situated near the manor house at Silver Hill, and not on the site we know today. A canon of Beauchief Abbey climbed the knoll each day in order to celebrate mass at the chapel, and say the Lord's Prayer for departed souls, including the soul of Ralph de Ecclesall's father. He did this in return for the corn mill at Millhouses. The Abbey, founded in 1183 would be dissolved by Henry VIII in 1536, and this of course resulted in the closure of the modest manor chapel, which sadly fell into disrepair and remained closed for many years. It was restored in 1622 by the Vicar of Sheffield, Thomas Toller, and the town's Puritans. Toller's son-in-law, Edward Hunt was appointed as the first minister of Ecclesall.

The eighteenth century would see significant development of Ecclesall, largely due to the opening of the turnpike road from Sheffield to Manchester, and the Ecclesall Parliamentary Enclosures, which took place between 1779 and 1788 when building began on the moor. During the 1780s the chapel became inadequate for Ecclesall's growing population, thus Enclosure Commissioners were appointed to allot the available land and some was set aside for a burial ground and a new chapel. The foundation stone of the building which stands today was laid on 27th June, 1787 on the Carter Knoll and opened for worship in December, 1788. It was consecrated in August, 1789 as a chapel of ease under the Parish Church of Sheffield. Further significant changes took place during the nineteenth century, when in 1843 Ecclesall became part of the borough of Sheffield and its church underwent immense alterations, whilst becoming 'aesthetic' rather than 'utilitarian'.

In 1849 Ecclesall became a parish, and by the early twentieth century – amid an increasing population – it was no longer regarded as rural, and further alterations would take place. Indeed a foundation stone for the new East End of the church was laid by Lady Stephenson on 27th June, 1907. The event was reported in the 28th June edition of the *Sheffield Daily Telegraph*:

'The Bishop of SHEFFIELD said they were gathered on a historic occasion. A hundred and twenty years ago that day, possibly that very afternoon of June 27th, 1787, there was being laid the foundation-stone of that Church, of which there was to be laid the extension that afternoon. A hundred and twenty years was a long time to look back, and it was rather difficult to imagine the scene. One of the most eminent Churchmen of

Sheffield, the late Sir Henry Stephenson, said of Ecclesall Church that it was not worthy of the Churchmanship of Sheffield. They were now doing something to make it worthy of that Churchmanship [. . .]. The foundation stone was laid by [Sir Henry Stephenson's widow], Lady Stephenson, to whom there was presented for the purpose a handsome silver trowel, suitably engraved, and a polished wood mallet.'

Evidently the new foundation stone was laid in 1907, and the extension unveiled. Two world wars would come to pass, and Sheffield was significantly affected by the Blitz in 1940, yet Ecclesall's church escaped potential damage and continued to receive its ever faithful congregation. This is perhaps a fitting moment to pay tribute to those who perished in the Sheffield Blitz, and one of Francis Buchanan's granddaughters and her husband were among them.

It was possibly the removal of the galleries in 1907 that resulted in the nave roof becoming unstable by the 1960s, but a new one was swiftly installed. The late 1990s saw extensive modernisation to the church building, making it more practical and more welcoming – especially to families, which is how the church remains to this day. The churchyard meanwhile – partly incorporating the original land granted during the late eighteenth century, but also land acquired later – amounts to nine acres of grassland and burial ground. It was here that Margaret and I meandered among burial sites sprinkled with primroses, all the while deliberating potentially appropriate spots for an avid poet such as Francis to be positioned with pen in readiness. The site is much altered since the late nineteenth-century, and on the occasion of Francis' visit, this hill upon high was in the midst of winter, which was not overlooked.

For Francis perhaps it was a familiar hideout – the church, with terrain he knew and loved – or a favourite stroll. The vicar of 1881, the Rev. George Sandford, may have been known to my great-great-grandfather. It is perhaps not beyond the boundaries of possibility to suppose that Francis and his family attended services or ceremonies held by Sheffield's oldest clergyman. With still many years ahead of him, this popular and highly respected vicar of Ecclesall was to hold the position until only death would command his retirement in September 1898, by which time Reverend Sandford had reached his 82nd year.

Francis was inspired by winter; and the poem – though powerful – requires minimal analysis or explanation. The setting intensifies his words, for only an historic and serene spot such as this might enthuse a poet to describe seasonal events and surroundings so proficiently. The boisterous turbulence, 'the loneness of the sacred tombs' and the lettered floor are rhythmically defined, as he imagines the dead beneath are listening all the while to the moan of the gusty wind. And as the wafting snow dances to the music of the wind, the reader catches its high-pitched wail.

With a watchful eye on the weather as the seasons inevitably changed, maybe Francis regularly visited the churchyard, and rhyme would flow effortlessly from his pen. In later years the burial ground was to become the final resting place of one of Francis' beloved sons, David Lloyd Buchanan – though sadly the plot, devoid of a memorial stone, bears no inscription. He was interred there in 1927, and his wife Emily Julia in 1934. By then Francis had long since departed this life, but his ode to the harsh, yet glistening winter of 1881 lives on . . . as does Ecclesall Churchyard.

As a final point . . .

My forebear's highly atmospheric verse written in Ecclesall Churchyard does not overlook the bracing weather, as my own words intimated. But that was before I discovered mid-January, 1881 was one of the coldest episodes on record. Indeed the poem's opening line implies it was a 'Stern winter'. Parts of England endured bitterly cold temperatures, frost, ice, heavy snow, blizzards, and widespread disruption. Nonetheless, as the *Sheffield Daily Telegraph* of 17th January reported, some local residents made the best of it:

'THE SEVERE WEATHER
SHEFFIELD

On Saturday and yesterday the frost was as severe as ever, and skaters had a lively time of it. Merchants who deal in skates, filled their windows with these articles, for which there was a brisk demand.

Yesterday Little London dam was, in local phraseology, "a sight." Several thousand people were on the ice or by its margin; and skaters and spectators made up a crowd for whom vendors of roast potatoes, cocoa and coffee, oranges, apples, and the inevitable "lemon drops," catered most successfully.

People of all ages and sizes, as well as of both sexes, from the servant girl to the uniformed representatives of our brave defenders, cut out stars and figure 8's, or came to grief in the attempt [. . .].'

Little London dam is mentioned in *The Land We Live In – A Pictorial and Literary Sketch-book of the British Empire*, published in 1849 by George Knight, London. The backdrop and the dam itself are portrayed as pleasing to the eye: 'One of the most picturesque roads from Norton to Sheffield is Derbyshire Lane. The view [. . .] descending into the valley of the Sheaf is surprisingly beautiful. At the foot of Meersbrook-house is a fine sheet of water, called Little London dam.' The water occupied a more than adequate spot between the River Sheaf and the railway line – adequate that is, for skaters. Indeed during the winter months large numbers of people would flock to the frozen dam with skates at the ready. Local newspapers promoted the skating events, which took place for many years and rather astonishingly, it was customary to hold cricket matches on the very same ice.

Later amid swiftly changing times, the surrounding area became industrial, and the popular dam was eventually filled in during the 1970s, but a painting of the dam survives, making it possible to appreciate the site. Christopher Thomson (1799-1871) captured the 'fine sheet of water' and its surroundings beautifully, and his work can be viewed online at Art UK. If one were to follow the road which sits nearby today (Little London Road in actual fact) it would lead to a sizeable car park surrounded by a range of establishments. And challenging as it may be, once a vision of the fine-looking long-forgotten, ice-covered dam is firmly visible, it might just be possible to make out distant echoes of the gliding click-clack of skates, amid excited laughter and screams of delight.

It seems Francis purposely dated his poem written in Ecclesall Churchyard, January, 1881. Perhaps he felt certain many would remember the month, the year . . . the harsh winter weather. His call on the churchyard and the ensuing poem likely occurred once open-air conditions were less severe. Be that as it may, when unable to bear the enduring coldness any longer, (despite presumably being clad in warm clothing) and possibly distracted by compelling flashes of inspiration concerning the preceding weeks – he may have returned home to record the swiftly evolving stanzas. Francis may have returned home to create 'King Frost'.

9

'KING FROST

THE King has condescended
To visit us again;
And from his throne, in the far-north zone,
His icy breath to the south hath blown,
To spread his ermine train.

He shakes his hoary ringlets,
And laughs his hoarse guffaw;
And over the sea, in savage glee,
On the whirl of the north wind's majesty,
He rides in his mighty awe.

His eyes are red and bleary,
His brow is cold and white,
And his cheeks puff out, with a roar and a rout,
As he tosses the blinding snows about,
In his madness of delight.

He sings his shrillest trebles,

And his hollow basses groan,
Over the vane of the church's fane;
And, hark! you can hear thro' the streets again,
His full-pitch'd baritone.

He shivers with his rattle,
The iron-staunchion'd pier;
And he laughs outright, at the baffled might
Of the engine hissing its steamy spite,
Up thro' his ten-feet drifts of white,
When no man's help is near.

He hurls his foamy thunder,
High on the rumbling beach;
And to anxious friends, the death-shriek he sends
On his roaring blast, as the stout ship rends
Almost within their reach.

He whirls around the mountain,
And howls adown the dell;
And beneath his heap, he buries the sheep,
Down in the snow-drift, huddled and deep,
On the lonely heather fell.

He wreathes thro' his snorting nostril
His misty rimes of grey;
And he shouts, ho, ho! as unfortunates go
Into the brooklet's overflow,
That they thought was far away.

He stuns the lordly mansion,
And shakes the lofty hall;
And the lowly cot, with its greenwood plot,
'Mid the frosted brake is not forgot,
In his dire carnival.

He racks the frames of thousands,
And his ally, Death, is near;
To help with a will, to puzzle the skill
Of the potent leech and the potent pill,
And over the beds of the weak and ill,
They gibber and laugh and jeer.

He binds with glassy fetters,
Like a Kaizer's bonds, as strong,
The onward glow of the river's flow,

And the trees like the branching coral grow,
And 'tis silence all, above and below,
For he's froze the songster's song.

Go back to the North, thou tyrant,
To thy ancient waste of glooms;
Take thy glittering chains, and thy frozen rains,
And thy catalogue of aches and pains,
Back to thy arctic-outpost domains,
Where nought but weirdness blooms.'

Francis Buchanan

Much of this poem has been written in limerick form. Of the twelve verses a typical example is a five-line stanza – a verse essentially defined as a quintain, and on occasion referred to as a quintet – the limerick being the most recognised case in point. Such verse requires the author to ensure the rhyming of specific lines – usually the first, second and fifth, but also lines three and four. However, there is always room for disparity and for sure, a poet is armed with autonomy concerning choice of words, their well-defined message and the length and style of a verse. As master of his own creations, Francis was perfectly entitled to form a poem in the style of his choosing, with verses of varied length and rhyming arrangements to his liking. In fact a limerick is generally short and frequently humorous, if not nonsensical. It is the kind of verse that effortlessly flows from the pen with remarkable speed to thenceforth be cited in a parallel fashion, *and* the kind of verse to be based upon rude comedy, which has widely been in circulation for ever and a day! As to the origins of the limerick, several notions exist and some believe it was dreamt up in either the city or the county of Limerick in Ireland, but nothing is known for certain.

Thus 'King Frost' is loosely based on limerick form. Timeworn strategies concerning the layout and methodical use of rhyme have narrowly been observed, and the poem unquestionably comprises humour. There are however, slightly serious undercurrents, which although principally at the forefront have nonetheless, been somewhat camouflaged by the introduction of descriptive and atmospheric content using both simple and impressive language, rhythm and humour – all of which strongly stir the imagination. A select few lines of 'King Frost' would undoubtedly stir the imagination of a child, and though the date it was written is unknown, perhaps Francis recited some of the lines to his children – wondrous words only to be relished with a thrilling mixture of delight and fear! It is of course very likely my great-great-grandfather composed verse specifically for his children, and I imagine him spending time with them as he reads aloud from the written word, spontaneously delivers new lines, or simply recounts verse from memory. No matter which method Francis adopted in conveying his poetry, such gatherings were undoubtedly vibrant and enjoyable for all concerned. And as Francis delved into the past, his own family may have eagerly awaited intriguing tales of Scotland and all that shaped their father's life, perhaps accompanied by lyrics from his Scottish counterparts – only complementing those from his own pen.

It is worth noting that skilfully rhyming and rhythmical poetry is often humorous, entertaining and enlightening – as well as a time-filling guaranteed method of distraction concerning youngsters! Being fortunate enough to have been on the receiving end of some truly wonderful poetry from a very young age, I for one bear testament to just how valuable and joyous the poetic form of literature can be. Early introduction often leads to a lifelong love of poetry and reading, which in turn steers the way to an inherent desire to write, and possibly become an author.

The author in this instance is Francis Buchanan, and in his Sheffield collection are two poems concerning wintertime. 'King Frost' however, is the antithesis of 'Lines Written in Ecclesall Churchyard', which tells of 'trees . . . jewelled o'er with glittering white'. The serene and beautiful surroundings are enhanced by the white, crisp, yet delicate coating of frost. All in all it displays elements of a pleasant and inspiring winter's day. 'King Frost' on the other hand, is a clearly unwelcome visitor – *himself* being a truly severe onset of winter, equipped with all the usual nasty conditions. The consequences of such chaos bring glee and merriment to the presiding King, who stridently laughs at his ill-fated prey. This is fundamentally, a rather unpleasant poem I suppose, for it portrays (without restraint) the huge and hostile impact of adverse weather conditions . . . and neither man nor beast is safe.

This forbidding account actually brings a chill to anyone reading it! Rich with captivating atmosphere, its use of description and powerful expression is remarkable. Yet despite its almost pulsating, vibrant energy and tragic connotations, there is room for fun and amusement. And as I mentioned earlier, it is a poem that strongly stirs one's imagination. It is therefore by no means challenging for a reader (of any age) to envisage almost cartoon-like images of a roaring and guffawing angry presence, as it brings about unwarranted levels of distress and destruction. Arguably, what Francis describes brings to mind a huge and terrifying figure with an unfavourable face, a long and unruly wizard-like silvery mane, and eyes which express sheer gratification – only to be enhanced by highly animated, vicious and harmful deeds! The author of this poem succeeded without question in ensuring his readers would fully appreciate that King Frost is none other than a menace!

First-hand experience of harsh winter weather and the disagreeable memories it shaped, may have provided Francis with inspiration. I feel quite certain he endured several challenging King Frost episodes during his years in Scotland. Indeed wintertime in Yorkshire proved to be equally unkind at times. The callous, and dare I say it . . . *icy* character he created in order to articulate the perils of bitterly cold, wintry weather and all it yields, demanded potent imagination and wonderful use of evocative language. I believe (and hope you agree) in this Francis triumphed, and more than one hundred years later, right before your eyes is the masterpiece that is 'King Frost'. What further proof do you need . . ?

10

'SHEFFIELD'S SCENERY
THE VALLEY OF THE DON A.D. 1580

IT gives a pleasure thus to dream
And ponder on the silent past,
In refluence to track the stream
That time hath overcast:
When Hope's dimm'd Orb hath almost set,
Then memory soothes the soul's regret.

Ah, Fancy, bear me on thy wing
Back o'er the ruins of the past,
And as a bird mid'st blossoming
Finds food and rest at last;
So tho' around be desert here,
Thy oasis is fair and clear.

'Twas on a balmy morn of June –
(The empress of the vernal year) –
When in meridian, Nature's tune
Trills loud upon the ear,

And flowers all their sweetness fling
Upon the Summer's quivering wing.

I stood upon a green-topp'd height,
O'ershadowing the limpid Don,
With Fancy borne in mystic flight
Three centuries agone;
Now where thou see'st that mart beneath,
Was then a forest bound by heath.

The pheasant and the thrush were there,
And water lilies gem'd the sheen,
Thatching the troutlet's sylvan lair
With crowning leaves of green;
And o'er the ripples, plashing by
Glanc'd in his gold the dragon fly.

In bush and brake the linnet loud
Caroll'd his song in ecstasy,
And from the morning's amber cloud
The lark sent his reply;
And all the quire in lusty glee
Thrill'd wood and wild with minstrelsy.

Great oaks and elms were here supreme,
And winding thro' the wooded plain,
The waters kiss'd the trembling beam
And flash'd it up again,
In circlet rays a hundred-fold
Up to the roof of blue and gold.

The hill-encircled valley lay
In peaceful beauty; all was love,
As if God thro' his gate of day
Breath'd glory from above;
The joy there was as gentle rain
Refreshing earth with heaven again.

Far as my eye could reach, the scene
Was flower and foliage, slope and mound,
A wavy majesty of green,
With dazzling sunshine crown'd;
And graceful deer and tripping hare
Were fearless in the joyance there.

The beauty had a rapturous charm,

A charm that kill'd to give new breath,
As a brave spirit scoffs the arm,
And triumphs over death:
Such had that Eden over me,
So blissful was its purity.

I saw a little cottage there
Embosomed in its belt of trees;
The blossoms of the plum and pear
Decoy'd the passing breeze,
And from its porch the rose's bloom
Enamour'd morn with its perfume.

The river played its sweetest tune
Upon the reeds beneath the bank,
And flowers in the idle noon
The fairy music drank;
While corded elms and chestnuts tall
Sent down a song as musical.

There comes a hidden holiness
In whispers of the breeze along,
Soft trills as if celestial bliss

Was echoing Heaven's song –
Ah! surely such strange power is given
To draw us nearer unto Heaven.

Again, in dreamy listlessness,
Just as the sun his zenith gain'd,
When shade was nearly shadowless
And nature's silence reign'd –
Almost as hush'd as night would be
Beneath her purple canopy.

I looked, and saw a castle grim,
Its gloomy grandeur, cold and grey,
(Making the noonday haze look dim)
In turreted array;
Upstanding like a menace there,
Amidst the beautiful and fair.

The Don flowed with a darker wave,
As it embraced the chilling gloom;
The waters slower seem'd to lave
The basement of a mighty tomb:
Their brawl was check'd, their song less free,

The stoney marge more shadowy.

And so it was: it seem'd to me
As if a blackness rear'd between
The glow of bright tranquillity
And night's more dubious sheen;
And the dusk-shadows frown'd below,
As if sweet hope was dimm'd with woe.

E'en so it was: the portals there
Frown'd dismal in the summer day;
The banner trail'd from middle air,
'Shamed of it gaiety –
In those dark towers a lovely queen
Was dreaming over what she's been.

The warder from the turret grim
Look'd down on Don's erratic flow,
His hour of wardship was to him
No more than lagging slow;
But hours to her were as long years,
Furrow'd with grief, and drench'd with tears.

The very breeze was slowly sighing,
　Around the Talbots' hoary pile;
The darken'd day was now denying
　Its noon-accustom'd smile;
Sleek Perfidy, with her pois'nous breath,
　Had double-barb'd the shaft of death.

Ah, me! And where are they, I said –
　The Stuart and the Tudor too?
The headless queen – the Royal Maid,
Whose lips blanch'd as the missive sped,
　Graved with the words "I slew."
　Ah, where are they? quoth Reverie,
　　And Echo said, ah, me!

And where are all the warrior-men?
　Where all the fortresses of old?
Where the high emprise that was then
　Earn'd neath the banner's fold?
Where is the wisdom? grey-beards cry;
"Life's but a dream," is Death's reply,
　I wake ye when ye die.'

　　　　　Francis Buchanan

joyance – a joyous feeling or festivity, marge – border, margin, edge, quoth – said

Set amongst the pages of *Sparks from Sheffield Smoke* (1882) are two poems penned by Francis, and relating to the Valley of the Don – this being the River Don's neighbouring expanse across the Pennines and South Yorkshire. The two verses appear independently – indeed an additional poem can be found sandwiched between 'The Valley of the Don A.D. 1580', and 'The Valley of the Don A.D. 1882.' They are however, noticeably linked, and each poem proclaims a clear, powerful message – only to be described as partially alive with echoes of the past, yet wholly awash with loss, displeasure and passion. Francis forlornly reflects on the valley of the sixteenth century, which he claims was prized for its profuse natural surroundings, thriving wildlife, scenes of splendour and almost inaudible stillness. Yet three hundred years had elapsed when my great-great-grandfather composed with meaningfulness, two heartfelt poems portraying a principled account of significant transformation and detriment. His words reveal all he had learned from history, and how he envisaged the terrain by the River Don in the year 1580. Three centuries later, Francis' impassioned thoughts and receptive pen responded fervently to what appeared before them. What transpired was 'The Valley of the Don A.D. 1882', and what it *interprets* is a deeply conflicting poetic narrative, which rather more mildly reflects on the peace and beauty of long ago, whilst shifting the focus to the conflicting scenes of the late nineteenth century with a sense of forfeiture, sorrow and regret.

Applauded by some and reviled by others, change on a colossal scale had befallen the Valley of the Don . . . solely at the hands of man. In *my* edition of *Sparks from Sheffield Smoke*, Francis' poems relating to the spoiled valley have purposely not been separated, for I would like my . . . *our* readers to become immersed in the sheer intensity of the preliminary changing times – witnessed by my forebear almost 150 years ago. This was just the beginning, and as the two poems become one, you will find yourself confronted with a frank and formidable account concerning authentic occurrences and localities. Francis proclaimed how pleasurable it was to ponder the silent past of the valley adjoining the River Don. He pointedly gave one of the poems a general title – 'Sheffield's Scenery'. On balance, it appears this is the case in question. My forebear believed the silence and magnificent backdrop within the valley had vanished amid the ravages of time, and clearly asserted his reasoning through poetic verse. He observed how the dense forest of bygone times had been replaced by a market – a scene unbefitting for thriving great oaks and elms, flowing streams, and wildlife. It was once a valley encircled by hills, and captured by serene beauty – rich with raw and striking colour. What stood amid Sheffield's scenery in the year 1580 was its castle, and within its walls was imprisoned the intensely anxious Queen of Scotland. Agreeable as it was, Francis' vision of the Valley of the Don's Elizabethan terrain was overshadowed by impending doom. My Scottish forebear's poetry speaks of Mary Queen of Scots' confinement once more, yet both Queen and castle had long since perished by 1882.

The oncoming changes foretold in Francis' candid verse have overwhelmingly come to pass. Significant transformation to the region by the River Don was addressed by way of a poetic account of what he saw before him in 1882 . . . and the words cascaded from the pen of a man before his time. As a twenty-first-century successor of Francis, I lost count of the number of times I read with astonishment (and with a shiver down my spine), lines which clearly foresee the repercussions of man's evolution . . . man's intervention. The words were written with a huge sense of foreboding loss, regret, concern, and fear for what he realised was happening in *his* lifetime . . . and fear concerning the future. Francis' words convey a very insightful message – particularly in view of the current climate, (*climate* being the operative word, you understand!) – whilst not overlooking the woeful certainty that events of the nineteenth century were just the beginning. Thus both poems relating to the Valley of The Don, created at the hand of my shrewd ancestor, are fitting beyond measure. Of course Francis was a poet. He was an individual with gargantuan observation skills, boundless imagination, and sentiment.

On 10th January, 1884 the *Sheffield Independent* was to encapsulate such portrayals by referring to a piece about Mr F Buchanan of Sheffield, which had appeared in the *Glasgow Weekly News*: 'Mr Buchanan is evidently of a reflective and philosophic turn of mind. He loves to muse on things past and present, and draws a moral from some hard and stony subjects [. . .]. Like all true poets, he has a keen eye for the beauties of nature, and he revels in descriptions of natural scenery [. . .].' Without question this was Francis in a nutshell, for all the while he mournfully pondered how the beautiful scenes of Sheffield's valleys continued to fade, he mused over 'what is grasping man [. . .] who lays his plans and builds his towers / Who speculates with greedy eye / The gains of future hours.' He deliberated how the greed of mankind brought with it factory smoke, sulphurous fumes and putrid vapours, when once the land was occupied merely by woodland, wildlife and the trill of bird. And though the River Don continued to flow, its shores were largely bereft of enchantment. As ever, Francis skilfully ensured his words rhymed, whilst creating for his readers a cumulative effect.

I think all that remains concerning 'The Valley of The Don, A.D. 1882' is to ask oneself whatever would be going through Francis' mind if he were present on this earth today? Note the poem's emphasis on 'Time', and in view of that I will leave you with some final words from Francis' verse, as it contemplates the activities of man: 'Mistakes he (so it seems to me) / Brief time, for an eternity [. . .] On Self-adhering to his store, / (As if earth was an evermore,)'. Food for thought, to be sure.

'THE VALLEY OF THE DON A.D. 1882

THE sun was coursing to the west,

And all his golden path was drest

With curling flakes of yellow guise

That floated o-er the burnish'd skies,

And thro' the gauzy screen his ray

Intensified the deep'ning gray,

Throwing long shadows o-er the plain,

From factory and sacred fane;

And over all the vale of Don,
From the hill-bounded horizon,
A fan-like glow was spread,
As if God threw a crimson pall
Adown on things terrestrial,
To vouch hope was not dead.
I gazed, and as I gazed methought
That wisdom was not dearly bought,
If from this wooded slope mine eye
Had power to view this galaxy –
Had power to grasp the glory given,
And soul enough to rise to heaven,
In wafted prayer, for blessings lent,
Up to the great Beneficent.

Out o'er the prospect far and near
My vision dwelt on wood and weir –
On wrinkled hills and dells between,
And fallows brown and meadows green;
On rocks, and hollows deep in shade
That long ago old waters made,
In epochs yet before the blow
Of death gave life to life below:

Erst when this varied culture then
Was jumbled waste of sea and fen,
Before Time 'gan to count his years,
Or distribute his smiles and tears.

An age there was, years long ago,
When tangled forest stretch'd below
In wavy tracks of brown and green,
With here and there a tower between,
In yonder valley, where you see
The belching smoke of factory,
Twisting its pillar dense and black
Up into cloudland's azure track,
Blotching the ether's concave sea
With murky wreaths of industry;
Where you can faintly hear the steam
Keep time – with thud and flashing gleam –
As with a calculating blow
The engine shapes the mass below,
And from the roof the belted wheel
Makes eye to quail and brain to reel;
Where brawny men, seen by the flashes,
Work, sweat, and toil, 'mid cracks and crashes,

And breathe the sulphurous fumes withal,
And those in Hades' capital,
Who, we are told, roast in the States
Presided over by the Fates.
Who would believe that heretofore
This clutter was a breezy moor,
Clothed with the purple heather bell,
Where grouse and pheasant loved to dwell?
And where, far from the smoky loom,
The foliage made the only gloom,
And all the disagreement heard
Was whirr of partridge – song of bird,
And where the stag from covert trees
Sniff'd freedom in the scented breeze,
And shook his horns in lofty pride
As, wind-shod, sped he far and wide.
The Don still winds his sluggish stream,
Still glitters in the western beam,
And throws adown the vale below
His quicken'd wave, and idler flow,
Still sings his anthem as before;
But from his sparsely wooded shore,
The chorus comes not as in yore.

The haunted groves and oaks have vanish'd,
And fays and songsters have been banish'd,
To come back never more.
And lint-white Time laughs at his freaks,
And miser-like chinks days and weeks
Against the heavier days and years;
And he doth chuckle as they rattle
Amidst earth's ever jostling battle.
An hour, a day, a year, a span,
A dole for toiling, scheming man,
To nourish hopes and fears,
And what is grasping man? Mused I,
Who lays his plans and builds his towers,
Who speculates with greedy eye
The gains of future hours;
Mistakes he (so it seems to me)
Brief time, for an eternity.
What all this art-triumphant scene,
Yon structures of terrestrial power,
Built with the dust of what hath been –
The nothing of an hour –
Power, gold, fame, pride, sith what are ye?
Froth-bubbles swirling on life's sea!

Thro' summer's sun and winter's frown,
These everlasting hills look down
On palsied vice and grumbling wants,
On poverty and pageants,
On Self-adhering to his store,
(As if earth was an evermore,)
Clutching the dross with skinny hand
While from his feet Death digs the sand.
As on this old oak stump I lean
And look upon the sunset scene –
The red ray glinting far across
The valley, stream, and moorland moss,
O'er glade and glen, and rich champaign,
And meadows low and fields of grain;
O'er streaky belts of wooded green,
With creeks of waving grass between,
Just cresting like a mimic sea
Round island banks of forestry.
I ponder, as I turn my gaze,
And follow the expiring rays
Which gild the apex of yon spire,
That rears above the smoke and fire.
They gleam far through the dusky lane,

Where Hunger gnaws to fatten Gain,
And from the alley, court, and street,
The dull red walls reflect the heat;
And from the river slowly rise
The putrid vapours – Fever's prize;
Want shakes her rags, Lust spreads her toils,
And grinning Death bags all the spoils.
Close by the windings of the stream,
Huge boilers fret, and ingots gleam,
And ponderous hammers thunder;
And mighty clanks, as from huge chains,
Suggestive of a Titan's pains,
Writhing in fetters under.
The incongruity of sounds,
The reeling faculties astounds,
And stuns the ear with wonder; –
Stuns Muse and matter from the brain:
And Fancy, with the whirling strain,
Flies from the light to shades below,
To surging fires and brimstone flow,
Where lava-rivers smoke and hiss,
Down through the measureless abyss,
Boiling to burst asunder.

Strange sight, for contemplative mind,
This trade-inferno of mankind;
Sweat-basted, bakes the human swarm,
Arms fashioning for good or harm –
Steel emissaries, for King Death
To quicker let escape Life's breath;
Shot, shell, and guns, to play the games
Hell-born ambition oft proclaims;
Steel plates that float in every sea
Where floats the banner of the free;
Protection offering to the world,
Where'er the honour'd flag's unfurl'd.

Strange Time, thy evolution brings
With every year new offerings,
As thy ephemeral hours glide by,
Their dust and ashes multiply.
Piles on the piles of other days,
Rise up to feed thy gaunt decays;
The worms above, the worms below,
As ever gnawing as they grow.
Science and beauty – dust to dust –
Earth to its earth, crust to its crust;

What are thy greatnesses that be?

Motes – tossing to eternity.'

Francis Buchanan

drest – older version of the word dressed, Erst – Old English for first or at first, Hades – the Ancient Greek God of the underworld known as God of the Dead and the King of the underworld, roast in the States – the earlier industrial revolution of the United States spread throughout Europe, sith – one's journey of life, experiencing one's lot, also an archaic word for since, Motes – particles, spots, specks.

11

'PARKWOOD HILL

To sing of Cooper's ridgy hill

How sweetly Denham tuned the lay;

How Grongar's height awoke the trill

Of Dyer, sweet as song in May;

How Richmond charm'd the harp of Young

With melody of beauty rare;

But thou, my Muse, hast never strung

Thy lyre to sing this prospect fair.

Give power to my untutor'd skill

To limn the view from Parkwood hill.

Awake my strain, the morn is bright –

With Nature's harmony unite –

A rural theme demands thy lay –

Fair Parkwood be thy song to-day.

Join in the joyfulness that swells

Above the belted woods and dells,

From charm to charm rove as the bees,
New fragrance seeming more to please,
With plenteous love diffusive fill
My heart, on breezy Parkwood hill.

Ah! what a splendour spreads below,
What tints of green and golden glow,
Can eye more lovely scene survey –
More hill and dale enamell'd gay?
More beauties at a single glance
Than from this wooded height entrance?
Shut out from, (yet so closely near)
The dun that would the fairness sere,
From sounds which would awake thee still
With clanks of labour – Parkwood hill.

Say, silvery Don, who onward flows,
Hast thou in all thy wand'rings seen
A loveliness of such repose –
A valley more serene –
Than this that thou dissectest now,

Ere into blackness fallest thou?
Now thou art radiant with the hue,
Of such a heaven of streaming blue;
But all thy beauty's glow will chill,
When thou art hid from Parkwood hill.

Here from this height mine eye surveys
The hamlet grey amidst the haze,
The hills that seem by distance blent,
Deep in the azure firmament;
The river's flow, and sparkling fall,
The 'broider'd lawn and ivy'd hall,
The farm in patches brown and green,
The quaint old village spires between
The chequer'd uplands – dam and mill,
From thy retreat – dear Parkwood hill.

The valley never tires the sight,
So lovely are its tints of light,
So delicate the pencilling.
And blue-mist wreath, like floating screen,

Endraping rock and shadowy tree,

With gossamer transparency,

That shifts and shimmers in the sun,

As o'er the fields light shadows run,

And arrowy beams upshoot until

They crown thy crest, fair Parkwood hill.

Upon the threshold step of toil

Thy beauty rests, and thou the while

Art dreaming in thy solitude,

Unconscious that one little rood

Divides thee only from the roar

That surges at thy outer door;

On thy bright face the critic eye

Nor stain nor blemish can descry,

So near, but all enshrined still,

From smokey turmoil – Parkwood hill.

Come ye who want a peaceful day,

When early morning throws its ray,

Or when the western shadows fall,

Low in the wood's cathedral;

Come in the spring, in summer come,

Or when the autumn sheds decay.

When winter's frost may thee benumb,

Here thou'lt be warm'd in wisdom's way,

Thou'lt learn the dullest thoughts to kill,

Upon the slopes of Parkwood hill.'

Francis Buchanan

On the 21st of September, 1882 the *Sheffield Independent* announced in its Literary Review the publication of the original *Sparks from Sheffield Smoke*. A selection of lines from 'Parkwood Hill' were met with admiration: 'Like a good painting, Mr. Buchanan's poems are full of atmospheric effect [. . .].' On describing the view from Parkwood Hill, clearly my forebear's intention was to create verse comprising some exceptional description – equal to that of the seventeenth-century poet Sir John Denham, and his great work 'Cooper's Hill', also John Dyer's celebrated 'Grongar Hill'. Perhaps the critic of the aforementioned review believed Francis had achieved his objective. The eighteenth-century Welsh poet and artist, Dyer captures in 'Grongar Hill' the glorious outlook from the Carmarthenshire hill-top. The hugely popular, lengthy poem is commonly read and re-read. Uunfortunately, I present to my readers only a few inaugural lines:

'GRONGAR HILL

SILENT nymph! with curious eye,

Who the purple ev'ening, lie

On the mountain's lonely van,

Beyond the noise of busy man,

Painting fair the form of things,

While the yellow linnet sings;

Or the tuneful nightingale

Charms the forest with her tale [. . .]

Grongar Hill invites my song,

Draw the landscape bright and strong [. . .].'

John Dyer

I consider 'Parkwood Hill' to be one of Francis' most reflective, and beautiful poems. In my view the author realised his intention. Indeed the considerable atmospheric description generates a sense of being present on the hill, by his side. Nature, wildlife, signs of human activity, the River Don, outdoor splendour, and a treasured retreat are central to the verse. The author characteristically refers to the nearby unwelcome smoke, roar, and chaos, but 'Thou'lt learn the dullest thoughts to kill / Upon the slopes of Parkwood hill.' You may find yourself longing to read and re-read *this* poem! Interestingly, the final line refers to the 'slopes of Parkwood hill'. Francis could not have known that more than a century later, an impressive dry ski slope would be erected on the site known as Parkwood Springs . . . only to be destroyed by fire.

Selected sites of beauty in the Sheffield area are featured within these pages. It is hoped my interpretation (together with wonderful poetry from bygone days) not only authenticates their charm, but lays emphasis on the importance of such locations. My book acknowledges those devoted to protecting and preserving them, whilst involving the community. It introduces dedicated teams of volunteers concerned with the conservation of settings around the city – appreciated by them, and by my poetic forebear. The matter in question is no exception. Indeed Friends of Parkwood Springs was founded in 2010, with one goal . . . to make it a better place for all. Francis' poem entitled 'Parkwood Hill' is beholden to this very spot.

What was once a Deer Park, is today widely regarded as a country park in the city. Woodland, heath, fruit trees, beautiful gardens and wildlife attract residents – who are invited to volunteer gardening assistance, enjoy a walk, or appreciate the birdsong and far-reaching views across the city. Others may choose to simply unwind in the calm serenity, explore the historic Wardsend Cemetery or participate in organised events. Further information is available at www.parkwood-springs.org.uk

As well as Parkwood Hill, located in the vicinity of Parkwood Springs was once a village inhabited by local people, and labourers from further afield. It is almost impossible to believe the thriving community ever existed, but indeed it did. Barbara

Warsop was born in the village during the late1930s, where she lived happily for 26 years. With a desire to ensure memories of the village – its history and its people – would not fade into obscurity, she asked former residents to contact her via a local newspaper. Tales of life experience amid a wonderful community between the 1920s and1960s, were gathered from those who responded and Barbara embraced the opportunity of sharing them in a book. *The Lost Village of Parkwood Springs* is a most interesting and enjoyable read, which comprises the history and development of the village.

You may remember me referring to the destructive storm of December, 1894 which affected Wincobank Hill and surrounding areas. South Yorkshire undoubtedly experienced a number of ferocious storms over the following years – certainly the *Sheffield and Rotherham Independent* recounted details of a 'GREAT HURRICANE IN SHEFFIELD', which struck on 16th December, 1873. Described as the worst tragedy since the Great Flood of 1864,* it caused immense destruction to property and tragically, loss of life. Though not as badly affected as some localities, Neepsend and Parkwood Springs were victims of the gale's relentless fury, and the newspaper correspondent chose to adopt a rather light-hearted approach concerning the situation: 'There are few houses in the higher part of Parkwood Springs with whose slates or chimneys the wind did not make free. The damage to some of them is very considerable; and the temper of many a tidy housewife was sorely tried when she found her carpets covered with rubbish, and her furniture smothered with dust.'

* Many local people will undoubtedly have heard of the Great Sheffield Flood of 1864. It caused widespread disruption and sadly, significant loss of life. Books from Sheffield authors describing the tragic event include *The Dramatic Story of the Sheffield Flood* by Peter Machan, illustrated by Eric Leslie and published in 1999, and more recently in 2014, *INUNDATION The History, the Times and the People of The Great Sheffield Flood of 1864*, by Mick Drewry.

A pleasantly diverse compilation entitled *Ballads, Poems and Recitations* was composed by E. Darbyshire of Sheffield, and printed in 1885. The volume includes some memorable poems – the village of Parkwood Springs being central to one of them. My forebear clearly saw the rhyming potential of the title and subject of his poem 'Parkwood Hill', as did Darbyshire concerning Parkwood Springs:

'JEALOUS JIM AND THE CHAP THAT CURED HIM

JIM Prince, a young farmer, as rich as a king,
Wed a smart country lassie from Parkwood Springs,
And, proud as a peacock, he took his fair bride
To be queen of his farm up at Grenoside.
Just seventeen summers the lassie had seen,
And Jim, quite a lad yet, was scarcely nineteen [. . .].
Jim loved his wife Jessie, not well, but too much;

That is, he was jealous, and without any cause,
A wrong way of loving as too many knows.
Now the first time she spoke of the sweethearts she had
Before she knew him, the poor fellow went mad;
And among many other ridiculous things,
He cursed every young chap in Parkwood Springs [. . .]

[and] he said, with a leer,
"Tha'd better not av them chaps comin 'ere [. . .]."

Much sooner than dreamt of:- It was Christmas eve,
The first of their wedded life, I believe,
Jessie came down to Sheffield to purchase some things,
And called, on returning, at Parkwood Springs,
Just to see the old folks and the young ones at home,
And when she reached Grenoside darkness had come.
There Jim had been waiting, impatient, for full
Two hours, as wild and as mad as a bull.
But she chanced to pop in, as Jim had popped out
To see if the mare and dog-cart was about;
And so, to surprise him on some future day,
She put all the nice things, she had bought, safe away.
And scarce had she done so, when in entered Jim,

She saw in a moment the plight he was in.

He looked daggers at her, and said with a frown,

"Then thah's called at t'owd neighbourhood comin thro' t'ahn."

"Ah did," she replied, "An ah'll tell thee another thing,

Ah've brought a young chap wi me thro' Parkwood Spring."

"Thah's wot!" shouted Jim, "then weer as ta put him?"

"Weer 'av ah put him?" she echoed, "why i't cellar Jim!" '

Assuming Jessie expected him to go away for a few days and had hidden the young man, Jim recklessly grabbed his gun and fired it into the cellar. With great alarm Jessie cried "Jim! Jim! as'ta gon off thee head?" She hurriedly explained that the chap in the cellar was a lifeless pig, and another chap had brought him home for her. Suddenly feeling foolish, her husband calmly replied, "[. . .] what a jackass ah've been, An ah'll nivver be jealous, wi'aght cause, any more."

"Then thah'll nivver be jealous," his wife said, "ah'm sure."

There's little now left of my story to tell,

Save this, they spent Christmas jolly and well;

And a party they had to let in the New Year,

And lots of old faces from Parkwood was there.

And there, on the table among other nice things,

Was the chap she brought with her from Parkwood Springs.'

E. Darbyshire

All ended well for Jessie and Jim, but not for the ill-fated pig! Edward Darbyshire was born in Sheffield during the 1840s, and it was perhaps inevitable that he would, like most of his family, aspire to become an optician. And perhaps inevitable that he would create a catchy little song with the title 'If There Were No Opticians'. But there is another poem I would like to share with you. The optical expert cum versifier may have planned to relocate, as a parting message appears in his book. He did in fact remain in Sheffield, and the lines I have selected emphasise his love of Sheffield . . . love of natural surroundings, and disapproval of pollution. Does it remind you of someone?

'SHEFFIELD, FAREWELL!

OLD Sheffield, my birthplace, I'm leaving behind me,

Her forest of chimneys now fade from my view;

I would not desert her, but fortune, unkindly,

Tells me, in tears, I must bid her adieu [. . .]

The city of sulphur that strangers have found thee,

And black as thy smoke were the tales that they told;

Had they but climbed on the hills that surround thee,

> They'd know thy black mantles have trimmings of gold.
> Here are thine outskirts, oh, what can be fairer?
> These sweet hills and dales know no factory din;
> While cottage and villa, and palace of splendour,
> All speak of the home-joys that labour must win.'
>
> E. Darbyshire

Another delightful poem created by my great-great-grandfather is **'Lines Written in Shirecliffe Hall Lane'**. It was published in *Sparks from Sheffield Smoke* of 1882, and a review in the *Sheffield Independent* – as mentioned earlier concerning 'Parkwood Hill' – believed the poem contains 'some genuinely beautiful bits of description'. Here are some of its finest lines:

> 'AH, what a lovely scene below!
> Rest awhile amidst the bloom,
> Feast thine eyes with sunset's glow
> From old Nature's drawing room;
> From her curtain'd frontal view
> Colours rich of every hue;
> Wavy tops of vernal trees,
> Sheening rays, like sunlit seas –
> Panoramic loveliness,
> Which the breezes soft caress.
> All the fields are gay with flowers,

Foliage clothes the sylvan bowers;
Hyacinths, in shady woods,
Dangle to the fledgling broods,
And the dandelion's hue,
And the humble daisy's too,
And the golden buttercup,
All are genial looking up.
Joyous birds and joyous flowers,
Let your joyfulness be ours.
Where the scenic beauty ope's
Wider, to the purple slopes,
Threading thro' the fields below
See the idle Dona flow,
Basking in the warm sun,
As if too languid to run.
Nearer I can see a dell,
Garnish'd with the purple bell;
From hence seeming like a lake,
Flowing round its bramble brake;
And yonder windows 'neath the rays
With twenty orbs appear to blaze,
Throwing up a garish glow,
As if a furnace burn'd below.

And see the Barracks frowning there,
Soldiers marching in the square;
And from thence the faint tattoo,
Sounds like huntsman's far halloo.
Wider still, and yet more wide,
Spreading up to Grenoside –
Far around the circling hills,
What a wealth of beauty fills
Dingle shade, and hoary rock,
Meadows speck'd with tree and flock;
Windy summit, steeple grey,
Misty moorland far away;
Stannington uprising high
Like a village in the sky;
Quaint, and as if fresco'd there,
On the color of the air,
Wadsley, in the vale below,
Grey amidst the yellow glow;
And its asylum's ruddier beam,
Suggestive of a wilder gleam.
Up from Malin's pretty bridge –
From Rivelin to Bradfield's ridge,
Gather in thy teeming crop

Of charms, from vale and bluey top.

"Silent nymph, with curious eye,"
Thy treasures here do multiply.
When thou look'st before, thou sees
Grandeur, for new ecstacies;
When thou turn'st around, new dreams,
Give my muse a flow of themes [. . .].'

Francis Buchanan

Interestingly, Francis quoted the first line of John Dyer's 'Grongar Hill' in this poem, and the words of Dyer – "Silent nymph, with curious eye," cleverly rhyme with those introduced by my ancestor: 'Thy treasures here do multiply'. Clearly an admirer of the eighteenth-century poet, my forebear utilised his own work to demonstrate this. On reading Francis' poem I visualise the restful spot from which a scene of nineteenth-century 'panoramic loveliness' was visible. The verse appears to accurately portray the scene described by historians, authors and poets of his era, and in the preceding years.

I have uncovered a fine example of this: *The Illustrated Guide to Sheffield and the Surrounding District* by the Sheffield editor and historian John Taylor, which refers to the precise location encountered by Francis. The informative guide was principally designed for visitors to the town and offers readers a thorough, structured guide to some of its districts, neighbourhoods, streets and buildings, as well as much of Sheffield's rich and captivating history. Considered a popular reference book it has been published a number of times. Indeed 1971 saw an edition comprising a new forward by the local historian and archivist, Mary Walton. However, for the purpose of this book I am quoting from an earlier copy dated 1879, which suggests one may

'[. . .] turn up Shirecliffe-Lane, at the top of which, on the left, are the gates of Shirecliffe Hall, once the seat of the ancient family of the Mounteneys, but now the residence of the Watsons. A little beyond the gates there is a fine view of the adjoining country, reaching out as far as the villages of Handsworth and Laughton-en-le-Morthen. Still higher we reach a point from which, overlooking the Osgathorpe and Wincobank hills, Norwood, Page Hall and Firth Park, in the near foreground, we see a fine expanse of country east of Sheffield, prominent objects in which are Keppel's Column and Hoober Stand, described in our account of Wentworth Woodhouse and the seat of the Fitzwilliams.'

Francis' poem refers to Shirecliffe Hall Lane. It is however known simply as Shirecliffe Lane, and still survives. The original Shirecliffe Hall, built by the De Mounteney family was situated there (the reason behind my great-great-grandfather's choice of title, I presume). And the hall built during the nineteenth century was positioned close to the highest point of the lane, at the other side of today's Cooks Wood Road and just inside the entrance to Parkwood Springs. My forebear would have been well aware that Henry Edmund Watson, a retired solicitor, reputable local figure and member of the aforementioned family, had resided at the hall for many years. In fact the original *Sparks from Sheffield Smoke* was published 'Under the Immediate Patronage' of several notable figures: The Right Hon. The Earl of Wharncliffe, The Right Hon. A. J. Mundella, M.P., (see chapter entitled 'Francis'), C. B. Stuart Wortley, Esq, M.P., (Charles Beilby Stuart-Wortley), Worshipful MAYOR of Sheffield, M. Hunter Jnr., (Michael Hunter Jr., Mayor 1881-1882, and brother of Joseph Hunter, the antiquarian), and Sir John Brown of Endcliffe Hall. Henry E. Watson, Esq., of Shirecliffe Hall was amongst them, and Francis' book indicates there were more unidentified patrons. According to the 1881 census, two of Henry Watson's sisters also lived at Shirecliffe Hall along with a Lady's maid. And the hall's team of domestic servants included a footman, housemaid, cook, kitchen maid, and two gardeners.

The hall was demolished during the twentieth century, but it is possible to follow the lane leading to where it once stood; possible to follow in Francis' footsteps. The inspiring scenes may be somewhat altered, yet one may envisage all he observed by simply enjoying his enchanting lines of poetry. On reaching the top of Shirecliffe Lane, crossing over Cooks Wood Road and entering Parkwood Springs, the curious wanderer may follow a trail which heads towards Francis' beloved Parkwood Hill.

12

'THE DYING POET

HE is sitting at a table, and a tallow candle's sputter,
As it crackles to exist amidst the gloom,
Throws a baleful sort of glimmer, and the shadows dance and flutter
On the wretchedness that floats around the room,
And a pallid face within that dusky room.

Thro' the attic's dusty lattice streams a midnight glory, beaming,
And it struggles to alight upon the floor,
Just beneath the chair and table, where the poet in his dreaming,
Is enshrined amongst the treasurings of yore –
The lovings that are dead, and gone before.

Far from that squalid garret, where the fever-hag is breathing,
He is soaring, upward soaring, thro' the vast,
And the king is busy gnawing, as the garlands are en-

wreathing
Round the shadowy memorials of the past –
The far off gleaming-duskness of the past.

The batter'd clay is shrinking, and the candle's wick is blinking,
As it moves the dreary shadows on the wall;
And nearer to the table, the impressive face is sinking,
He is dying of starvation – that is all –
Jostled, from life's busy cycle – that is all!

"Home, home," the poet murmurs; "they are beckoning and waving,
And I see beloved faces all a-smile;
And the tassel'd broom is golden, where the summer brook is laving,
By the stepping-stones, beneath the rustic stile –
It is but," he whispers softly, "but a mile."

"Ah, the flowers of May their tribute to my weariness are bringing,
For they loved me, as they love the golden light;
And I hear the dear old voices, as they welcome me with

singing."
'Twas the tempest, singing dirges to the night –
Singing death-songs as his eyes were meeting light.

He is roaming, in his fancy, where the mountain straineth higher,
Bonneted with snows of ages in the blue,
And he looks upon the emblem, as his soul is getting nigher,
To the purity that streameth on its view;
To a *something* that is gladdening and new.

And the silver ray is creeping, tho' it seemeth to be sleeping,
On the coldness of the bare and boarded floor;
And the poet's soul ascending is amongst the golden reaping,
Which they're garnering within the mystic door,
Where the weary are at rest for evermore.'

Francis Buchanan

'Born in a cellar . . . and living in a garret'. That's how the original saying goes isn't it . . ? Or at least it was before becoming more commonly known as '*starving* in a garret'! I am in little doubt Francis was aware of the phrase coined by the eighteenth-century Cornish writer Samuel Foote, which was in all probability the inspiration behind this astutely written poem.

Known for his satirical writing, Foote liked to base his parodies on people and situations and was not afraid to ridicule. This well-known idiom relates to those of a creative disposition – generally artists and writers – who at times become so utterly immersed in the transpiring canvas or literary stroke of genius at hand, that the minutes and the hours are voraciously consumed. The necessity to eat is entirely forgotten.

A garret is typically a cramped and dismal space to be found at the top of a house, below the roof – for the most part offering a sloping ceiling. By definition the garret would hardly be considered an abode of high esteem, thus prompting it to be deemed the only choice accessible to the impoverished and solitary, creative mind – an occurrence considered romantic by some! Likewise, within the *family abode* a garret (or an attic) might serve as the ideal hideaway to undertake such a resourceful, yet reckless quest.

Be it rolling hills, wooded glens, the marvels of an ancient edifice, or the thought-provoking sights and sounds amid Sheffield's streets, my great-great-grandfather was a poet to rejoice at not only the beauty of nature, but the peculiarities of life. This is from where his poetry surfaced, thus it is with a wry smile that I endeavour to picture him sitting at a desk in a murky garret, as poetry flows from his pen. I am more inclined to believe he would take every opportunity to embrace the vastness and freedom of the open-air. It seems quite clear that Francis happily deposited himself in Ecclesall Churchyard amidst the bracing wintriness, and what followed was to be one of his especially introspective and atmospheric poems. What is more, I doubt he roamed the land surrounding Haddon Hall only to swiftly return home or relocate to an oppressive corner somewhere, in order to transcribe into verse all he had observed.

In spite of this, on becoming acquainted with 'The Dying Poet' an initial thought flashed through my mind: could the poem have transpired as a consequence of Francis himself facing accusations of hiding away in a garret, or some such space – accompanied only by his thoughts and his poetry? Though good-humouredly of course . . . and with no sign of affront! In truth however, such a scenario seems rather unlikely. I suspect my forebear's idea of a solitary space was more liable to be set within a secluded spot surrounded by green and pleasant land, than a garret offering only dreary incarceration and dimness. Since no-one is around to enlighten me of Francis' customary approach to composing verse, I will regrettably, never learn of it. Accordingly, I fancy (a popular and charming choice of term to emerge throughout Francis' compendium of poems) that he produced some of his lines at home, albeit amidst family and business commitments, whilst seizing every opportunity to devote his free time to an alfresco setting of serenity, where he could comfortably write. And with slight amusement I ponder Francis' reaction to the knowledge that his great-great-granddaughter is attempting, more than a century later, not only to scrutinize his poetry, but unravel precisely how and where it was written.

Francis' poet is dying in a garret-like solitary, threadbare and grubby room, and I believe he is dying of starvation from the outside world, as well as malnourishment. As he rises upwards to be greeted by long lost loved ones, it is with a sense of ambivalence that I endeavour to comprehend the meaning of these words. Perhaps as his body and mind are starved and death rapidly approaches, he begins to hallucinate, or maybe he *is* happily reunited with beloved family members. He joins them in a heavenly place of splendour, joyfulness and peace which, it transpires, lies close to a brook 'By the stepping-stones, beneath the rustic stile' and all is bejewelled with the flowers of May, so dearly cherished by my forebear. Unsurprisingly, what appears to be my predecessor's image of heaven is within reach, for it is 'but a mile' – quite possibly all the distance required if one were to leave behind the town's smoke and racket in search of a tranquil scene of beauty, embellished with nature.

13

'FAITH

HERE cometh meek and noble Faith,
The lowly one who fears not death;
Brave 'midst the scorn of wicked men,
She lives, to die, to live again.
She sees the treasures unreveal'd,
And pants for the Elysian field;
Nor doubting fears distract her mind,
She turneth not to look behind.
Of purity she is the soul,
Her actions sanctify the whole,
In sweet simplicity of charms,
She points to Christ, and soothes alarms;
Cheers the dark mind, and smooths the way
To endless peace and endless day;
Faith is the twin of Charity,
Of rarities – the rarity.'

Francis Buchanan

This most profound and skilfully written poem does not allude to a person or people who act in accordance with their faith . . . it is concerned with faith itself. Francis describes faith as a humble entity with no fear of death, which bravely continues to survive amidst contempt. The poem emphasises the significance of faith in humanity – indeed faith accepts with certainty the presence of a person's hidden values, which it yearns to encounter once the soul is finally at rest. Francis' words define faith as a feminine philosophy, which turns away from doubt – refusing to be distracted by it. And faith brings with it pure and calming thoughts, which exist simply as a result of knowing Christ . . . making the pathway clear to interminable harmony. I do believe religious faith was important to my great-great-grandfather, and imagine he and his family regularly attended church or chapel. Which begets the question: was the entire family committed to a particular congregation in Sheffield? I long to know, but simply do not have the answer. Nonetheless, faith was present throughout Francis' life, and I am able to reveal what is known.

It began with his Baptism on 7th April, 1825, which took place at a Church of Scotland – the old Kinnoull Parish Church in Perth. The church was situated at the old burial ground (see chapter entitled Francis) and largely demolished in 1826. The new parish church was built on another site in Perth in 1827, and can be located on Dundee Road. I assume that in his formative years regular church attendance was a mandatory, yet joyous occasion. Later he would secure places of worship wherever life took him. Certainly on 6th December, 1852 Francis and my great-great-grandmother Susannah Lloyd were married at the Cathedral Parish Church in Manchester. Born on

21st December, 1826 in Oswestry Shropshire, Susannah was baptised at the town's ancient Anglican Church known as St. Oswald's. And I simply must remark on the somewhat pleasantly surprising coincidences uncovered, concerning names and events: My parents were not only to name me Susannah, but they too were married on 6th December – over one hundred years later!

My great-great-grandparents' children were baptised at Anglican Parish Churches in Manchester and Sheffield. Two of the ceremonies took place at the Sheffield Cathedral Church of St. Peter and St. Paul during the 1860s. Now generally known as Sheffield Cathedral, the Grade I listed building is steeped in history and welcomes Church of England worshippers. In his book *A Popular History of Sheffield* (1978), J. Edward Vickers states that the nineteenth century saw a growth of religious practice, as increasing numbers of churches and chapels were built throughout the city. And in addition to Catholic and Protestant places of worship, sacred philosophies relating to other denominations widely emerged.

Francis and his family settled in the Pitsmoor area of Sheffield for some time, and I was thrilled to discover a most enlightening newspaper article dated 28th June, 1894. The 'ROUND THE TOWN' columnist with the *Sheffield Daily Telegraph* known as Rambler, was delighted '[. . .] to note the promotion of a Pitsmoor old boy, who will be remembered by Mr. Chorlton's congregation. Mr. T. R. Buchanan, for three years accountant in the bank of New South Wales, is about to leave for Sydney.' Indeed 'the son of Mr. Francis Buchanan' had been with the bank since 1883, and was to engage in a new role at the head office. Thomas Richard and other family members may indeed have known the Vicar of Pitsmoor, Mr Samuel Chorlton – who would in due course become a Canon of the Anglican Church. My ancestors may have regularly attended his service at the church known as Christ Church on Pitsmoor Road. Built in 1850, it still survives and is in fact a Grade II listed building. Ecclesiastical parishes inhabited by my ancestors included Brightside and the Wicker, and it was their home on Fowler Street (now known as Fife Street) that was situated within the parish of Pitsmoor. Although the family moved home several times, the census was recorded every ten years – making it impossible to know of their whereabouts at all times. Though I can confirm that the family drapery and hosiery at 40 Spital Hill was occupied by the family during the 1870s.

Some of my great-great-grandfather's poems give a clear indication of his devotion to religious faith. Two examples being 'Love' and 'Wincobank Hill', which present divine existence as fundamental to life, and rejoice at how the natural world flourishes. Francis, in defiance of doubters, did on no account attempt to veil his devotion. Indeed he would occasionally utilise his poetry as a means of articulating its worth. All things considered, it seems clear that faith was of great importance to Francis. It was something to be cherished, together with his beloved family and crafted verse.

14

'A SHEFFIELD WORTHY

THERE'S a decent old man with a primitive stall,
Who stands all the day with his back to the wall,
With a vesture that's brownish, and a napless old hat,
And his whiskers are grey as the patriarch rat.

He is up in the morn with the trill of the lark,
For his spice must be made, be it daylight or dark;
And while with old Somnus young snorers are laid
This worthy old merchant his stuff has purveyed.

You can see him down there, by the arches that span
The Wicker, midst rattle of lurry and van;
Like a Cerberus, watchful he stands at his post,
Be it sunshine, or moonshine, or starshine, or frost.

He wears all before him an apron of white,
And sleeves of blue chequer, clean, comely, and dight;
With a neckcloth to match round his wrinkled old chin,
But nary a wrinkle the neckerchief in.

A portly umbrella – a shadowing wing –
Above him, though clouted, its benefits bring,
For it keeps off the rain-drops, the dust, blow, and glow,
As a minaret's dome shades its relicts below.

'Tis a noble old fellow, as honest as gold;
Confiding as childhood, tho' wither'd and old,
With a generous heart neath his well worn coat
(From humbleness, greatness is not so remote).

His age? Well it's drawing to eighty and seven,
A milestone, you'll say, near the confines of heaven.
The hint may be faint, but it still may express,
The harder the toiling the nearer the bliss.'

Francis Buchanan

In Francis' Sheffield collection 'A Sheffield Worthy' is one of my favourite poems. Those familiar with the Wicker Arches will surely experience little difficulty in visualising the old character, firmly established in his chosen spot. Having witnessed inordinate changes and events in Sheffield and no doubt, in the day-to-day undertakings on the thoroughfare known as the Wicker, the old railway arches stand today as prominent as ever. They form part of the Manchester, Sheffield and Lincolnshire Railway viaduct built in 1848, and the generous focal arch above the through road is complemented at either side by two lesser arches for pedestrians.

If indeed this captivating personality was real, Francis obviously came into contact with him regularly – perhaps on a daily basis – whilst clearly becoming engrossed in his appearance, livelihood and sturdy commitment: 'He is up in the morn with the trill of the lark [. . .] watchful he stands at his post, / Be it sunshine, or moonshine, or starshine, or frost.' This verse tells a story, and such detail in the description of the gentleman's garments, essential paraphernalia and bodily features, completes the visual image for the reader. Thus the man who 'stands all the day with his back to the wall' appears as authentic as the setting – an age-old Sheffield landmark. And it doesn't end there. Francis' sharp, and at times humorous rhyming tale is bursting with clues relating to the street character's . . . well . . . erm . . . *character!* The reader becomes mindful of his virtues, for this decent old man is a noble fellow, as honest as gold. Use of the term 'worthy' has over time become somewhat abandoned, but fundamentally, implies that an individual is deemed a pillar of society. Francis clearly recognised this local figure as 'A Sheffield Worthy'.

He simply *had* to be a genuine character! On reading 'A Sheffield Worthy'*,* Francis' street-seller, or 'hawker' comes to life, and I became convinced my forebear not only knew his subject, but was unable to resist the need to convey him in verse. The clues were there, and they would surely lead to the discovery of this curious soul, whose '[. . .] spice must be made, be it daylight or dark [. . .].' Naturally when one thinks of 'spice' being prepared, spicy foods and seasonings spring to mind. But perhaps not so much in Sheffield (and indeed other areas of South Yorkshire) where in the past, sweets were generally known as spice – a term still in use today. This might be because sweets were once made with spices as well as sugar, and were even used to aid indigestion. But whatever the reason, during the latter part of the nineteenth century, it appears there was a dear old man with a familiar face, regularly selling his spice beneath Sheffield's Wicker Arches.

Local newspapers printed decades later, provided the answer to his authenticity. The *Sheffield Daily Telegraph* occasionally published letters and comments from readers, concerning local well-known characters (usually historical), and they would generate public interest. Local people who shared their memories could generally tell a tale or two, and this is what led me to 'Spice Billy'. One letter published in the aforementioned newspaper appeared on 20th July, 1925 and reveals that the street hawker stood against the Wicker Arches whatever the weather, and depending on which direction the wind was blowing, his chosen spot alternated between the Walker Street side and Spital Hill. He sold butterscotch (which was of course home-made) from a wooden tray, suspended by a leather strap around his neck, and wore an old top hat, a clean apron and white sleeves. His true name – as local papers would verify – was William Reynolds. I couldn't wait to meet him!

Now equipped with a name, further details of his description, and of course his age: '*Well it's drawing to eighty and seven*', locating William on census records was a painless task. *Sparks from Sheffield Smoke* was published in 1882, comprising poems written, if not during that very year, certainly in the preceding years. As anticipated, an 86-year-old 'Spice Hawker' named Mr

Reynolds resided in Sheffield in 1881, and I discovered he was boarding with an Irish widow named Mary Noon.

I uncovered the following (entirely unforeseen) news story, that was widely reported and appeared in the *Sheffield Daily Telegraph,* on 6th October, 1881: Mary Noon and her lodger – the very same William Reynolds – became embroiled in an almost scandalous and unfolding incident. William, an honest and reputable citizen, took what he believed was the right course of action, but there would be dire consequences for Mrs Noon, who found herself named and shamed. Recognised as a pauper, Mrs Noon was in receipt of funds from the Parish amounting to 2s. 6d. per week, until it emerged that huge quantities of monies had been squirreled away inside her home. She had been claiming relief for approximately three years, but Mr Jackson, the Parish relieving officer responsible for making her payments, held suspicions concerning her eligibility.

It was the woman's lodger, Mr Reynolds who would prove there were indeed grounds for suspicion, when he paid Mr Jackson a visit, taking with him 32 gold sovereigns rolled in sugar paper. He had discovered the gold (which was incidentally, rather old, rather dirty, and had in fact been withdrawn from the precious metal currency) in a clothes chest at her home. When a second sum of money was discovered by Mr Reynolds, once again rolled in paper, and amounting to £16 10s. – making a grand total of £48 10s., Mr Jackson visited Mrs Noon at her home. Reports claim that once the funds had been discovered, Mary became 'deranged' and events had 'turned her brain'. Furthermore, it seems she had lent the sum of £20 to a relative, which was not repaid – an incident which contributed to her condition. As a result of these events, Poor Mrs Noon found herself at the Wadsley Asylum. Meanwhile, Mr Jackson reportedly repaid the Parish £16 7s. (relief funds 'falsely' claimed by her), and arranged to pay 10s. to the funds of the asylum as long as the money lasted, and Mary remained there.

Newsprint coverage and use of language could perhaps be construed as rather unkind, if not hostile. In the course of my research it did not go unnoticed that this 'old dame', became widely regarded as a wealthy, or miserly pauper or at the very least, a 'destitute female' – which can only be described as blatant suggestions of mockery. Indeed Mrs Noon's old clothes chest became her 'treasure-box', and whilst it is certainly possible that deception lay behind these events (which cannot be overlooked), it might be important to consider the wider picture surrounding the circumstances that warranted a place in an asylum. Was this woman afflicted with a condition which affected her mental health? Was it all down to confusion and absent-mindedness . . . or did she succumb to a 'breakdown' as a result of her activities being exposed? It is impossible to know. You and I were not around and almost 150 years have passed, but uncertainties surrounding the story do raise further questions. Was Mary Noon unaware of the stash of funds? It may have been well hidden for decades and long forgotten – perhaps a likely scenario, considering the state of these largely obsolete treasures. Why was Mr Reynolds rummaging through his landlady's clothes chest . . . and *why* on his discovery, did he 'blow the whistle' without hesitation? Was it the right thing to do? Perhaps . . . but I'll leave that for you to deliberate. In any event, the moral standards of William Reynolds, or 'Spice Billy' were duly noted, and according to some, should not have gone unrewarded. Whether he *was* in fact remunerated remains to be seen, but one is forced to assume the popular street-hawker did not anticipate further popularity. His humble disposition and simple livelihood had already gained him an enviable reputation.

I feel sure Francis was aware of these events. Indeed this was probably what he was alluding to with his words 'as honest as gold' not to mention his choice of title, for surely no-one could deny that 'Spice Billy' had earned the accolade – 'A Sheffield Worthy'. No-one that is, who supported this sincere little man, amidst probable diverse opinions. But when all said and done, the majority vote secured his reputation.

Two years later, on 27th October, 1883 to be precise, it was reported by the *Sheffield Daily Telegraph* that

'A WELL-KNOWN Character, who has inspired a poetic soul to graceful verse, has gone. William Reynolds, better known as "Spice Billy" is dead. For years he stood at the Wicker Arches, the most familiar face in all that dreary quarter. There he coupled with a knowledge of comfits "the correct tip" for every race to be run by man or horse. Great as was his learning in the lore of the turf, it could not keep him out of the Workhouse, for there he found himself on 24th June, and there he has died at the ripe age of 88.'

In fact William Reynolds sadly departed this life on 24th October, 1883 at the Sheffield Workhouse in Pitsmoor. The 'Hawker' of Spring Street died of 'Fenectus', which, I am led to believe, is the Latin expression for 'old age' – in itself, a remarkable accomplishment in the midst of Victorian Britain. His weary old bones were laid to rest on 26th October at a site known today as Saint Michael's Catholic Cemetery in Rivelin,

Sheffield. William was buried in the St. Vincent's section of the cemetery, and the following piece of information about the burial site appears on its website. The Parish Priest, Father Patrick Walsh has kindly granted permission for me to quote these informative, yet moving words: 'There are no headstones to locate any of the graves in St. Vincent's section (which appears to include some random graves around the various walls of the cemetery – all with no headstones to locate them) [and which] was for paupers who were buried in very cheap coffins in common graves, some holding unbelievable numbers of totally unrelated persons [who] often came from the 'Union' or Workhouse [. . .].' Thus a rather grim expiration for 'Spice Billy', and perhaps hardly befitting for a 'Sheffield Worthy', but was it for anyone – or simply a sign of the times? He would have been missed. The space he once filled at the Wicker Arches was now redundant, surplus . . . vacant. No headstone stands where he lies, and it seems only poetic verse holds his memory dear. But what of Mary Noon . . ? (I hear you say). Alas she was admitted to Sheffield's Middlewood Hospital (a psychiatric hospital) in 1881, and died there in 1883 . . . preceding William Reynolds by three months.

As previously pointed out, readers of the *Sheffield Daily Telegraph* would from time to time – by way of a 'Letter to the Editor' – recollect local historical characters, which in turn inspired others to share their own memories. One such letter published in 1925 was submitted by a reader named W. T. Gent, who had in fact known 'Spice Billy' and remembered that about fifty years ago a poem about him was published in the newspaper. Remarkably, he recalled a few lines from the poem, which he believed was written by the late John Hall of Norbury.

Of course you and I are familiar with Mr Gent. You might cast your mind back to my piece about Wincobank Hill, where it became clear that William Thompson Gent knew of John Nixon – the local gentleman who composed a poem about it. Mr Gent was clearly aware of John Hall and his place of residence, and both were successful businessmen. Would it be unreasonable to imagine the two were acquainted?

A further poem about 'Spice Billy' – this was an exciting find! Indeed John Hall's poem appeared in the *Sheffield Daily Telegraph* on 23rd May, 1874 – 51 years earlier! Mr Gent could of course have kept a copy, discovered the poem again more recently, or owned a volume of Hall's poetry (more about that later). However, I feel certain he genuinely remembered the poem, and had not stumbled across it for many a year. Here is the poem in its entirety, taken from Hall's published volume:

'A STREET CHARACTER,
DAILY VISIBLE

A little old man, with a sallow face

And a shrivell'd, parchment skin,

With a batter'd hat, and a seedy coat,

And an apron up to his chin, –

Stands all day long by the Railway Arch,

Selling his simple wares –

Butter-scotch, toffy, and India rock,

On a wooden tray he bears.

Winter and summer, there he stands,
   Counting his half-penny gains,
   With an ancient gig umbrella,
   To shelter him when it rains;
   Around him you will often see,
   Stray loungers of the street,
   For he is a public character
   Whom idlers love to meet.

And you will hear him there descant
   On politics and laws –
Trades unions, and workmen's strikes –
   Their remedy, and cause;
For while he has been standing there
   These fifteen years or more,
He has studied human nature well,
   And gather'd wisdom's lore.

Go ask him how his business pays –
   He answers with a smile,
"Although the dividends are small,
   Thank God, *they're free of guile*;

An *honest* shilling day by day
Is as much as it can do –
But on Saturdays, a trifle more
To serve for Sunday too."

"My wants are few; I eat and drink
As much as does me good;
There's more folks kill'd by *over much*
Than *over little* food.
I'm better off than many men
With wages ten times told –
I've neither servant, wife, nor child
To worry me or scold."

"I live in lodgings near at hand,
At half-a-crown a week,
Including fire on winter nights
And what small help I seek;
But that, thank God, I seldom want,
Altho' I'm nigh fourscore,
For I have rarely ache or pain,
And of health a perfect store."

"It's better earning something here,
Altho' it be but small,
Than moping upon parish pay,
Or in the Workhouse thrall;
And long as I have strength to stand,
I'll struggle on alone,
And gain a living for myself,
Dependent upon none."

God help thee, valiant little man!
I never see thy form,
Thy stoic face, and placid mien,
Serene amid the storm –
But I think of the great goodness
Of compensating Heaven
That to friendless age and poverty
So much content has given.

Though I do not say I envy thee
Thy humble lot and part,
Yet I envy much, thy patient soul,
Thy brave enduring heart;
And I learn from thee a lesson

Of manly toil and trust,

To make the best of circumstance

And own God's dealings just.

May 15th, 1874.'

John Hall *ALIAS* "J.H.J."

It becomes almost immediately apparent that the subject of this poem is none other than William Reynolds – or indeed 'Spice Billy'. The author's detailed use of description unquestionably reverberates that of Francis Buchanan's in his poem, 'A Sheffield Worthy'. John Hall's poem is relayed almost as if an interview had taken place, which ultimately tells 'Billy's' story in verse. Or perhaps the author simply listened and observed – employing his memory and rhythmical skill to ultimately create wonderful, authentic verse. Clearly another admirer of the familiar street hawker, Hall does not conceal his strong sentiments, and local readers of the time no doubt relished authentic verse relating to Spice Billy, as it would only confirm what they already knew. More than a century later, the very same words are introducing the intriguing fellow to my curious readers. Following extensive research, I have become very familiar with Spice Billy and William Reynolds . . . who are of course, one and the same.

John Hall was not only regarded as a Sheffield Worthy, but a Sheffield Literary Landmark. In addition to his deep involvement in Sheffield's public life, he was elected as a Town Councillor and was widely regarded as a shrewd, and highly successful businessman. Indeed he was the senior partner in the firm John Hall and Son – colonial and continental produce merchants and sugar millers of Granville Hill, Sheffield. The compassionate philanthropist was a valued and respected citizen and his son, the Reverend George Walker Hall was vicar of Norton for many years. Another son, Charles Edmund Hall gained recognition from the publication of his novel, *Hathersage A Tale of North Derbyshire*, published in 1896.

A correspondent with the *Sheffield Evening Telegraph* published an enlightening tribute to John Hall on 13th December, 1907, following his recent death: '[. . .] one evening, sitting by the fireside at Norbury, his son [. . .] looking after his comfort, he told the story of his life to one who jotted down the particulars stipulating that nothing he then said should be published till he had "crossed the bar".' It transpires that he loved to be outdoors, being very familiar with Derbyshire – particularly Chatsworth and its stately home. Writing prose and verse was an outlet – taking place once business affairs were over. He began to write editorials relating to the countryside and for a time, contributed to the *Sheffield Mercury* using his initials, J. H. which, in order for readers to make a distinction between him and his good friend and fellow columnist John Holland, became J. H. J. – presumably John Hall 'Junior', as his father was also John. He declined the offer of becoming a paid contributor to the *Sheffield Daily Telegraph,* but became involved with the Literary and Philosophical Society (and in time became president) after being introduced by Holland. Hall had his poems published for private circulation: 'Everyone was asking for a copy and [. . .] I had them published properly.'

The work John Hall 'had published properly' was his delightful little book *'Thoughts and Sketches in Verse'* (1877), which he dedicated to his wife – the sharer of his thoughts, and critic of all his sketches. Here are a few words from the introduction to his book: 'Should the casual reader of these "thoughts and Sketches" in future years find pleasure or amusement of any kind, or recall pleasing memories and associations of the past, their rescue from oblivion by publication will not have been altogether in vain.' And on delicately leafing through my own cherished copy of Hall's work, I discovered a tribute to John Holland: '[. . .] shall not Hallamshire break forth / In grief for her departed son – / Her bard – and last remaining one – / Whose muse for half a century long / Has hymned her praise in ceaseless song'.

John Hall loved his beautiful home, Norbury Hall and his impressive library included great works by Charles Dickens, Sir Walter Scott, Tennyson, and Wordsworth. After his death family members continued to reside there for a number of years, before it fell into other hands. During the early 1920s, the hall, situated on Barnsley Road in the area known as Pitsmoor, became the property of the West Riding of Yorkshire Territorial and Auxiliary Forces association and functioned as an establishment for units of the Territorial Army. It would undergo many structural changes, and be occupied by military for decade, though I like to think Mr Hall would have heartily approved of this worthy arrangement. The building still stands, having experienced much transformation and tenancy. For further details see *From Bailey to Bailey – A Short History of Military Buildings in Sheffield* by Stephen Johnson.

John Hall's homage to 'Spice Billy' is of course encompassed in his published collection of verse, and his poems relating to Haddon Hall and Chatsworth are featured in this book. 'JHJ' and my great-great-grandfather were like-minded people. Both were passionate poets who loved nature, and both were very observant! I like to think they met – or were at least aware of each other's presence and rhythmical flair. It is in fact very likely. Finally . . . nestled somewhere amongst Mr Hall's notable collection of poetry at Norbury Hall, and taking up very little shelf space, there may have been a small volume entitled *Sparks from Sheffield Smoke.*

15

'ROTHERHAM

DOWN by the foot of yonder hill,
Where Rother mingles with the Don –
Just where they join and murmur on,
By factory and clacking mill;
Where hissing steam in gauzy curls,
Deafens old Dona's gentle purls;
Where Naysmith hammers thump and thud,
Like living things of bone and blood,
Stunning the ground with awful batter,
That frightens Echo with the clatter;
And sparks, against the darkness seen,
Spread showers of violet, blue and green –
A pyrotechnical display,
That makes the blackest night look gay.
This pandemonium of noises,
Revels dissonant, and rejoices
Where nature tuned her many voices:
And here ranged England's Robin Hood,
Where smoke o'er-canopies the town,

And fiery engines groan and frown;
Where column'd bricks rear to the sky
(Great smoking tubes of industry);
There Saxon Cedric's stronghold stood.

The old romance is dead and gone,
The serf, the franklin and his tower
Gone, all have had their little hour;
And, as before, Don warbles on,
Singing along his placid way;
Now in the sun, now in the shade,
Now stealing past a fertile glade,
Now glistening 'neath the summer moon,
Now sweltering in the fervent noon,
Now plashing on his pebbled shore,
He frets and gurgles more and more,
And longs to go, and longs to stay.
Now dancing past an aged hall,
Now sweeping round a wrinkled rock,
Now tumbling over weir and lock,
His waters whirl and seeth below;
And stunn'd by the unkindly fall,
He froths in anger from the blow,

And slowly bends with graver flow,
Around yon bark'd old garden wall.
Now murmuring where the children sing,
Stringing their daisy necklaces,
As from his marge they downward glance,
Down to their images that dance
Beneath his bright expanse;
Laughing to the sun-brown'd faces,
Ringleted with golden graces;
By the cowslip bank, and the blue hare bell,
He slippeth along half-dreamily,
Around the roots of that stately tree
(That he hath known a century),
The broad-crowned monarch of the dell;
A big hearted, sheltering, honest oak,
Who when a sapling, planted there –
To mark the advent of an heir,
Grew on the brink so slim and bare,
Swaying its arms, in boisterous spring,
A desolate and trembling thing,
As if the heavens it did invoke.
The heir has long since gone to earth,
And heirs who had from him their birth,

All in the ground are mouldering;
Still the old river crawls along,
And the old tree holds up its head,
A sovereign in the sylvan throng;
While generations three are dead,
From peasant up unto the king.
Man, last of all created races,
How few in years art thou!
Death judges well the pale steed's paces,
And wins the race, I trow;
Thy three-score years and ten, how short,
To get prepared thy full report.
In this calm hour of evenglome,
I love to let my fancy roam,
Unfetter'd, o'er the trackless main –
Yon hazy field, without a name,
Where solitude and silence reign
Joint sovereigns o'er the vast domain;
Yon far untravers'd horizon,
Engirdling round the concave blue,
Reflects the glory of the sun,
In pale mysterious, flitting light,
That gleams the threshold of the night,

As bidding it adieu.

These hills of leaves still hold their own,
Tho' denser foliage they have known;
And where the Red rose tinged the White,
And where the White rose paled the Red,
Pale labour fights for daily bread.

Away, by Wentworth's avenues,
The noble forest blooms its hues;
And ancient trees nod 'neath the stars,
Which blink and wink the same to-night,
As when they twinkled down their light
On gash'd and ghastly scars;
As when they saw the murder done,
And how the fight was lost and won,
And how the ranks were riven;
As now they see with watchful eyes,
The meek and smooth hypocrisies,
While smiles insulted heaven.

As when they looked down thro' the night,
Down thro' the blue bespangled arches,

> On cunning circumventing right,
>
> And plotting counter-marches;
>
> As then, so now, yon starry lights
>
> Look down on wrongs usurping rights.'
>
> Francis Buchanan

What might be looked upon as akin to the flowing river portrayed in this verse, are the imaginative and poetic words to 'gush' from the pen of my forebear as the River Don leaves behind the banks of Sheffield, and joins the nearby town of Rotherham. Francis' poem implies that Rotherham can be found 'Where Rother mingles with the Don', and though the town sits by the Don, never distant is the glistening River Rother. It rises in Derbyshire, and flows through Chesterfield as it readily replenishes its canal, progresses onwards to the ever popular Rother Valley Country Park, on through the Sheffield districts of Beighton and Woodhouse, before joining the Don in Rotherham. And the presence of the River Rother is of course what contributed to the town's name, whilst bringing about an appropriate title for the Rother Valley Parliamentary Constituency.

Some tome ago I wrote a newspaper article concerning nineteenth-century Rotherham. It predominantly addressed the 1850s, and my research was to uncover a wealth of information. The town was simply bustling with inhabitants engaged in active livelihoods – of one form or another. What I write on this occasion contains only a modicum of detail. In a somewhat theatrical manner, the River Don tells the story by means of Francis' poem.

I consider this poem to be beautifully written, and such is the power of its atmospheric words that the reader not only voyages alongside the River Don, but encounters a variety of scenes along the way. The sights and events both river and reader chance upon, form only a taste of the hive of activity that is Rotherham. Bustling with toil and drudgery amidst mills and factories, is Francis' animated portrayal of a town vigorously creating batter and clatter, amid a variety of raucous reverberations. A 'pandemonium of noises' is all one can hear amid the cascades of colour generated from the sparks of productiveness. And it seems the sharp, bright colours are sufficiently spectacular to warrant the author's use of the term pyrotechnical! In employing vibrant, eloquent language to poetically describe scenes he finds abhorrent, my forebear has demonstrated skill. Perhaps his use of language is somewhat derisive, for in truth Francis deemed such *wondrous* sights as anything but! Unless of course, by way of his customary rhythmical manner he spontaneously logged all he could see before him, despite his fundamental lack of approval.

The compelling lines of rhyming verse take the reader on a tour through the town alongside the River Don. Following a dynamic introduction to the neighbourhood, the poem briefly turns its attention to legendary tales and historical facts, figures, and fortresses of old. This turn of focus serves to highlight that the town has been steadily and irrevocably transformed by man's yearning necessity for industry. Yet at the heart of abundant change and time evolving, the River Don merrily continues its journey. The reader becomes aware of magical lyrics and a hurriedly growing pace. Indeed the poem's strong sense of rhythm represents the surging performance of the river, and thus assumes a cumulative effect – an expressive style occasionally favoured by Francis.

The Don literally runs into numerous unidentified regions and establishments, which may or may not be fictional consequences of Francis' breath-taking imagination. I am particularly taken with his use of intense detail concerning the drive and response of the river as it adapts to the ever-changing surroundings. Readers might just catch the splashing and babbling foamy river . . . and visualise it slipping swiftly through the town. Having hinted at the poem's potential inclusion of fictional ideas, I have not disregarded the fact that some may be genuine – not forgetting of course, how very little escaped my great-great-grandfather's powers of observation. As river and reader pass by an aged hall, I ponder the likelihood of its existence and consider possible contenders. The small chapel on Lady's Bridge has been ruled out; for although it prevails over the River Don, is mighty ancient and imbued with history, it could not be looked upon as a hall.

A more probable possibility is Aldwarke Hall (original spelling Aldwark), which stood in the area known as Aldwark/e, close to Parkgate, in Rotherham and the lock on the Sheffield, Rotherham and Doncaster canal by the River Don. On 13th November, 1886 the *Sheffield and Rotherham Independent* published a piece about Maritime Rotherham, which featured a drawing of the hall close to the lock, and facing towards Rotherham. Current times brought about many changes, but in bygone years a spacious plot by what is known as Aldwarke Lane was occupied by an imposing mansion with surrounding land and stables. There is mention of the hall in John Holland's collection of accounts relating to tours of the River Don. The mansion to replace the original construction was demolished during the late nineteenth century, but was still standing when Francis turned his thoughts, and his pen towards Rotherham.

The popular local historian, author, Alderman, and prosperous businessman John Guest (1799-1880) produced a book in 1879 entitled *Historic Notices of Rotherham: Ecclesiastical, Collegiate, and Civil*. It explains that 'Aldwark was one of the many patrician residences and towering-strongholds which quickly bestrewed the banks of the Don in the olden time. It was a spacious many-gabled building, with extensive wings, and ample means for state occasions. It was noted for its unlimited hospitality [. . .].' Guest, a distinguished Rotherham citizen is also recognised as one half of the town's pioneering, and once thriving brass works partnership Guest and Chrimes – originally established during the nineteenth century by two of the Chrimes brothers, and later managed by John Guest and Richard Chrimes, who met through the Temperance Movement. Like many factories of its kind, the brass valve works operated close to the river – in this case the River Don, which during the industrial revolution provided water and steam.

Another contender, Ickles Hall was situated in the hamlet of Ickles on Sheffield Road, close to the Rotherham district known as Brinsworth. It stood beside a corn mill and more notably, by the River Don. The hall and its land lay claim to a long history – in fact the hall was rebuilt several times over hundreds of years. As is often the case, I am unable to date Francis' poem relating to Rotherham, but it was almost certainly created sometime between 1860 and 1882. Ickles Hall and its surrounding land continually offered a home and work base during those years, and was eventually demolished during the 1930s to make way for an expansion of the steelworks.

I previously revealed that my forebear loved to roam amidst Kinnoull Hill's beautiful woodland as a youth, and so enamoured, so powerfully drawn was Francis, it would not be unusual to spot him there when he occasionally evaded the schoolroom! Far from Scotland, and not all that many years earlier, another budding poet could often be found playing truant from school – preferring to explore the splendour of the countryside surrounding the little town known as Rotherham. His name was Ebenezer Elliott, and many may be familiar with his life and work. In later years he attributed his success as a poet to spending a great deal of time admiring scenes of nature. He became quite a political figure, and his ardent crusade against the Corn Laws, coupled with a reputation as a popular poet gave rise to him being widely recognised as the 'Corn Law Rhymer'. During the early to middle years of the nineteenth century laws imposing tariffs on imported goods were introduced. The purchase of grain was simply unaffordable, leading to poverty, hunger . . . and the publication of Elliott's volume of verse entitled *Corn Law Rhymes*.

A great deal is known about Elliott and his statue proudly stands in Sheffield's Weston Park. But he was actually born at Masbrough's New Foundry in the parish of Rotherham in 1781, where his father was employed for a time as a clerk at the Walker Foundry. Ebenezer himself would later become a factory owner, and when his business in Rotherham failed he relocated to Sheffield. I am particularly drawn to his early life in Rotherham and what inspired him to write poetry, and would like to share extracts from an interesting article published in the *Sheffield and Rotherham Independent,* dated 27th February, 1847:

'The manufacturing town as well as the country has found its Burns. As Burns grew and lived amid the open fields, inhaling their free winds, catching views of the majestic mountains as he trod the furrowed field, and making acquaintance with the lowliest flower and the lowliest creatures on the earth, as he toiled on in solitude; so Elliott grew and lived amid the noisy wilderness of dingy houses, inhaling smoke from a thousand furnaces, forges and engine chimneys, and making acquaintance with misery in its humblest shapes, as he toiled on in the solitude of neglect [. . .].

[. . .] the spirit in both was the same. They were men of the same stamp, and destined for the same great work; and therefore, however different were their immediate environments, the same operating causes penetrated through them [. . .].

[there was much] thunder of machinery, and a din of never-ceasing hammers; but amidst the chaos of sounds there were heard – not songs, but groans. It was then that Elliott was born, and there that he grew, in the very thick of this swarming, busy, laborious, yet miserable generation.'

Although published a number of years before Francis' poem, the newspaper article's description of Rotherham's early industry bears striking similarities.

Clifton House is a rather grand Georgian building positioned by Clifton Park in Rotherham, and is the home of the town's museum and archives. Joshua Walker and his wife Susannah had the house built in 1783 and owned the neighbouring land that was to eventually become a public park. Former family members founded the Walker Foundry – a Rotherham-based business of iron and steel production in Masbrough, as I briefly mentioned earlier. The business prospered and expanded, but was sold in 1833 after making a loss. However, Henry Walker – son of Joshua remained active and influential as a member of the town council, became a local magistrate, and let it be known he was in support of the anti-slave trade. Though now residing at another property – Blyth Hall in Nottinghamshire, Henry and his family continued to gain respect in Rotherham. Henry Walker's wife Elizabeth Abney, was a writer of poetry, which I feel should not be overlooked. A collection of her work was published in 1821 and given the title *Poetry and Prose. Including some Original Correspondence with Distinguished Literary Characters.* An extensive list of subscribers includes her husband Henry and several other members of the Walker family. The poet James Montgomery secured three copies! The author's given name is simply 'Elizabeth', and the book begins with an 'ADDRESS' to readers. What follows is an excerpt:

'Should a work so unpretending, meet with effectual patronage from those who may be willing for once to try the merits of a publication, which promises nothing for itself, and offers them nothing but an opportunity of showing kindness to a stranger, who dare not even disclose her name to her benefactors, – those benefactors may be assured, that, though they may not have done it to one who is worthy of their regard, they have done it to one who will be unfeignedly and unceasingly grateful for the least token of their benevolence.'

Some of Elizabeth's verse reveals her abhorrence of the slave trade. 'Invocation to Liberty' is listed in the contents page of Mrs Rawson's *The Bow in the Cloud* (see 'Wincobank Hill') and the author's given name is Mrs. Henry Walker. Today she is often referred to as Elizabeth Abney Walker. Here is a selection of lines:

'INVOCATION TO LIBERTY

ALL hail, sweet Liberty! thy cheering ray

Gives promise of a bright – a glorious day –

Soon may it burst in dazzling splendour bright,

Chasing the *long*, *deep* gloom of Slavery's night!

Unloose the fetters! – set the Captive free! –

Bind up his wounds! – and soothe his agony!

Shed the blest influence o'er the hapless Slave,

And shew him *thou* has found a heart to save!

Let him at length the hallowed vision see

Of Peace, – of Hope, – of Joy, – of Liberty!

Wave thy bright banner! mount it up on high!

Unfurl thy standard to the gorgeous sky!

Enroll *thy* name there, – *Briton, brave,* and FREE!

'Tis a fit emblem of thy *Land,* and *Thee!*'

ELIZABETH

Pioneering individuals and indeed families, employed men in their multitudes and produced vast quantities of merchandise – all the while enhancing their own wealth and lifestyle. And who could blame them? But intense industrial activity brought about a vast array of changes – not all of them constructive. Those who protested were largely concerned about the cost to the environment – the loss of eye-catching foliage, open air spaces, woodland and wildlife, amid ever increasing noise and pollution. The numbers concerned may have been marginal, and justifiable motives were perhaps open to debate, nonetheless, there is frequently opposition to unwelcome change . . . indeed 'twas ever thus. But alas, the devastation these age-old objectors prophesised would in the fullness of time, come to pass. The rhymesters among us aired their passionate feelings of loss, sadness and disapproval with pen in hand. Such a powerful, yet peaceful method of protest may be prised and chronicled for immeasurable time – possibly making it all the more effective. The Industrial age will doubtlessly always attract differing opinions, and has perhaps never been more controversial than today. There is more from the pen of my predecessor concerning this unsettling, yet contentious theme in his incredibly thought-provoking poems relating to 'The Valley of the Don'.

By the second half of the nineteenth century it became clear that pollution was poisoning the River Don and its surrounding waters. It was poisoning the river which tells us a story . . . the river to escort us on a tour of the town, as it surges splashing and bubbling through Francis' poem. The pollution problem was making the news, and in 1864 the *Sheffield Daily Telegraph* reported on 8th December, that a meeting of the

Local Board of Health in the Rotherham area raised deep concerns about the district's mortality rate, and '[. . .] in the years 1862 and 1863 the medical officer from the Health Department of her Majesty's Secretary of State twice visited Rotherham, and inquired into the state of health and especially with reference to the outbreak of typhoid fever [. . .].' It was concluded that '[. . .] the natural situation and state of Rotherham to be such as will not account for the sickness and death which have prevailed; but [. . .] being situate on the River Don, which flows from Sheffield, brings down an immense quantity of sewage which falls into it at Sheffield and is deposited in the bed of the river near Rotherham, polluting the stream, and poisoning the air, is mainly the cause of the sickness and mortality [. . .] and which [. . .] cannot be accounted for in any other way.' The need for a bill of Parliament was voiced in order that the discharge of sewage into rivers and streams may be prohibited.

Local newspapers regularly reported cases of river pollution caused by sewage and animal farm waste. Coal washing by collieries was an additional source of contamination, and regarded as an offence by the 'River Pollution Prevention Act'. Streams flowed into canals, which in turn greeted our rivers, as human disregard and ill-informed actions increasingly resulted in perilous waterways. During the early 1890s concerns were raised over the state of the River Don by firms whose operation relied on steam, as polluted water was harmful and ultimately impractical. There were tales of businesses making huge losses as a result of boilers becoming corroded, and insurance companies discontinuing policies. And not discounting the vulnerable wildlife – poisoned or deprived of their habitat.

Methods of water pollution prevention were continuously high on the agenda during the late Victorian era – an occurrence which continued (though with varying foundations), well into the twentieth century and beyond.

In the face of innumerable challenges, calamities, and uncertainty in this ever changing world, the River Don remains an unwavering presence in Rotherham and surrounding areas. Or in the words of my insightful forefather: 'And, as before, Don warbles on . . .'

16

'SHEFFIELD MANOR

STOP, for the ground is holy here;
Tread softly o'er this eminence,
Where time hath almost driven hence
The beauties I revere.

Sad memory contemplates the past,
And Fancy sighs for lost romance;
For demolition's grim advance
Hath wrinkled with its blast.

Here stood the Talbots' princely piles,
And in their paths the deer and hare
Heard the nightingale's sweet tune;
And the pool, at midnight there,
Imaged the brightness of the moon –
Now a black pit defiles.

Here Mary* sat, her wistful eye
Out-gazing o'er the broad expanse,

Watching the dark cloud-shadows dance
Across the sunny woods below;
Poor Queen, thou dreamt of future woe,
In thy captivity.

Now the Castalian spring is gone,
And gone are the Castalides,
And Fancy groans her vain distress;
The great oak trees and elms are dead,
And where the grand old chestnuts spread,
'Tis now a muddy lane instead,
Where beauty is unknown.

Romantic Fancy images
The buried past of other days,
(Like Endor's witch) her spells upraise;
She reconstructs the Manor-hall,
Where the dejected Cardinal†
Mourn'd greatness that was his.

She fires the yule-log in the grate,
She spreads the board with haunch and loin,
And sparkles rimmers of red wine,

As knight and squire and ladye gay,
Swell music to the roundelay,
Nor miss the beggar at the gate.

She stimulates the stirring dance,
Where this old hybrid chaos stands;
And here, brave fingers press'd fair hands,
And lips breath'd softly in the ear,
Where now a bumpkin sells his beer;
And where hung tapestries of grace,
The miner hath a dwelling place;
Grim craft usurps old elegance.

* Queen of Scots   † Cardinal Wolsey'

Francis Buchanan

Castalian refers to the characteristics of a spring named Castalia that was sacred to the Muses in Greek mythology. Castalides are the Muses associated with that spring.

The ancient dwelling portrayed in verse by my great-great-grandfather is Sheffield's sixteenth-century Manor Lodge, which during his era only partially survived as a ruin not too dissimilar to the remnants of today. It once stood proudly amid picturesque parkland alive with deer, and was built for the landowner, the 4th Earl of Shrewsbury George Talbot, to provide him and his family with a country retreat. In later years it would serve as the ideal location to hold a person captive.

An enlightening piece was published in the *Sheffield Daily Telegraph* on 1st July, 1912 entitled 'THE IMPRISONMENT OF MARY QUEEN OF SCOTS', who was indeed the prisoner I alluded to. The article is concerned with archaeological interest in the site, nonetheless, 'Memories of ill-fated Mary Queen of Scots were revived in the course of a pleasant ramble over the ruins of Sheffield Manor, in which some forty or so members of the Hunter Archaeological Society participated [. . .] under the leadership of Mr. Thomas Winder.' The gentleman explained that Sheffield Manor was '[. . .] the country mansion or summer seat to which the Earls of Shrewsbury retired when the sanitary conditions of their Sheffield Castle [. . .] became too bad for continued habitation. The Manor was situated in the midst of a beautiful park of gigantic oak and beech trees, extending over an area of about 2,462 acres.' However, 'In 1706 it was dismantled by Thomas, Duke of Norfolk, and [. . .] gradually degenerated into small cottages and a few public-houses, which were destroyed only about forty years ago.'

In its secluded spot, the early Lodge was thought a most suitable location for the confinement of a Queen who posed a threat to the English monarch. The measures endured by the Scottish Queen are widely documented. Indeed the Earl of Shrewsbury was commissioned to keep Mary well-guarded, and when Queen Elizabeth I anxiously inquired after the accomplishment of measures implemented, the Earl's son wrote to his father relating his words of assurance to Her Majesty. In his book *The Picture of Sheffield*, or *AN HISTORICAL AND DESCRIPTIVE VIEW OF THE TOWN OF SHEFFIELD* published in 1824, the poetic historian John Holland recreated events as he transported his readers to days of yore. A hostile environment was creating acrimony amongst Britain's great rulers and Mary, now Queen Elizabeth's prisoner '[…] was removed from Sheffield Castle to the Manor House [. . .] and was kept under the same cruel restrictions as before, "good numbers of men continually armed, watched her day and night, and both under her windows, over her chamber [. . .] so that unless she could transforme [sic] herself to a flea or a mouse, it was impossible that she should 'scape." '

John Holland composed a sonnet concerning Sheffield Manor – using the term which describes this arrangement as its title – and it was published in his selection of poetical pieces, *Flowers from Sheffield Park* in 1827. He clearly resisted any temptation to permit lines of atmospheric description and unsettling historical events to flow from his pen on this occasion. It seems he had other things on his mind:

'SONNET

WRITTEN NEAR SHEFFIELD MANOR, AFTER VIEWING A CONSIDERABLE PART OF THE RUIN WHICH WAS BLOWN DOWN DURING THE NIGHT OF JANUARY 14, 1824

PILE of the Talbots! through thy ruins long

Have furious tempests raged, and storm winds driven:

Yet like some giant-rock, firm-based and strong,

> Wedded to earth thou stoods, and braving heaven:
> I've thought, should I sink to the earth before thee,
> These walls, which first inspired my youthful strain,
> The green fields round, the proud hill top that bore thee,
> Might be my record: ah, wild wish, and vain!
> Orphan, and heir of centuries! Had grey Time
> Been left to its slow rightful conquest o'er thee; –
> But hands, more barbarous than our northern clime,
> Have smote, and left me vainly to deplore thee, –
> Have by one day's dilapidating rage,
> Achieved the proud spoliations of an age.'
>
> John Holland

The lyrics are powerful, expressive, and emotive. Holland clearly struggled to suppress his feelings of sorrowful loss and fury, and he explains why:

'Many readers [. . .] will probably remember the "ivy mantled tower," which was standing at Sheffield Manor in their youthful days, and which was blown down in the night of March 2, 1793.' He then informs his readers that in recent years thoughtless visitors – whether poets, painters or historians – had damaged the walls, leaving behind a mass of architecture suspended in the air. Unsurprisingly, during a recent storm the stonework collapsed '[. . .] with a tremendous crash, amidst a gale of wind [. . .]. Thus [. . .] this interesting ruin has become a mere shell, and a few more winters will probably deprive this neighbourhood of one of its most interesting and far-conspicuous features.'

Decades later – on 3rd December, 1914 to be precise, the *Sheffield Daily Telegraph* encompassed a Literary Supplement featuring 'Sheffield and its Poets'. The early nineteenth-century poet Mary Hutton was one of them, and a short biographical piece defined her as the '[. . .] wife of a Sheffield working-man [. . .]' who seemingly wrote verse '[. . .] to keep the wolf from the door.' One learns that life for her and her husband was a struggle, as both suffered ill health. Mary's poetry provided their sole income, though she left it on record that '[. . .] she would gladly have kept a gentleman's lodge, or done anything else whereby she "could have earned honest bread." ' This is a thought-provoking statement, yet I am not entirely convinced.

Indeed one is forced to deliberate whether Mary, a skilful poet, did in fact delight in creating verse, and often felt compelled to scribble down thoughts. Her volumes of poetry such as *Sheffield Manor and other Poems* published in 1831, and *Cottage Tales and Poems* (1842) were well received, and 'In spite of her humble position in life, she must have had some knowledge of current literature.' I tend to agree – for not only did she know who John Holland was, but must surely have been mindful of her own talent and genuine possibility of publication when she approached the local versifier for assistance. The account of actual events was published in John Holland's biography – *The Life of John Holland* by William Hudson. Mrs Hutton left her poetry at Mr Holland's home, along with a letter describing her circumstances and her hopes of it being published with his assistance. What transpired was her first volume of verse, and its subscribers were well aware of

Holland's compassion, generosity, and participation in the publishing arrangement for a humble woman he considered quite ingenious. I did indeed unearth an advertisement which appeared in the *Sheffield Independent* on 22nd January, 1831: 'In the Press, and speedily will be published . . . Price Three Shillings . . . SHEFFIELD MANOR AND OTHER POEMS . . . by MARY HUTTON.'

Considering Mr Holland's distinguished popularity as a human being and a poet, I would not be at all surprised to learn that Hudson's account was not only eagerly anticipated, but flew off the shelves, so to speak. The tale of Mary Hutton's plight, and the measures to assist in her objective evidently gained the support of Sheffield people. Hutton's poem 'Sheffield Manor' is exceptionally lengthy, and tells a remarkable tale of historical figures of supremacy, whilst the Scottish queen finds herself once again imprisoned. Like much of Mary Hutton's work, the theme evidently ranked highly in her reasoning, and it seems rather unjust to reduce it in length and narrative, but reduce it I must. In any event, her poem ensures that two women – whose lives were destined to be diametrically opposed, and who nonetheless, faced hardship – will not be erased from our minds:

'SHEFFIELD MANOR

HERE as I glance around my tearful eye,

Where Shrewsbury's turrets once so towering stood,

My sad heart pays the tribute of a sigh,

While memory weeps, and terror chills my blood.

These splendid ruins strike with holy fear,
Their pensive minds, by contemplation led,
Who in the twilight slowly wander here
To meditate on the illustrious dead:

To meditate on ages long gone by,
When pilgrim bard sang forth his various lays,
Attuned his loudest strings of minstrelsy,
To celebrate their noble chieftain's praise.

Oh, had these ancient mouldering walls a tongue,
They would a tale of dreadful woe unfold; –
Would tell of ROYAL MARY, fair and young,
Whose beauteous form seem'd scarce of earthly mould;

– Would tell that here she spent her nights in tears,
Her weary days in sad and hopeless sighs;
Confined by envy, nineteen tedious years
The hapless victim of calumnious lies.

Methinks I hear her deep heart-rending sighs,
Methinks I see her agonizing woe;
Methinks I hear her sweet and plaintive cries

In undulating murmurs soft and low.

These ruin'd walls, that shake with every wind,
Did once in splendid pomp their heads uprear:
Now scarce a vestige tells the inquiring mind,
That Shrewsbury and his vassal-train dwelt here.'

Mary Hutton

Amongst the residents of Sheffield to appeal to the public on behalf of Mary Hutton, were the Scottish poet James Montgomery (justly mentioned in this book previously), and Samuel Roberts, a prosperous man of business. A native of Sheffield, Roberts was known for his fascination with the incarceration of the Scottish Queen, and a few years after Hutton's book was published, he had the 'Queen's Tower' built in memory of the hapless prisoner. Many years later, at a time when Mr Roberts' son (also Samuel) resided at the property (in fact his father would never inhabit his own creation), the *Sheffield Weekly Telegraph* published on 3rd October, 1885 an informative piece concerning the well-known construction: The building sits '[. . .] on a most commanding site overlooking Sheffield. It is a handsome and picturesque edifice, forming a striking and pleasing feature in the landscape on the wood-crowned ridge of hills which bounds Sheffield on the eastern side.' The article reveals the tower was positioned approximately one mile from the ruins of the Manor, and Samuel Roberts was known as an enthusiastic apologist of the said queen. Indeed '[. . .] when the Manor was crumbling away he rescued a portion of the old wall and the mullioned window through which it is supposed Queen Mary looked out from her prison apartment.' It was positioned in the beautiful grounds of the Queen's Tower, along with a small marble tablet displaying his tribute to her, and what follows is a short passage: 'Alone, here oft may Scotia's beauteous Queen, / Through tears, have gazed upon the lovely scene [. . .].'

I feel certain my great-great-grandfather was aware of the Queen's Tower, which he unquestionably observed. Amongst other things Samuel Roberts of Sheffield was a manufacturer of silver and plated goods, man of property, and philanthropist. As a writer and supporter of the abolition of the slave trade, who also opposed the use of climbing boys to sweep chimneys, he held principles equal to those of James Montgomery and the two were closely acquainted. Mr Roberts was a notable person of Sheffield, and on his death in 1848 the *Sheffield and Rotherham Independent* of 29th July acknowledged that 'He was a character. Shakespeare's phrase – "We ne'er shall look upon his like again," is often quoted in regard to very [. . .] commonplace personages. But it is truly applied to Mr. Roberts.'

His preoccupation with the Scottish Queen's captivity in Sheffield, perhaps had some bearing on at least one of his daughters. It may have inspired Mary Roberts to create *The Royal Exile*. This incredibly lengthy (some might say epic) series of verses is a collection of imaginary Epistles, powerfully transcribed by Mary Queen of Scots during her captivity at Sheffield's Castle and Manor Lodge. It was published in 1822 – only a few years before Mary Hutton's contribution, and there are two volumes – the first of which largely comprises Samuel

Roberts' detailed biography of the said queen. *The Royal Exile* was reviewed under 'Sheffield Poetry' in the *Sheffield Independent* of 24th December, 1824. It is defined as 'The first, and indeed the only work by which Miss Roberts is known to the public, and the largest poetical performance published by a native of Sheffield [. . .].' The piece continues with 'Not any of her predecessors have discovered the same compass of thought, and the same versatility in the execution, that she has manifested [. . .].' The evaluation ends with 'Another particular, which is highly creditable to the best feelings of humanity, and which ought not to be omitted, is, that the profits arising from the work are devoted to the funds of an "Aged Female Society" established in Sheffield; to which nearly £40 have been already presented.' Indeed it is proclaimed early in Volume I that: '[. . .] the profits of this publication are designed to alleviate the sufferings of deserving females, afflicted with bereavements, the infirmities, and the too frequent neglects of old age, – with poverty and want, sometimes with ignorance and evil habits, tottering on the brink of the grave [. . .].'

In *The Royal Exile* a section entitled 'Lines Introductory to Mary, Queen of Scots' Letters' includes lines which emphasise the disparity concerning how Sheffield Manor House was experienced by Queen Mary, and by her captors:

'And the nymphs and the Naiads who flit round yon seat,

   The home of thy sorrows, their favourite retreat – *

     Oh, still let them linger to grace the wild scene,

       And hallow the region *where MARY has been.*

* The Manor House in the Park.'

Mary Roberts

In the book entitled *Memoirs of the Life and Writings of James Montgomery* by John Holland and James Everett, it is proclaimed that

'Miss Mary Roberts says she "is not the authoress of the 'Royal Exile,' " a poetical production, the credit of which has always locally been identified with her name; but of course, her explicit disclaimer, however seemingly delayed, must now be admitted. Who, then, did versify the imaginary trials of Mary Queen of Scots in the "Royal Exile?" Montgomery himself, who not only printed the work, but revised the [manuscript] always spoke of Mary Roberts as the writer.' It is then pointed out that her father, Mr Roberts claimed the poetical part of the book to be '[. . .] the production of a very young female now just starting (trembling indeed, but ardently) [. . .].'

There is no mention of Mary Roberts on the book's title page, only affirmation that the poems are *By a Young Lady* (a common way of describing a female author at a time when writing was deemed unsuitable for women – particularly 'ladies') and includes *by her father, The Life of Queen Mary,* which is of course Samuel Roberts. Though not at liberty to provide an answer to this mystifying declaration, I like to believe a young lady was indeed the author of such reputable and enduring work.

My book repeatedly refers to Joseph Hunter, whom the Hunter Archaeological Society was named after. It seemed inevitable

Sheffield Manor would not escape the curiosity and detailed exploration of a man fascinated by antiquity, and early structural sites. His published work *Hallamshire* provides evidence of this, with a stimulating description of the site. He believed 'It was not the practice of our ancestors to include much architectural ornament in their dwelling-houses. Ornament was reserved for the public and especially for ecclesiastical edifices.' Bearing echoes of Holland's standpoint, Hunter goes on to reveal his verdict concerning the condition of the nineteenth-century remnants. Indeed he felt certain only earlier portrayals would present a true image of the original Manor: 'Of the present state and appearance of the ruins the engravings here given from faithful and beautiful drawings will long preserve the memory, when the ruins themselves shall have perished [. . .] but no pencil, no pen could do justice to the magnificent panorama of distant scenery which spreads around the site of this edifice.' He almost rhythmically describes the view from Sheffield Manor, which encompasses 'The fir-crowned heights of Norton, the sweet vale of Beauchief, the purple moor of Totley, and the barren hills of the Peak, the thick woods of Wharncliffe and Wentworth, the widening vale of the Don, and the hills of Laughton and Hansworth, [sic] each distinguishable by its spire [. . .].' Hunter concludes that the once appealing structure must have created a remarkable and prominent spectacle, amid scenery from much of the surrounding expanse. John Holland's book (as referred to earlier) reveals an interesting quotation by him: '[…] there are many fairer towns than Sheffield itself is, yet its neighbourhood presents such a boundless variety of beautiful rural scenery as it is generally allowed that no other town in the kingdom is equal.' In all probability, Francis Buchanan cast his eyes over

Holland's heartfelt words, and despite his profound love of Perthshire, would surely have been in agreement.

My research has repeatedly uncovered groups of modern-day volunteers committed to preserving and maintaining sites of historical interest in Sheffield – sites favourably observed and noted by my forebear over one hundred years ago. In view of this I began to ponder his undisputable feelings of pride and contentment, if only he were currently an onlooker. Sheffield Manor Lodge is not merely a site highly esteemed by Sheffield and its residents, but a very important part of English and European history. My Scottish ancestor's poem compassionately addresses Mary, Queen of Scots' captivity within the walls of the gradually crumbling Manor, and I feel certain that despite his underlying sadness (or perhaps as a consequence of it) Francis would be of the same opinion as the group known as Friends of Sheffield Manor Lodge. It recognises the importance of chronicling events which shaped local and global history, whilst educating interested 'friends'. As a registered charity with more than 400 members, it works closely with the site managers, who address the restoration and preservation of the site. The Tudor Style Gardens are maintained, and seating allows visitors to relax and admire the beautiful meadows and wild flowers, whilst accessible historic costumes bring the past to life. David Templeman, an Elizabethan Historian and Speaker is Chair of the group, and his comprehensive book *Mary, Queen of Scots The Captive Queen of England 1568-87* offers a most interesting and biographical account. Further information about the group is available at www.fosml.org.uk

Those inspired to visit Sheffield's Manor Lodge might embrace what they see and endeavour to visualise bygone times. Whereupon poetry enthusiasts may be inspired to seek out profound versifiers, who once evocatively created lines conveying what *they* saw. Indeed wordsmiths such as my great-great-grandfather, and others presented in this chapter departed this world long ago . . . but their words will live on.

17

'WHARNCLIFFE

SHAGGY Wharncliffe, how I love thee,
With thy grey old crags above me,
Cresting high amid the trees,
Like bald rocks in emerald seas.
All thy old associations,
Are like intermediate stations,
On the refluent track of time,
Looming thro' its misty rime.
Sylvan Wharncliffe, in the spring,
With the sun illumining
Rock and streamlet, field and tree,
In a golden galaxy;
When thy waken'd life is teeming,
From its torpid wintry dreaming;
When the shadows chase the brightness
O'er thy slopes with fairy lightness;
When the snowdrop's spotless token
Tells that winter's ranks are broken,

That he now withdraws his legions
To his far Siberian regions;
Ah, tis then thy vernal gladness
Bursts its icy tomb of sadness.
Thy delicious smells and breezes
Give to life new terms and leases;
Thou, the best of all physicians,
Cures our spleens by sweet transitions;
Hail, dear Wharncliffe, hail thy wood,
Melody and solitude.
Hark; the lark is on the wing,
Morning anthem offering,
More mellifluous as he soars
Up to Heaven's sapphire doors,
Quiv'ring, singing, mounting, cheering,
Till he leaves our sight and hearing.
Is it instinct? is it reason?
Or the changing of the season?
Or a fond uxorious feeling
That is with his bird-heart dealing?
Or a song of gratitude
To the Giver of all good?

Tell me this, ye learn'd sages,
Who read Wisdom's sacred pages.
Tell me this, thou transient thing –
Man-moth, with thy reasoning,
What impels the bird to sing?
In the shadows listening
To the voices of the spring,
It is good to wander here
With the childhood of the year.
Joyful heart and joyful chatter
Cares of mind and troubles scatter;
Hark, the red-wing'd merle sings
Mid the bursting blossomings,
And the finches, spinks, and linnets
Warble to the merry minutes.
Hither to soliloquise,
As the morning dews arise,
Slowly up to meet the light –
Gems of day and tears of night,
Glist'ning tears in moon-eyed roses,
Weeping when the night reposes,
Brilliants in aurora's lustre,

When the dancing sunbeams muster,

Hither, let us come to wander,

Through the mazy woods meander,

Hither from the city's bustle,

From the hum and from the hustle,

From the shoals, where hungry breakers

Hiss, like busy mischief-makers,

From the wheedlings and the warpings,

From the bickerings and carpings,

Here in solitude communal,

Give us grace for Heaven's tribunal.'

Francis Buchanan

With regard to their love of writing poetry and choice of inspiring themes, Francis Buchanan, John Holland, Ebenezer Elliott, and James Montgomery were likeminded people. I feel confident my readers will be of the same opinion; and it will surely come as no surprise to learn that Holland, Elliott and Montgomery have somehow found their way into my chapter entitled Wharncliffe! The setting lies just a few miles from Sheffield City Centre, with views overlooking the Don Valley, Deepcar, and Stocksbridge. The beautiful scenes of dense birch and oak woodland are known as Wharncliffe Woods. The River Don merrily flows by, and all is safeguarded by imposing ancient crags – a remarkable sight to behold. The peaks of the crags are largely crowned with heather, and the site has been of archaeological interest for centuries. Quarrying in the area produced quern-stones, which were fashioned into useful tools for grinding materials such as flour for making bread.

Not surprisingly, the area is bursting with foliage and attracts abundant wildlife. Holland chose to share its enchantments with readers in *The Tour of the Don* – the result of his rambles along the banks of the river, first published in the *Sheffield Iris* in 1836. It unveils a range of expanses in and around Sheffield, and other parts of Yorkshire – Wharncliffe being portrayed as a magnificent scene of splendid isolation, ever appealing to gifted versifiers. The copious leafy lushness is transformed into a wonderful richness of falling leaves during autumn, as it becomes ensconced with '[. . .] dark greens, deep yellows, rich browns [. . .].' Fine forests are shadowed by a mass of rocky mountain-like stone and adorned with rolling waters. Indeed '[. . .] a person might almost fancy himself for a moment as fully sequestered from the world [. . .].' However before long, one is reminded of civilisation by a well-used road, and '[. . .] that very antithesis of solitude – a well loaded bundling stage-coach!'

In his book *Hallamshire* the Historian and Antiquary, Joseph Hunter defines Wharncliffe as a woodland expanse offering '[. . .] a prospect rich, varied extensive, and beautiful as eye can behold.' This brings to mind inspiring scenes no rambling poet could resist. Indeed this was Holland's precise viewpoint: '[. . .] it is impossible not to be at once struck with the magnificent aspect of the scene before us, and the disheartening consideration, that it will be next to impossible to introduce a single new element into the description of a spot to which so many gifted pens have done honour.' Nevertheless, Holland's devotees (myself included) eagerly anticipate an array of charming verse concerning Wharncliffe in *The Tour of the Don*, but what emerges was composed by an author unknown to me:

'In all their pride still wave the Wharncliffe woods,

Still o'er their bowers the summer dews descend;

In freshness flow the Don's translucent floods,

High o'er whose banks the rifted rocks ascend;

Still all his hidden brooklets rippling wend

Through mossy banks, and murmur as they flow

Where pensile flowers, like bashful virgins bend,

To see their beauties in the waves below,

That kiss their perfumed lips, and in their blushes glow.

W. H. STERNDALE'

This new-found poet bearing gentle, eloquent verse, with an air of romance had caught the attention of John Holland. I discovered the excerpt was taken from a poem entitled 'The Lord's Oak' by William Handley Sterndale (1791-1866), and all eight verses were published in Joseph Hunter's earlier mentioned book. A volume of Sterndale's work was never printed, but his mother Mary Sterndale (née Handley) exploited her literary talent by having some of her work published. *The Panorama of Youth* (1807) – a collection of stories and poems for children, and her novel *The Life of a Boy* (1821) were justly celebrated; and it seems John Holland was acquainted with the author. Indeed momentarily distracted from his chronicled account relating to Wharncliffe, he pauses to introduce a new approach by proclaiming: '[. . .]why should I aim at a description of Wharncliffe, while the following glowing sketch – the-pen-and-ink painting of a lady too! – lies before me?

"Immediately on leaving Wortley, we descended a long and steep hill, and turning to the left, entered upon the vale. The road continued by the side of the Don, that emerged from its source in the moors above; but I am quite unequal to describe the sublime and beautiful variety which the succeeding seven miles presented. On the left, the wooded amphitheatre; on the right, hanging copses, tufts of wood, interspersed with sloping pastures [. . .]. We looked up to the circular rampart that crowned the summit for several miles; and when we were opposite the lodge, that like an eagle's nest, appeared perched in the sky, we scarcely could believe that we had soared so high, or the foot of man could have reached there [. . .]." – *[The] Life of a Boy*.'

Holland follows the extract with 'what boy? And who is the lady who writes in that style? As to the first question, I can only reply "read the book" – to the second, Sheffield responds, MARY STERNDALE. I am glad of this opportunity of naming with respect a lady whose presence always reminds me of the old school of female geniuses – if I may use such a phrase [. . .] and when I first spoke to the Sheffield authoress, I recollect congratulating myself on having talked with the lady who talked with the lady, who had talked with Doctor Johnson [. . .]. But whither am I rambling? *from* the banks of the Don certainly: well, then, I will conclude this chapter with good wishes for the welfare of the author [. . .] who has chosen [. . .] one of the prettiest spots.'

I simply adore Holland's style of writing! Indeed what a delightful introduction to the eighteenth-century English writer, poet, and critic Samuel Johnson. He is of course famous for publishing in 1755, a very well received and hugely influential Dictionary of the English Language, incorporating a number of literary quotations from celebrated wordsmiths like Shakespeare; and for which he was given a doctorate – hence the title Dr. Johnson.

As John Holland rambled along the River Don he became preoccupied with the ancient lodge that Mary Sterndale alluded to in her novel, and thenceforth continued his account with some enlightening details. He describes a '[. . .] bold ridge of broken rocks, which crests the summit towards Wortley: [beyond which] Wharncliffe Lodge appears, to keep up our smile, not unlike a vessel at anchor amidst the sylvan surges.' He does however consider it to be of a 'mean appearance', but on entering discovers a comfortable and old-fashioned scene with tasteful accessories about the place. 'This house was in fact, during one period, the temporary residence of the Wortley family – here dwelt the celebrated Lady Mary Wortley Montagu; and this scene of the paternal domains seems to have remained as a verdant spot in the memory of this singular woman [. . .] for when writing from Avignon, in 1743; after describing the situation of that place at the junction of the rivers Rhone and Durance, she says: "Last summer, in the hot evenings, I walked often thither, where I always found a fresh breeze, and the *most beautiful* land prospect I ever saw, *except* Wharncliffe [. . .]." ' The sixteenth-century lodge, now a Grade II listed building still stands at Wharncliffe.

A fictional tale interwoven with historical truths accurately defines Sterndale's *The Life of a Boy*. A brief, unexpected call on Wharncliffe is described in a letter by the narrator, who relates a recent unanticipated delay in Sheffield during a trip to London with her husband. Hence '[. . .] recollecting that Wharncliffe Lodge, near Wortley, was in the vicinity, I was desirous of seeing the place where the celebrated Lady Mary Wortley passed the [. . .] first years of her married life [. . .].' A visit to the lodge ensued, and the awestruck character exclaimed in her letter: '[. . .] I would rather live at Wharncliffe Lodge, than any place I ever saw.' Then 'Turning to the west-end of the building [. . .] the grandeur of Wharncliffe burst upon our view. Woods, and rocks, and sky, deep valleys, and distant moors, in all the gorgeous display of a fine October day!' The English aristocrat, Lady Mary Wortley Montagu was born in London in 1689. She was the progeny of the Peierrepont family of wealthy land owners, with connections to estates such as Thoresby Hall in Nottinghamshire; and she was a poet. As a child she frequented the family library with a mind to 'steal' her education. Indeed she taught herself Latin, and began to write – creating two volumes of poetry and a short novel by the age of sixteen. She married the diplomat Edward Wortley Montagu and travelled alongside him through Europe. Later she became recognised for her literary achievements.

There is more to tell concerning Wharncliffe and its rocky crags. Some may be familiar with the legendary tale of The Dragon of Wantley, and surprised to learn that Wharncliffe was once known as Wantley. According to the legendary tale, a dragon dwelt in a cave amongst the crags and terrorised the locals, devouring all in its path. It was slayed by a knight claimed to be More of More Hall, and believe it or not, the hall – a Grade II Listed Building dating back to the fifteenth century or earlier – still stands directly below the crags in the locality of Stocksbridge. To the best of my knowledge, the entrance to Sheffield Town Hall bears a wall sculpture of the knight slaying the Dragon, and since the 17th century the tale has been portrayed by way of a ballad, an opera, and a novel.

Ebenezer Elliott's contribution concerning Wharncliffe resulted in verse of a contrary theme – though not alive with nature, as one might expect. It is a tale of love, betrayal and murder – intensified by supernatural influences. 'Night. A Descriptive Poem' (1818) is presented as four books – four unrelated poems portraying events which occurred during the night, and Book II is entitled 'Wharncliffe. A Legend'. More than fifteen years later, in his book *The Splendid Village: Corn Law Rhymes; and other Poems*, Elliott asserts in the preface to 'Wharncliffe' that 'WE have all heard of the Dragon of Wantley: but as I neither believe in dragons, or intend to become the historian of the prejudices of the human mind, it may be proper to explain, that this tale [. . .] originated many years ago in a dispute with a friend [. . .].' Concerning poetry, his friend considered some subjects unsuitable. But Elliott was not convinced, and he '[. . .] determined to attempt a practical refutation of my friend's assertion; and the result was "Wharncliffe," *"the ne plus ultra of German horror bombast"* – MONTHLY REVIEW.'

It tells the story of Striga, an enchantress who has murdered her husband and loves the husband of her own sister. She calls for her paramour to kill his wife, but he refuses. Enraged with fear and jealousy, Striga approaches evil spirits and demands they intervene. But her plans go horribly awry. The following selection of lines from Elliott's 'Wharncliffe' describe its appearance during the hours of darkness, which evocatively sets the scene:

'[. . .] the hard rocks dip their rugged feet

In Don's dark wave, and billowy heights ascend, –

Surges eternal, silent, motionless, –

As if th' Almighty's hand had still'd and fix'd

The waves of chaos, in their wildest swell!

Bid thy winds sleep; and bid thy calmest moon,

With each fair star, and fairer planet, look

On Wharncliffe of the Demons! Tranquil scene!

Lonely and beautiful! yet, oh, how wild!'

Ebenezer Elliott

Among the countless versifiers eager to poetically convey what they saw before them at Wharncliffe, was (unsurprisingly) Sheffield's celebrated bard, James Montgomery. His poem indulges the reader with lines eloquently describing what was present on earth beneath the little cloud he observed. I have selected one of the numerous abridged versions, and my choice is taken from *Poems of James Montgomery*, edited by the Rev. Robert Aris Willmott in 1860. He is known for producing a number of edited collections of poetry by celebrated poets, and *A Journal of Summer Time in the Country* (1849). Like Elliott's extraordinary contribution, Montgomery's verse was composed in 1818, and I expect Francis was mindful of both. Although necessary to shorten Montgomery's lengthy poem for the purpose of this book, it loses little charm:

'THE LITTLE CLOUD

Seen in a country excursion among the woods and rocks of Wharncliffe and the adjacent park and pleasure-grounds of Wortley Hall, the seat of the Right Honourable Lord Wharncliffe, near Sheffield, on the 30th day of June, 1818.

THE summer sun was in the west,

Yet far above his evening rest;

A thousand clouds in air display'd

Their floating isles of light and shade, –

The sky, like ocean's channels, seen

In long meandering streaks between.

Cultured and waste, the landscape lay

Woods, mountains, valleys stretch'd away,

And throng'd the immense horizon round,

With heaven's eternal girdle bound;

From inland towns, eclipsed with smoke,

Steeples in lonely grandeur broke;

Hamlets, and cottages, and streams

By glimpses caught the casual gleams [. . .].

> One little cloud, and only one,
> Seem'd the pure offspring of the sun,
> Flung from his orb to show us here
> What clouds adorn *his* hemisphere;
> Unmoved, unchanging in the gale,
> That bore the rest o'er hill and dale,
> Whose shadowy shapes, with lights around,
> Like living motions, swept the ground,
> This little cloud, and this alone,
> Long in the highest ether shone [. . .].'
>
> James Montgomery

I really didn't know what to expect from this chapter . . . or more precisely, 'Wharncliffe'. Contributions from notable literary characters (indeed old friends!) have proved invaluable. If my forebear did not stumble upon the magnificent splendour of Wharncliffe during one of his rambles, he may have become entranced by Holland's roam along the River Don.

In any event, on reading Francis' poem his affection for the setting is clear from the outset. It was predominantly written by means of the rhythmical structure of couplets, when two lines recurrently rhyme and the steady sense of tempo is unbroken. Accomplishing this requires skill and foresight, as the composer must maintain the style, but focus all the while on aspects of the rhyme. See how it metrically rhymes continually, as the reader is indulged with descriptive language. I particularly like the way he describes the aged and worn crags – ever cognisant of the changing world around them. Also the colours of the changing seasons and their influence on nature. The author believes thanks should be given for all he sees around him that is good. And baring echoes of some of Francis' other poems, Wharncliffe describes the haven of peace and serenity he so desired, where the plenteous birds are joyfully singing in gratitude. As he wandered far from 'the city's bustle' my predecessor may have become quite overwhelmed by nostalgias of distant woodland . . . the refuge of his youth, which not only inspired his poetry, but ultimately led him and his readers to Wharncliffe.

18

'HADDON HALL

ONE morn, I sat by yonder hall,
Where thou may'st see the turrets tall,
O'er tree-tops rear so grim and gray
In battlemented old array;
Beneath me rippled tortuous Wye,
With slow and muffled music flowing,
And 'neath the sun's inspiring eye,
The rustling woods with gold were glowing,
And thro' the far withdrawing glades
The trees made vista'd collonades.
Old oaks with many a gnarled knot,
Hoar relics of an age forgot,
And mighty beeches whisper'd there
The mystic language of the breeze;
Like spirit sighs from upper air,
Awakening kindred sympathies,
Wafting my soul on Fancy's plumes,
Through gleaming light and pensive glooms.

I'm roaming away thro' the forest glade,
With the knight and the squire, the dame and maid,
In the long ago, in the long ago,
O'er the dewy green by the river's flow,
And crashing thro' bracken end bramble;
Down the slope and the dell, with the Avenel,
To the tinkling of the goshawks' bell,
With a gallop, a shout and an amble;
Haloo, my fancy, hark to the horn,
Stirring the halls of the rosy morn;
And the deep-mouth'd bay of the churlish hound,
As the stag springs out with the noble bound.
Behold in his pride the fugitive
Pressing away thro' the tangled greave,
Tearing adown thro' the ferny dell,
Scorning the shout and the whoop and yell!
With his stately antler'd head upright;
Strong in his courage, swift in his flight,
Shod with the wind, in his terror he flies,
Great in his terrible ecstasies;
Spurning contempt to the yelping pack,
Who are bringing him death on his track.

Come, my Fancy, pilot be,
Let us change the fantasy;
See you yonder gleaming towers?
There the ballroom cheats the hours,
With its minstrelsy.
Tripping feet and laughing faces,
Pioneer to love's embraces,
And its ecstasy.
A wall of darkness lours
Around the woods and bowers;
And thro' the darkling night
A pair of eyes are gleaming,
A ray of hope is beaming;
And Love's puissant light,
From that high hall a sigh,
Sad and fearfully
Mixes with the trembling air,
Kindred sigh and whisper'd prayer,
Making bold the watcher there;
Hark to the minstrels pealing,
Look at the dancers wheeling,
As thro' the woods are stealing,
Sir John and his Dorothy,*

And the ready steed is ringing

His hoofs o'er the stony way,

As lone Philomel is singing

Her midnight roundelay.

* * *

Ho, Fancy, art thou napping,

Dost thou not hear that rapping,

On Haddon's studded gates?

Hear'st thou not the brazen clang,

And the cannon's thunder bang?

The Queen of England waits. †

The virgin queen is there;

Haddon bring out thy fair,

And, with chivalric bearing, man

Thy battlements and barbican;

Gaily let thy pennons stream,

Flash thy swords, thy lances gleam,

Morning, ray thy orient light,

On each helm and corslet bright,

Lend thy auriferous beam.

Thro' the gloomy portals' arch,
Sturdy steel-capp'd warriors march;
And the stony slope adown,
Knights and barons of renown
Prance their glittering steeds;
The idle river gurgles on
Heedless, 'neath the bridge of stone,
Playing with its reeds.

And the silver trumpets sound,
And the hundred echos round
Mimic with their empty measures,
Airy pomps, and fleeting pleasures;
And giant Time counts grains of sand,
Trickling thro' his bony fingers,
And the river, happy ever
By the water lilies lingers,
Whispering to the weeds.
And Beauty's glance and Passion's sigh
Are linking golden chains,
That oft corrode if Passion's gust
Leaves only stings and pains.

> The retrospect has vanish'd now,
> The mystic wreath falls from thy brow;
> The pageantry has fled.
> That wither'd monument of gloom,
> Shrined in its wilderness of bloom,
> Gleams like a sunset from the past,
> – A twilight glory lingering,
> Subdued, ere overcast
> With clouds of Time, whose fingering
> Brings down thy hoary head.

* The celebrated Sir John Manners, who eloped with Dorothy Vernon, from Haddon. † Elizabeth.'

Francis Buchanan

On limestone banks overlooking the River Wye, not far from Bakewell in the Peak District, stands Haddon Hall. This splendid Fortified Medieval Manor House was originally built as a Norman Fort during the twelfth century and is renowned for its wealth of history, alive with legend, romance and mystery. The ancient hall, with its archaic contents and alluring gardens attracts vast numbers of visitors each year. Eager day-trippers arrive in anticipation of a memorable outing at this enchanting Grade I listed wonder, and they are not disappointed. For at the very least, the hall boasts Medieval and Tudor architecture, ancient gargoyles, household furniture, terraced walled gardens that cascade downwards to the river, and a lower garden with wildflowers and pond life. Potential visitors are presented with a choice of tours which appeal to those seeking adventure, together with an intensely realistic experience of the hall and its history.

Robert Smythson was a celebrated early Elizabethan Architect, and his work at the hall includes the Long Gallery and the garden's fountain terrace. The tour named after him explores his great accomplishments. An impressive collection of English, French and Flemish tapestries warrants a tour designed to behold them. And those with a fondness for outdoor pursuits might wish to engage in activities which took place at Haddon Hall for centuries – such as archery, fishing, picnicking and walking, all of which utilise the estate's historic parkland and ancient forests. Particularly fascinating is the array of poems and signatures etched onto glass over centuries, by masons and visitors alike. Furthermore, the ancient architecture and scenic surroundings make Haddon Hall an ideal location for filming, and against the backdrop, period dramas such as Jane Eyre and Pride and Prejudice have proved to be both dramatic and authentic.

As Haddon Hall's popularity grows, today's sightseers tend to arrive in a range of motor vehicles, including coaches. But in former times callers would make their way to the hall by other means of transportation. You may be surprised to learn that as a tourist attraction, Haddon Hall was extremely fashionable during the Victorian era. In fact its status grew around the mid-1830s, when organised outings were big business. Numerous groups and associations were attracted to what the hall had to offer. Indeed I fell upon this notice, published in the *Sheffield Daily Telegraph*, on 15th August 1857:

'SHEFFIELD YOUNG MEN'S CHRISTIAN ASSOCIATION.

EXCURSION TO HADDON HALL AND CHATSWORTH.

The Members and their Friends propose Visiting Haddon Hall and Chatsworth, on WEDNESDAY NEXT, August 19th. Tickets may be obtained from LOXLEY BROTHERS', and the Newspaper Offices. LADIES ARE RESPECTFULY INVITED.'

(And very pleased I am to *see it!*)

The following advertisement was published in the same newspaper, on 25th July, 1868:

'OMNIBUS DAY TRIP to BASLOW and HASSOP (for Monsal Dale, Bakewell, and Haddon Hall) on WEDNESDAY next, July 29th. For Particulars see small Bills, at the Sheffield Carriage Company's Offices, 5 Waingate.
J.W.UNWIN, Manager'

Notices like these, promoting jaunts to Derbyshire's historic residences would regularly appear in newspapers. It seems the Victorians never grew tired of them. In truth planned excursions continued for decades, and tourists journeyed from far and wide, as they began to take advantage of the train. On 3rd July, 1880, the *Burnley Advertiser* printed the following:

'ALTHAM'S DAY EXCURSIONS [. . .] Arrangements have [. . .] been made for parties who wish to secure Conveyances to drive them from Rowsley Station – immediately on the arrival of the train – to Haddon Hall, 2 miles; Haddon Hall to Chatsworth, 5 miles; and Chatsworth to Matlock Bath, 9 miles. Fare, 3s. each person . . . the loveliest parts of the district can be viewed, and the Tourist will arrive at Matlock Bath about 3 p.m.

GENERAL INFORMATION. Haddon Hall [. . .] is open constantly. Usual charge for admission, 3d. each. A 'Bus runs to and from Rowsley about 11. a.m., 2 and 4 p.m. Fare 1s. each way [. . .]. A splendid walk and view can be had from Bakewell to Chatsworth [. . .].'

The village of Rowsley lies just minutes from Haddon Hall, and during the nineteenth century its railway station provided a convenient pause for those with sights set on the Hall, and other historical locations. No matter where their voyage originated, passengers would disembark at Rowsley, having previously organised a further mode of transport to escort them to their final destination. The Derbyshire Peak District has always been considered an especially scenic route by train, and the line to Rowsley, which initially opened during the 1840s as part of the 'North Midland Railway' became known as the stop not far from Haddon Hall. However, the line was prevented from following its intended route by opposition from the Duke of Devonshire, who was against the railway running through Chatsworth Park. Likewise, the Duke of Rutland of Haddon Hall refused to allow the railway to cross the estate on the surface, forcing the company to go underground and build Haddon Tunnel. But being on average only 12 feet deep, the 'tunnel' was merely a shielded approach.

During the 1970s the Peak Railway Society was formed by a group of enthusiasts, following the closure of the railway in 1968. The society is still in operation today, and as I write, its aim is to recover the line that runs between Matlock and Buxton. The northern terminus is currently at Rowsley, and steam trains run throughout the year between Rowsley South Station and Matlock, Platform 2 – a distance of four miles. My great-great-grandfather may have made his way to Haddon Hall by means of an organised day trip involving use of the train via Rowsley station. On the other hand, as I ponder Francis' deep affection for rural landscapes – notably the enigmatic woods and forests, which offered inspiration for his written verse – I envisage him rambling through splendid terrain adorned with trees, and harmonious with birdsong . . . eventually arriving on foot.

Growing interest in the Hall resulted in a number of poems and fictional works emerging from enthused authors – who, amidst rumours that Jane Austen had written part of her commemorated *Pride and Prejudice* within the shadows of Haddon Hall, and Sir Walter Scott based some of his novels on this striking setting (though nothing has ever been proved), – were keen to turn out in replica and proudly create their masterpieces. I believe Francis was present at the Hall, where surrounded by beautiful scenery and driven by insight, he composed his own adaptation of historical events, bursting with rhyme and romance.

At the root of the growing interest in Haddon Hall during the nineteenth century, lay enthralment surrounding the sixteenth-century legend of Dorothy Vernon's elopement. Many will be familiar with this tale, accompanied by the copious literature and dramatic performances it stimulated throughout the centuries, and across the world. Today Haddon Hall is home to Lord and Lady Edward Manners. Lord Manner's ancestors Sir John Manners and Dorothy Vernon, though deeply in love, were forbidden to see each other – possibly as a consequence of conflicting religious beliefs or uncertain financial prospects. Sir John was the son of 1st Earl of Rutland and Dorothy's father, Sir George Vernon, descended from a long line of Vernons and previously de Vernons, who owned and occupied the Hall for centuries. Resolute in defying their fathers' wishes, the two of them absconded and were married, whilst legend flourished alleging that on her quest to meet with Sir John Manners, Dorothy silently crept away from a crowded ball at Haddon Hall. Subsequently, however, the couple were to inherit the Haddon estate on the death of Dorothy's father, Sir George Vernon, and it has remained with the Manners family ever since.

Francis Buchanan may have been familiar with the work of Samuel Rayner, a well-known artist and author of the early part of the nineteenth century. His work of 1836, *History and Antiquities of Haddon Hall* explores its architectural details, the gardens, and naturally the tale of Dorothy Vernon. Celebrated as an artist, Rayner encapsulated Haddon at a time when the property had been deserted for almost two hundred years, when the Manners chose instead to dwell at Belvoir Castle, in Leicestershire – another Seat of the Dukes of Rutland. The Haddon estate, with its mixture of architectural styles from different eras, was left unaltered during the Georgian and Victorian periods of modernisation. Therefore, Haddon Hall was largely untouched, and preserved for perpetuity . . . and for its welcome guests to cherish as they step back in time. During the early part of the twentieth century the estate was significantly restored by the 9th Duke of Rutland.

My great-great-grandfather found himself 'one morn [. . .] sat by yonder hall' with its view of tall turrets above the tree tops, and the 'muffled' sound of the River Wye. By means of deeply eloquent words, he takes us with him – so we too are able to brush against the marvels of Haddon Hall. This lengthy composition begins with detailed rhyming verse, which depicts Francis' picturesque surroundings, with pleasing views reaching out beyond the ancient trees and relics – archaic and grey with age. Moved by what he sees, Francis begins to daydream as he roams aimlessly 'In the long ago, in the long ago' through the forest, alongside imaginary characters from bygone times. As his fanciful notions take charge, events become more dramatic and the flowing river begins to crash 'thro' bracken and bramble' as suddenly, an ensuing hunt is galloping by, as it reaches its target . . . which signals the end of the noble stag.

The mood changes, as in twilight we enter the ballroom amidst frenzied music and dancing: 'Tripping feet and laughing faces', as Francis relays events surrounding the legend of Dorothy Vernon and Sir John Manners as 'thro' the darkling night [. . .] A pair of eyes are gleaming / A ray of hope is beaming.' The pair slip away, leaving behind the hordes of excited guests as they take one last 'Look at the dancers wheeling [. . .] as thro' the woods are stealing, Sir John and his Dorothy [. . .].'

My forebear's powerful imagination is once again revived, with the thunderous entry of Queen Elizabeth I and her entourage via

'Haddon's studded gates 'as the estate, unprepared, scurries to welcome them in procession as [. . .] the silver trumpets sound [. . .].' These ancient Tudor times are in the past, and 'The pageantry has fled' – though memories linger at Haddon Hall, as it stands like a monument which 'Gleams like a sunset from the past [. . .].' This profoundly atmospheric and theatrical poem, overflowing with historical events – legendary or otherwise – is crammed with colourful, ingenious detail. It delivers a truly tangible (if not magical) experience of Haddon Hall's uninterrupted past, leaving the reader with a lasting impression, together with a thirst for ancient wisdom embroidered with intrigue and romance. During the late nineteenth century, those who devoured Francis' imposing verse relating to Haddon Hall (not to mention the rhythmical creations by other wordsmiths of the time) were no doubt eager to hop on board a train to Rowsley Station.

*   *   *

Haddon Hall never failed to entice droves of ardent poets with a need to satisfy an intensely powerful yearning to see it . . . to breathe the air . . . to touch its permeable stone walls. Indeed much of what took place before those walls has, with some resourcefulness, been recurrently interpreted by way of beautiful verse. I was thrilled to discover that John Hall and John Holland (habitual guests within these pages – if not familiar friends!) were among them, and happily share their verse with you. The following selected lines are from a 'sketch' composed by John Hall in 1849:

'HADDON HALL

A SKETCH – DESCRIPTIVE OF A SCENE WHICH TOOK PLACE JUNE 15TH, 1849.

'Twas noon; – and Sol's meridian ray

Gleam'd on old Haddon's ruin grey;

Each dusky tower, each gloomy height,

Was bathed in floods of golden light,

Whose radiant beams, of lightsome hue,

Around the pile their lustre threw;

Flinging anon its sombre shade,

In darker contrast, o'er the glade,

Where, deeply shadowed in the grass,

It lay, an elongated mass,

Stretching its prostrate limbs afar,

Like a huge giant slain in war,

Till in the Wye's adjacent flood,

Broken at last, the image stood.

But not alone was Haddon's pile

Illumin'd by the sunbeam's smile, –

Not only turrets, walls, and towers,

But woods, and streams, and fields, and bowers
All shared the glorious god of day,
And gladden'd in his bounteous ray!
Above, dark groves of ancient trees,
Wav'd their green branches in the breeze;
Below, the Wye's meandering stream,
Gush'd through the mead with silvery gleam;
Around, as far as eye could view
The landscape glow'd with brightest hue:
The rocky glen, the rising wood,
The smiling vale, and crystal flood,
The towering hills of moorland heath,
And peaceful hamlets couch'd beneath,
All, gaily garbed in summer's dress,
Shone forth, mid Nature's loveliness,
And blended, in one beauteous view,
Colours of every shade and hue.

But Haddon saw another sight,
By the same sun's discursive light;
For while the noontide splendour shone
O'er the horizon's glittering zone,
Stray wandering beams anon would pass,

The narrow casement's clouded glass,
Gliding through gallery and hall, -
Scaring the bats on roof and wall;
But when at length they pierced the gloom,
That filled the ancient banquet room,
(Where, ages past, the proud and great
Of England's barons ruled the fête,
But where the tattered tap'stry now
A melancholy change doth show),
Strange was the scene those beams beheld;
Strange was the picture they reveal'd!
No longer desolate and void,
The room was filled from side to side –
The tables set, the banquet spread,
The ample sirloin at the head,
The dishes filled with fruit and kine,
The goblets crown'd with ruddy wine;
While round the ancient room of state,
As fair a company there state,
As Haddon in her proudest day,
E'er saw at wake or holiday;
Nor ever till that hour, I ween,
Was such a group of beauty seen:

The maidens all, like rosebuds rare,
Were beautiful, and passing fair, –
The matrons too, with charms mature,
Failed not to dazzle and allure;
While both, on that eventful day,
Held, as of old, triumphant sway;
And as they sat around the board,
Methought the grim and bearded lord,
Whose picture hung upon the wall,
Smiled, as he looked down on them all;
Wond'ring, no doubt, again to see
Such scenes of life and gaiety,
And hear the blythe and merry strain
Of human voices once again,
Filling the halls with festive roar,
As in the feudal days of yore;
When he, perchance, the living lord,
Presided at the welcome board,
And saw around, on every hand,
The first and fairest of the land,
Join in the merriment and glee
Of English hospitality.

But, as he gazed, with kindling eye,
The vision changed as rapidly;
Awhile, the merry sounds were heard,
Awhile, the busy footsteps stirr'd,
Awhile, the gay and happy throng
Filled the old hall with laugh and song;
Then all was hushed: the clanging door
Creak'd on its rusty hinge no more;
The music and the laugh were quelled,
And solitude sole empire held;
The merry company had fled,
And all was silent as the dead!
Again the ancient room of state
Was left all void and desolate;
The owlet and the bat again
Resumed their interrupted reign,
And the grim picture on the wall
Was left sole tenant of the Hall!'

John Hall *ALIAS* "J.H.J."
Thoughts and Sketches in Verse (1877) Sheffield

Mr Hall was clearly unable to resist the lure of another of Derbyshire's popular scenes . . . Chatsworth. His poem was probably written during the 1840s, and I am delighted to share it with my readers:

'CHATSWORTH

WRITTEN AFTER A VISIT ON WHIT-MONDAY, THIRTY YEARS AGO

Hail, Palace of the mountains!
Hail, land of wood and flowers!
Of rills and sunny fountains!
Of groves and fairy bowers!
Of hills, and vales, and rocky dells,
Enchanted by a thousand spells,
Of landscapes bright and gay, –
Whose varied scenery among,
The silver Derwent winds along,
Its mead-meandering way!

Ah! with what charms attended,
Hath Nature's lovely Queen,
With Art here sweetly blended
To grace the glowing scene:
The stately Hall, – the rising wood, –
The placid lake, – the mountain flood,
The rich luxuriant mead;

And Park, wherein the wandering deer
In herds gregarious appear
Beneath the sylvan shade!

Here Flora, too, hath chosen
Her fair and honour'd seat,
With lavish hand disclosing
Her beauties at thy feet;
From east, from west, from lands afar,
Where flowers the radiant landscape star,
And gem the shining plain;
Here, to this highly favour'd spot,
The first and fairest she hath brought,
Of all her glittering train!

Ah! lovely scenes! what grandeur
And beauty ye display:
Where'er my footsteps wander,
Fresh charms adorn the way!
Where'er I turn my feasting eyes,
New prospects there before me rise
With bright and varied gleam;
So rich, so fairy-like, – the whole

> Would seem to my enraptured soul
>
> The phantom of a dream!'
>
> John Hall   ALIAS "J.H.J."
>
> *Thoughts and Sketches in Verse* (1877) Sheffield

John Holland's poem concerning Haddon Hall begins with a description of the condition of the hall at the time of his visit, and is presented as follows:

'ADVERTISEMENT

HADDON HALL, a mansion belonging to the Duke of Rutland, is finely situated on the River Wye, about two miles from Bakewell, in Derbyshire. The building is, at present not only uninhabited, but stripped of the greater part of its furniture and pictures: it is, however, in a state of perfect preservation, and exhibits one of the most characteristic specimens of the ancient domestic architecture in this Kingdom, probably in existence.'

The poetical sketch is centred on one of John Holland's Derbyshire 'pilgrimages' – on this occasion, a pleasant walk in the company of three friends, from Bakewell to Haddon Hall, on 12th July, 1823. It was published in the *Sheffield Iris* and Holland's *Flowers from Sheffield Park* and was written in two parts, the first being 'The Walk from Bakewell: We walk'd from *Bakewell* with unwearied feet / Hope in our hearts, and pleasure in our eyes, / And converse on our lips; for, wide around, / To every sense, the scenery was delightful [. . .] right before, in proud and gloomy grandeur, / Old *Haddon's* turrets greet the wondering eye.'

The second part is entitled 'The Mansion': 'At *Haddon's* ancient mansion, tree-embower'd! / And what, though all be solitude around, / And nought but empty silence reigns within – / Imagination peoples every space [. . .] Up stairs we went, and stroll'd through many a room, / Damp, cold, and comfortless; the walls time-stain'd.' In Holland's sketch, a guide is directing the group around the hall: "This," said our prompt conductress, "was the hall: / There, sat the master at his dinner board" [and] "This was the bower of *Lady Dorothy*, / And these her private walks." '

As this chapter closes, I feel unable to resist one more poem relating to Haddon Hall. This brief, yet rather profound contribution was written in 1830 by none other than a child of 11 years. It reveals a little of the imagination and preliminary literary skill of John Ruskin – whom I make reference to not for the first time within these pages. What follows was composed at a time when the lyrical journey of a fresh-faced Francis Buchanan (and pen) had barely begun. It appeared in *Volume I – Poems written in Boyhood* (1826-1835) – of *The Poems of John Ruskin* (1891):

'HADDON H.ALL

I.

OLD halls, and old walls, –

They are my great delight;

Rusty swords, and rotten boards,
And ivy black as night!
Hey, ruination and hey, desolation, –
Only created to spoil the creation!

II.

Dry ditch, old niche, –
Besides, an oaken table;
On't the warriors ate,
From a pewter plate,
As much as they were able!
Hey, ruination and hey, desolation, –
Only created to spoil the creation!'

John Ruskin

19

WAR POEMS

My great-great-grandfather's interest in global conflict (whether historic or relatively recent in relation to his era) and the lives and active service of soldiers, was formulated in a manner only a poet could embrace. Francis did in fact write several poems (and at least one song) concerning the military, and war, and there may have been more. Those which failed to escape publication appear in my forebear's original edition of *Sparks from Sheffield Smoke* (1882) and *The Crusader, with other Poems and Lyrics* (1848), as well as various newspapers, and anthologies of poetry.

The following selection of complete poems and excerpts are both graphic and dynamic. Some present to the reader an authentic account of actual events, with plausible experiences of soldiers, whilst others have been tailored to recount fictional tales based on warfare. I refer once again to the article published in the *Irvine and Fularton Times* of 24th October, 1884 (see chapter entitled Francis, and also the Epilogue), which has become almost integral to my book. It provides an excellent appraisal relating to two of Francis' war poems published in his Sheffield volume: '[. . .] he makes the Scotch bluid leap in one's veins in "Scotch Greys at Waterloo." The charge of the Greys and Enniskilleners at Balaclava, is also a good production, in which the actors, in high martial strains, and through the use of "sheer steel and sheer courage" do carry the day.'

The Royal North British Dragoons was a heavy cavalry regiment of the British Army, generally known as the Scots Greys. At the Battle of Waterloo in 1825, the said regiment, led by Sergeant Ensign Charles Ewart of Scotland (1769-1846) famously captured the regimental eagle of the French 45th Regiment of Line. What follows is a selection of lines from Francis' poetic version of those events:

'THE SCOTS GREYS AT WATERLOO.
THE CHARGE.

"CHARGE!" and the word pass'd down the line

And forth the horses sped;

The whirling sabres flash'd above

The dying and the dead;

One wild impulsive cheer rang out,

As Scottish men can cheer,

And then thro' smoke and fire they rent,

The column'd grenadier.

PART SECOND.
THE CAPTURE OF THE EAGLE.

AMID the shriek, the roar, the rush,
A stately trooper rides,
With reeking hide, and frothy flanks,
His plunging steed divides;
One flittering eagle rocks above
The sea of death below;
And Ewart marks it for his own,
Amongst the cordon'd foe.

PART THIRD.
THE RETREAT. THE CUIRASSIERS.

The corslets of these vaunted troops,
With Scottish sabres rang;
And many a blow on brazen helm,
Unhorsed them with a clang;
And many a cheer, in mid career,
Shook down both shriek and groan,
As the plated ranks of Bonaparte
Were crushed and overthrown.

> Indeed, it was a blood-red day,
>
> A day of glory too;
>
> The thistle's prickly head had daub'd
>
> The lily's spotless hue.
>
> Springs come and go, and summers glow,
>
> And autumns shed decay,
>
> But all imperishing remains,
>
> The triumph of the Grey.'
>
> Francis Buchanan
>
> *Sparks from Sheffield Smoke* (1882)

The Crimean War involving the Russian Empire and British, as well as French, Ottoman and Sardinian troops took place between 1853 and 1856. The Battle of Balaclava is one of the most famous battles of this war, and my ever vigilant predecessor clearly immersed himself in the copious newspaper reports of the time. Indeed the press throughout Britain and around the world regularly published details of war incidents – virtually as they happened. *The Illustrated London News* of 18th November, 1854 offers a reliable account of the actions of Britain's Heavy Cavalry Brigade against the Russians at Balaclava, on 25th October. The Heavy Brigade, otherwise known as the Scots Greys and the 6th Enniskillen's was commanded by the British Army Officer, Major General James Yorke Scarlett (1799-1871) and powerfully and raucously charged at the enemy – an occurrence quite the antithesis of the famous 'Charge of the Light Brigade' which came to pass on the same day. Before engaging with Francis' poem, I would like you to read the aforementioned London News article describing the charge of the Heavy Cavalry Brigade:

'[. . .] The Russian Cavalry, about 4000 in number, cantered down the hill with evident intention to attack our cavalry. No sooner was this perceived, than the bugle sounded the advance for our men, who instantly moved forward at a canter. As they approached the enemy and began to ascend the hill, the canter emerged into a charge, and the pace was terrific.'

The London press war news commentary goes on to describe how the Heavy Brigade charged directly towards the centre of the assemblage of Russian mounted troops and 'For a moment it was a glorious sight. The glittering helmets and weapons and varied uniforms of our fellows as they pressed forward to the charge, with sabres raised and lances levelled, made the mere spectacle beautiful; but accompanied with all its terrors, it was one of the most awful grandeur. The solid earth shook and reverberated with a sound like thunder, as a thousand horses, spurred to their utmost speed, went tearing up the hill, scattering the turf and grass like a cloud of sand behind them.'

It then recounts the response of the enemy, who were '[. . .] nothing loth to accept the challenge, and, indeed, they had little reason. For their numbers were as nearly three to one. In a line of two-thirds of a mile they swept down from the hill upon our men, meeting them about half-way up. The dull heavy noise with which they closed could be heard at a mile, and made the listener's blood run cold.' Hold that in your mind as you read the following poem. Though published in 1882, it may have been written considerably earlier:

'THE CHARGE OF THE "SCOTS GREYS" AND ENNISKILLENERS AT BALACLAVA.
OCT. 25TH, 1854.

I.

OUT flew the grey horses, and out flew the brown,
And the Scot and En'skillener thundered down;
And the gleam of their sabres flash blue in the gloom,
As the smoke-wreaths roll upward, like sea-wreaths of spume.

II.

Out over the gorse tufts, and red dabbled clay,
The chargers are champing and tearing away;
Right full at the centre the sword-blows have clash'd,
And as lightning thro' cloud-rifts, the red-coats have flash'd.

III.

The wings of the Russian are folding around,
But they meet to encircle the blood-frozen ground;
For the Britons have pierced the dark mass with a cheer,
And the Moskaw is shiver'd from van to the rear.

IV.

The Celt and the Scotchman are heroes to-day:
Sheer steel and sheer courage have won them the way;
In that terrible moment, tho' shaken and broke,
The fire of their Fathers hath heated the stroke.

V.

"They are lost now, God help them, what more can they do?"
The odds of the Russ are as twenty to two.
But the music of sabres on Muscovite steel,
Gives strength to the shoulder and nerve of the heel.

VI.

Lo, as they emerged from that forest of foes,
A shout o'er the morning from hundreds uprose,
As down thro' the vale like one bolt from a bow,
The Dragoon-guards and Royals have routed the foe.

VII.

The remnants are scatter'd and flying with speed –
The noble hearts saved in the hour of their need;
Full-well is remember'd the charge of the Grey,
And the Irish Dragoon, in that famous affray.'

Francis Buchanan

Sparks from Sheffield Smoke (1882)

The Charge of the Light Brigade is recognised as one of the most famous blunders to occur in military history; yet a most extraordinary act of bravery. The attack took place during the Crimean War's Battle of Balaclava in October, 1854. Major General Lord Cardigan was in command of the Light Brigade, equipped with smaller horses and lighter armaments; and with only six hundred mounted troops, they faced twice as many. Despite this, Cardigan ordered his cavalry to charge at the Heavy Brigade . . . with catastrophic results. It has been said there may have been some confusion – resulting in the order being misunderstood, and various leaders have been held responsible. My next choice of poem appears in its entirety, and relates to a soldier's experience of this famous incident, which he relives as he conveys events to the landlord of an Inn, and anyone listening.

The poem is a wonderful example of Francis' ability to relay an eventful, bygone account by means of another raconteur, as he simultaneously sets the scene pertaining to both crowded alehouse and battleground. Moreover, it is a somewhat alluring poem, which notably rhymes in a cascading fashion, affording (despite the subject matter) a most enjoyable read:

'THE SOLDIER'S TALE

I.

"Now, Landlord, fill this jug once more, we'll have another toss,

And then I'll tell you how I won this bright Victoria Cross;

And how we fought on that great day, and cut the

Russians down,
When the Light Brigade charg'd undismayed, for England and renown."

II.

The ancient warrior's eye lit up, up went the foaming tap,
And on the floor his wooden leg stub'd down with hollow rap;
And the roof-tree rung uproariously a goodly old refrain,
As the stout old English soldier fought his battle o'er again.

III.

"It was October twenty-fifth, in eighteen fifty-four,
About eleven o'clock at noon, I think it was no more;
When Cardigan rode down our line, and we cheer'd – once and again,
When he said we had, 'gainst fearful odds, to fight like Englishmen."

IV.

"To hear was to obey, and off we rode both neck and crop,
So eager were we for the fray, we did not care to stop;
Our sabres flash'd, as on we dash'd, all in that vale of death,
And not a pulse beat quicker then, nor shorter grew a breath."

V.

"The turf flew from our horses' heels – from right and left and front

Flew hissing down the iron shot, nor flinched we from its brunt;
'Twas game to see six hundred men – all told we were not more -
Face twenty thousand Muscovites, in that infernal roar."

VI.

"There was many a saddle empty then, before we struck a stroke,
And, with flashing steel above our heads, we plunged into the smoke;
No faltering there, nor bating speed, but onward thro' the dun,
And we cut him down on right and left - the gunner at his gun."

VII.

"Aye, 'twas a fearful sight to see – the bloody carnage there,
But we were demon-Englishmen, and nerved unto despair;
Revenge made giants of us all, and as we slash'd and slew,
We thought 'twas noble thus to die, before the wide world's view."

VIII.

"Our cheering was a death cry there to many a gallant heart,
And in the whirl of madden'd strife, we nobly did our part;
To emulate the featly deeds our fathers did before,
And on that day the Light Brigade compared with those of yore."

IX.

"Well, we returned, with glutted swords, and aching shoulders too,
We'd storm'd the battery in front, and smote the Russians through;
Back in retreat, thro' heroes dead – thro' seared and plunging horse –
And thro' a flanking fire of death, and thro' a column'd force."

X.

"We scatter'd it as Autumn leaves, when rustling down a dell,
Each shivers o'er its fellow leaf, till all are mixed pell-mell;
And English blood was scatter'd too, and English flesh and bone;
But I suppose, the deeds that day the blunder did atone."

XI.

"Again, we charged, again we turn'd, like stricken deer at bay,
The Cossack lancers flank'd our shreds, in twenty fold array;
Down came the grape shot from behind - from right and left – below,
And the coward volley swept to death both struggling friend and foe."

XII.

"'Twas here a Russian, with his sword, cut down my

gallant mate,
I clove the trooper to the teeth, it had to be his fate;
And as I loved my comrade well, I could not see him lay,
So from my horse I swung me down, and carried him away."

XIII.

"I cannot tell you how 'twas done, but what I say is true,
Through shot and shell, and cut and thrust, I bore him safely through;
And then our heavy horsemen came, to cover our retreat,
And we both were snatched from death that day, when Muscovy was beat."

XIV.

"'Twas thus I won the valour-badge, and saved my comrade's life,
And I am here to tell you all this chapter of my life;
God bless our gracious Queen, my boys – our fleet and army too,
And three times three, to all who love, the Red, the White, and Blue!" '

Francis Buchanan

Sparks from Sheffield Smoke (1882)

The Charge of The Light Brigade involved over six hundred men and approximately two hundred returned, rendering it futile and catastrophic. Just weeks later, the mid-nineteenth-century Poet Laureate Alfred Lord Tennyson (see chapter entitled 'To the Pimpernel') presented his well-known poem concerning the dreadful event, appropriately naming it 'The Charge of The Light Brigade'.

The final war poems and selected lines you are about to read, were written by Francis decades before those published in Sheffield. Indeed they appear in *The Crusader, with other Poems and Lyrics* (1848). 'The Crusader' is a tale in verse, of exceptional length – as is typically the case concerning narrative poems. Nonetheless, it boasts notable rhythm and rhyme. Francis may have selected it as the title of the said volume in view of its length, or it was a personal favourite. He possibly recognised how fine it is! The tale seems to be loosely based on the Third Crusade of the 12th Century – a battle involving European Leaders, including England's King Richard I (Richard the Lionheart) – and the scene is set at noon on an army camp in the Middle East, where the sun is beating down. They are prepared to fight Saladin, the Saracen leader, who opposes King Richard. A Page (or nobleman) named Edric is in attendance to the King, and ordered to take flight and join in battle with a noble knight named De Courtenay, for which he will be rewarded. When he triumphs, the King reveals that the boy was found by a Spanish soldier, who raised him as a son and taught him war skills – indeed 'how great fights were lost and won'. Richard the Lionheart took him under his wing and changed his name. Now the king is returning the young nobleman to his true father . . . De Courtenay. Although an ideal contender to appear in Francis' war poems, its magnitude allows for only selected lines:

'THE CRUSADER

The flower of English chivalry,
The heroes of old France,
Were there, to fight the Saracen
With many a well tried lance;
The Scottish broadsword too was seen
Beside the blade of Spain –
The battle-axe of Germany –
The falchion of the Dane.

'Twas in a gorgeous tent he sat,
The leader of this band,
In thoughtful mood, his lofty brow
Lean'd heavy on his hand;
A stalwart knight was he, I trow,
As ever couched a lance;
In peace his eye was mild – in war
A terror in its glance.

'Twas Richard of the lion heart –
The pride of England's isle –
The dread of Saracen and Turk
In deadly war's turmoil!
The sworn champion of the cross –
The first to take the field –
The bravest of that mighty host –
Last in the fight to yield!

He look'd upon some written scrolls,
That loosely lay around,
And from his couch he started up,
And paced the sandy ground;
He paused, and stood with folded arms,
Then mutter'd "Ha! 'tis well,
I'll mar his plot, and in his toils
I'll snare the infidel.

"Ho! Edric, here," the monarch cried;
And straitway in there came
A gallant youth, in page's dress,
Of an illustrious name;
With downcast eyes he silent stood

Within the royal tent,
Advanced, and kiss'd the royal hand,
As on his knee he bent.

"Now, trusty Edric, haste away
To our noble knight De Courtenay,
And tell him 'tis our command,
E-er yonder sun has sunk to rest,
To have ready, with steeds and in armour drest,
A thousand of his band.

Then away, away to our good Sir Knight,
And bid him prepare for the deadly fight,
E-er the moonbeam sport on the desert sand,
Be without the camp with his chosen band.
And hark you, Edric, by this I swear,
(And the monarch touch'd his baldric rare,)
E-er the morning rays on our banners shine,
A pair of silver spurs are thine;
For to-night you'll be of De Courtenay's train,
And win for thyself a knightly name."

And lowly his head young Edric bent,

> And swift he sped on his way;
> Nor stayed till he had reached the tent
> Of the gallant De Courtenay.'

The tale adopts a frenzied approach as Edric charges towards De Courtenay, joins the 'deadly fight', and triumphs in battle:

> 'Now Richard from his steed dismounts –
> They form a circle round,
> And youthful Edric forward comes,
> And kneels upon the ground.
> With glowing cheek and glancing eye,
> He slowly bent his head,
> As Richard with a naked sword
> Drew near with kingly tread;
> He gazed upon the aspirant
> Who wished a knight to be,
> And smiled as he prepared his blade
> To dub him such with glee;
> And now he lifts his princely arm,
> And touches Edric's head:
> And leap'd his ardent heart with joy
> As soon's he felt the blade;
> "Arise, Sir Edric, henceforth be

De Courtenay thy name –
Arise, and strive to emulate
Thy noble father's fame.
Come forth, my brave De Courtenay,
And here embrace your son;
His knightly name and silver spurs
I trow he's nobly won;
With my own hand I'll fix them on;
My own, too, they shall be,"
He said, and took them from his heels,
And bended on his knee,
And fix'd them mid the joyful shouts
Of every armed knight;
And press'd the youthful Edric's hand,
Whose eye beam'd with delight.
The brave De Courtenay came forth;
Surprise was on his face:
He gazed upon his long-lost son –
Hope of his ancient race;
And rush'd the youth into his arms;
The father's heart beat high;
As he embraced his noble son
The tear stood in his eye.

"Oh! tell me sire," the father said,
"Tell me how this can be,
That him I have bewail'd so long
Is now restored by thee?
While yet a child of seven years old,
He went with me to Spain:
I wish'd to use him to the field
Of battle and campaign;
One day I left him in my tent
To fight the foreign foe;
It was our fortune to be beat –
Our bravest men lay low.
Our camp was taken, and methought
A prisoner he was made;
And to this day I've wail'd his loss,
As one who has been dead." '

Now reunited with his father,
Edric is knighted by King Richard:

' "I've dub'd thee knight, and the spurs are thine,
Now let the beams on our banners shine;

> Shout forth, for to-day we'll feast with joy,
> Nor care nor sorrow shall bring us alloy;
> On, on to the camp, and let us prepare;
> We have beat the Saracen in his lair, [. . .]."
>
> The monarch said, and they dashed away,
> With long life to Richard Cour de Lion:
> And long life attend De Courtenay
> And his gallant son – his hopeful stay.'
>
> Francis Buchanan

Though not appearing here, 'The Crusader' also refers to Lord Byron's early nineteenth-century tales in verse – 'The Corsair', and 'Giaour', which undoubtedly inspired my forebear. His tale is of course fictional, but it seems there were genuine historical crusaders named De Courtenay.

'THE DYING SOLDIER

The din of mortal strife is o'er, and silence holds her reign,
Over the crimson'd field of death – the wounded and the slain;
But, hark! a groan assails the ear – a broken-hearted sound –

'Tis from a son of Albion's isle, stretched on the bloody ground.

The burning sun of India beats, on his devoted head,
The bold companions of his toil lie numbered with the dead;
His sunken cheek is ghastly pale, his lips are parch'd and dry.
His bosom throbs convulsively – the tears stand in his eye.

"Why did I leave old Scotia's heath for India's burning sand?
Why did I leave the braes and glens of my beloved land?
Alas! those dear romantic scenes I'll never more descry;
Far from my own – my native home, I'm fated here to die."

He spoke, a smile illumin'd his face, he raised his aching head
From the hot sand on which he lay – he look'd to heaven and prayed.
A shuddering tremor seized his frame, and then a struggling groan,
Told that the soul had winged its flight from its Terrestrial home.'

                        Francis Buchanan

20

PERTHSHIRE POEMS

'LINES

Written on Kinnoull Cliff, near Perth

Romantic scene! Again from thy proud steep,
Kinnoull, I view the landscape far below;
Stirred with the memories of the past I weep,
As I in my fancy boyhood's pleasures grow:
And even now I feel as I felt long ago.

Far down beneath me, in the summer sun,
Majestic Tay, impatient to be free,
Rolls his broad waters, sparkling as they run
Through many a lovely spot, towards the sea;
And at this height methinks I hear their minstrelsy.

Full many a happy hour I've roamed, I ween,
Upon yon verdant banks in days of yore,

Watching at even the silvery lunar beam,
Or listening to the ripple on the shore;
But ah! those hours are fled – the past returns no more.

Kinfauns* thy castle peers amid the trees,
Its turrets gilded as with burnished gold;
The crimson standard waving in the breeze
As it was wont when Longueville† the bold
With his retainers fought the southron 'neath its fold.

Dark Moredun± too, rears up his hoary head,
Where, long ago, Rome's legions from afar
Swept o'er his craggy height with thundering tread,
Equipped in all his barbarous pomp of war,
The spear, the sword and buckler, steed, and clattering car.

And thou I see grey Elcho, famed in lore
With daring deeds of noble Wallace wight,
Whose chivalry hath reached earth's utmost shore;
Whose giant arm asserted Scotia's right!
Who led her hardy sons triumphant through the fight!

Now thy stern walls are crumbling fast away,

And mouldering ruin seizes thee amain;
These moss-gaping chimes tell of Time's mighty sway;
And the mantle ivy, with its emerald train,
Seems to protect from waste thy tottering form in vain.

Far as the eye can reach, the verdant plain
Displays its gorgeous beauty, rich, serene:
There rears a noble mansion, here again
A clump of lowly cottages is seen,
And woods, and groves, dells, lawns and brooks fill up the scene.

Ah! Scotia, land of peace and happiness,
Of all the climes of mother earth the best,
Beneath thy soil, scenes of my early bliss,
I pray to heaven my weary bones may rest,
Where oft in youth's gay hour my foot the sword has prest.

Farewell, ye rocky steeps! sweet Tay, farewell!
Ye weeds, and wilds, ye solitudes, adieu!
Perhaps I'll ne'er again – ah! who can tell? –
Thus feast my eyes upon this matchless view:
Life's but a flickering lamp – our days are number'd few!

* The family seat of Lord Gray

† Ancestor of the family

± Hall of Moncrieff.'

Francis Buchanan

This somewhat heartrending poem was published in my predecessor's early volume, *The Crusader, with other Poems and Lyrics*. It was also selected to appear in Robert Ford's anthology of poems, poets, and biographical information entitled *The Harp of Perthshire* (1893). The poem was most certainly written during the 1840s, as my forebear's departure from Scotland was approaching. And my chapter relating to Francis includes a brief poetic quote concerning the view from Kinnoull Hill (or Cliff) taken from a later (slightly revised) version. Indeed the peak of the hill and its far reaching, remarkable outlook (to include the River Tay) is perfectly described in both poems, in which there is a sincere message. Though it will prevail in his memory, Francis will dearly miss his treasured hill, and yearn to see it once again.

Between 1880 and 1897 the justly named 'Friend of Scottish Poets', David Herschell Edwards published a series of books in sixteen volumes, which exposed a huge selection of verse penned by Scotland's minor poets. The author, poet, and printer was also the proprietor and editor of the Brechin Advertiser in Angus, Scotland. His anthologies include biographical sketches, critical remarks, and selected poems. Francis Buchanan is among those featured in the eleventh series of *One Hundred*

Modern Scottish Poets. I previously referred to my forebear's inclusion in *Modern Yorkshire Poets*, and he was perhaps delighted to find himself and his poetry encompassed in a Scottish version. Indeed Edward's account concerning Francis is decidedly complimentary, and alludes to both of his published volumes. It is similar to others I have read – all of which affirm his love of nature and solitude, his frustration at being apprenticed to a draper, and desire to become a sailor. The splendid appraisal could only be describing Francis Buchanan . . . only my great-great-grandfather:

He is a '[. . .] versatile writer, ever smooth and melodious; and though he has found a home in England, his heart still turns fondly to Auld Mither Scotland, his poetry showing how deeply the scenes and recollections of his early days are engrafted in his memory. In the words of a writer in the *Dundee Weekly News*, to which he is an occasional contributor, "Though his lot has been cast in the midst of the din and smoke of the great manufacturing town, he finds leisure amidst the rushing and crashing of machinery to evolve some bright poetic "sparks" to illumine the murky, stifling atmosphere by which he is surrounded." Mr Buchanan is evidently of a reflective and philosophic turn of mind. He loves to muse on things past and present, and treats his subjects in a clear and lucid manner, his lines having a smooth, pleasant, and healthy ring about them. Many of his poems are beautifully descriptive, and all of them indicate that the author is possessed of a cultivated and refined taste.'

Six poems from the pen of Francis appear in the Scottish anthology: 'The Dying Poet' was published in the original version of *Sparks from Sheffield Smoke*, and is presented within the pages of my adaptation. 'Maggie Lyle' also appears in *The*

Harp of Perthshire, and others are 'Labour', 'The Auld Thing Ower Again', 'O Stay Wi' Me', and 'Ready and Willing'. It seems my forebear was indeed 'an occasional contributor' to the *Dundee Weekly News*. The following poem was published in the said newspaper on 8th January, 1881 and those unfamiliar with Scottish terms should find it relatively easy to comprehend. Nonetheless, I will give you a head start . . . if you will excuse the pun. Of course Heid is the Scots word meaning head, and this head in particular is very sair (or sore) *indeed!* What follows is a selection of stanzas which may or may not be describing Francis' own unfortunate experience. And readers may wish to note that I believe nocht means nothing / naught, siller is silver / money, and micht is the Scots term for might / may:

'MY SAIR, SAIR HEID

I'm fairly tired o' life, indeed:

Nocht can I get to cure my head;

I've drugg'd mysel' till nearly deid,

And doctor's gain

My siller for what seems to feed

The cursed pain.

An' tho I often try to creep

Aneath the wing o' downy sleep,

That frae her influence I micht reap

Ease for a while,

She'll aye gae by wi' whirrin' sweep,

    An' me beguile.

That I am dwindlin' off my feet;

When wi' my frien's I chance to meet,

    At the first sicht o'me they see't,

        And say I'm thin –

    That there is scarce a pick o'meat

        Aneath my skin.'

                F. BUCHANAN

Another Scottish bard to be presented in Edwards' anthology (fifth series) is Henry Dryerre. Enchanted by Kinnoull Hill and the glorious scenery from its clifftop, he joyously busied his pen during Francis' absence. Though born in Edinburgh in 1848, he would eventually settle happily in Perthshire. The year 1884 saw the publication of his *Love Idylls, Ballads, and Other Poems*. The *Dundee Courier* of 7th October applauded it – describing the author as '[. . .] an ardent lover of nature in all her aspects, moods, and seasons [. . .].' If Francis was familiar with Dryerre's work, he would undoubtedly have been drawn to his lines addressed to a certain hill:

'KINNOULL

KINNOULL, Kinnoull, thou height most dear,

    Once more behold thy votary here!

On thy commanding brow I stand,

The monarch of a glorious land.

What richness greets my grateful eye,

What varied beauties 'neath me lie!

The Tay in silver silence softly flowing;

The kine on verdant meadows distant lowing [. . .].'

Henry Dryerre

*   *   *

Both poets treasured the River Tay; indeed Francis composed a poem devoted solely to the river, which was published in his early work. My predecessor perhaps thought it unseemly to present the poem to those possibly unfamiliar with Perthshire's landmarks. He thus submitted to his Sheffield publisher, a prudently revised version. But I found myself drawn to the original title, published in Perth. Sheffield's 'To the River Tay' replaced 'LINES, Addressed to the River Tay. After the style of Montgomery's Voyage Round the World', presenting irrefutable confirmation of my forefather's admiration for the renowned Scottish bard, James Montgomery.

There is of course mention of the 'Sheffield Poet' in this book, and the verse Francis was alluding to is actually entitled 'A Voyage Round the World'. My forebear clearly endeavoured to produce lines of a similar manner. Montgomery's verse is lengthy, and on reading it one is indeed taken on an extraordinary journey round the world – visiting what he refers to as 'Every shore beneath the sun'. His inspiration came from the sea on the North Yorkshire coast, which perhaps created in his mind sights and sounds of wonder from beyond. Montgomery's biographers – and essentially his friends – John Holland and James Everett, described in *Memoirs of the Life and Writings of James Montgomery Vol. IV.*, his whereabouts, activities and accomplishments during the closing days of 1826:

'Having attended one or two religious anniversaries at Whitby in December, he determined to go afterwards for a few days to Scarborough; the snow lying deep on the ground and himself, apparently, the only visitor in that fashionable locality at this ungenial season. The ocean, however, – which he had rarely seen without some interpretation of its voice, – was again suggestive; and he composed, while walking on the beach, the verses entitled a "Voyage round the World".'

It was written at a time when Francis Buchanan was but an infant. Hill scrambling, exploration, adventure and profound appreciation of his beautiful surroundings was yet to come. His twenty-third year would see the publication of some early work, comprising the river-inspired verse. Francis' poem follows the voyage of the River Tay alongside cherished ancient and familiar sights – as they are perpetually splashed, splattered and sprayed. I feel sure Montgomery would have been honoured to learn that my forebear had replicated his style, and in all likelihood he looked upon his fellow Scotsman with approval. His own work, and that of Montgomery may have prompted Francis to compose similar lines relating to the voyage of the River Don, in his poem entitled 'Rotherham'. What follows also appears in the original *Sparks from Sheffield Smoke:*

'TO THE RIVER TAY

Hail, all hail, sweet Tay, to thee,
Stream of my nativity,
You will aye remember'd be;
Glittering in the autumn sun
Bright as a tale of love you run
Onward to the broad blue sea.

From the western hills you flow –
Where the pines and birches grow,
Where the antler'd deer and roe
Watchful snuff and air around,
Fearing man in every sound –
Lightly down the dells you go.

Now adown the headlong height,
Flashing in the sunny light,
Dashing with impetuous might
Over black and frowning rock,
Stunning as with earthquake's shock;
On you rush in wild delight.

Now reposing, you are seen,
A waveless, dreamy, glassy stream,
Cheer'd not by the solar beam,
So deep thy course in woody glen;
Now in flashing light again,
Down you sweep the cliffs between.

Tired of madness and uproar,
Through the op'ning vale you pour,
More majestic than before,
Gliding through the fertile plain,
Grave and stately, to the main;
You have broke your mountain chain.

Scone* smiles in the autumn ray;
Kiss its shore with rev'rence, Tay –
It has seen a prouder day:
There old Scotland's kings were crown'd;
Murmur low, 'tis holy ground –
Then pursue thy merry way.

Join'd by Almond's gushing stream,
Roll you on with nobler mien –

Boast of Caledon, I ween;
Fair Sr. Johnston† greets thy view,
With her inch‡ of em'rald hue –
Lovely city peer'd by few.

Quickly through the arches wide,
Sweeps along thy ample tide;
Now by sweet Kinfauns‖ you guide,
Now 'neath fir-capp'd, grey Kinnoull,§
Haunt of raven, hawk, and owl;
Sparkle on, you can't abide.

Down through many a lovely spot,
Dear to memory I wot –
Noble mansion, humble cot;
Time worn Elcho¶ now appears,
Framed for deeds in other years –
Deeds which ne'er will be forgot.
Earnº pays thee homage due –
Mingle with thy waters blue –
A lovely bride, and meet I trew;
Now in might and majesty
Proudly roll a halcyon sea,

Ever joyous, ever free.

See thy noble frith-expands,
Fraught with ships from other lands –
Commerce o'er thee waves her hands;
Steamers on thy bosom ply,
Wreathing columns to the sky –
Nations' ensigns flaunt on high.

Pass'd is Dundee; on, on, you glide,
Crested waves kiss either side –
Seamews float upon the tide;
Broughty Castle on the shore:
Tott'ring keep, they warfare's o'er,
Lift thy head in strife no more.

All in the past. Hark! Ocean's roar
Echo'd back from Scotia's shore;
Yet thy waters onward pour –
Mingle with immensity,
With the deep unfathom'd sea,
Whose abyss thy rest shall be.

* Royal Palace of Scone.

† Ancient name of City of Perth.

‡ Large and beautiful play-ground call'd North Inch.

‖ Seat of Lord Gray.

§ Rocky cliffe, 600 feet high.

¶ Ruinous Castle

º Tributary stream.'

Francis Buchanan

My forebear also composed a song addressed to the River Tay. It was published in his early collection, and is profound and passionate. He is saying goodbye . . . and I feel his sorrow:

'A SONG TO THE TAY

Roll on, lovely river, roll on in thy gladness;

For ever and ever the sportive and gay:

The voice of thy waters, dispels all my sadness;

Thou'rt dear to my bosom, thou beautiful Tay.

How oft have I wander'd when summer was beaming,

In the spring-time of life, when from care I was free?

How oft have I sat me, when others were dreaming,

And tasted of happiness gazing on thee?

In the soft light of ev'ning how pleasant to wander
Along thy green banks, from mankind far away,
And list to thy ripple as onward you meander;
Or watch the moonbeam on thy bosom, sweet Tay.

But ah! I have seen thee when storms were impending,
Roll down thy clear waters all sadden'd with gloom;
When lightning was gleaming, and thunder was rending,
And nature took on the bleak hue of the tomb;

And as the bright sunbeam through riven clouds glancing,
When the tempest was o'er and had roll'd far away,
I've seen thy pure wavelets all merrily dancing,
More joyous than ever thou beautiful Tay.

They may boast of the Tweed, and of Clyde – classic river;
Though they be immortal in many a theme,
Yet can they compare with thee? never, ah, never!
Thou pride of auld Scotland, thou reignest supreme.

O sore is my bosom – e'er long must I leave thee,
Perhaps ne'er again by thy waters to stray;

> To bid thee farewell, oh how sadly 'twill grieve me,
>   My own native river, thou sweet winding Tay:
>
> But yet though far from thee, in other lands roaming,
>   I'll always remember, with fondest delight;
>   And as by some river I'll walk in the gloaming,
>   I'll fancy, I gaze on thy waters so bright.'
>   Francis Buchanan

* * *

The North Inch of Perth is essentially a large public park. Indeed you may have noted Francis' referral to the 'Large and beautiful play-ground call'd North Inch' in 'To the River Tay'. It sits opposite Bridgend, in the parish of Kinnoull, and the River Tay flows between the local community and green open space. Not unlike the smaller South Inch, the smooth grassland lends itself to prearranged outdoor activities, such as public assemblies or galas. For centuries it has been utilised as a sports ground (chiefly offering golf) and is popular with walkers, hikers and runners. The Perthshire poet Robert Nicoll (1814-1837) would rise before five o'clock each morning during the summer, and spend two hours at the North Inch, writing in the open air. As a local resident and aficionado, my great-great-grandfather would surely have been aware of Nicoll's work and distinctive practices. Francis also enjoyed the North Inch, and as you might expect, he produced a poem about it.

But before revealing it, I would like to introduce a gentleman who explored the site, and presented his findings in writing. Johann Georg Kohl (1808-1878) was a German historian, geographer, and travel writer. He devoted a great deal of time to his interest in the transportation and settlement of people. Much of his findings were published in book form – to include *England, Wales and Scotland* (1844). If my forebear cast his eyes over Kohl's interpretation of the appeal of Perth's North Inch, he would have read the following:

'I had heard much before my arrival of the "Inches" of Perth, and found with some surprise that they were nothing more than two perfectly flat pieces of land, lying, one north, the other south of the town, and called the North and South Inch, admirably adapted to all sorts of games and sports requiring level ground, but seeming to have little claim to the enthusiastic praise bestowed on them.' On arrival Kohl '[. . .] met the people streaming out of the gates towards the North Inch, to witness the performance of some feats promised by the clown of a rope-dancing troop, who wanted, as I heard it said, to "get up an excitement for their benefit," [. . .].'

Whether or not Francis occasionally mingled with the crowds, is of course unknown, but if curiosity won over, he would have witnessed quite a spectacle at the event portrayed by Kohl:

'The plan at present adopted, seemed well chosen to attract attention; the clown in full costume was to sail down the river in a tub, drawn by four geese, and had it been Juno with her swans, or Venus with her doves, the audience would scarcely have been so well pleased. The whole North Inch was covered with spectators, and in due time the adventurous navigator appeared, and embarked amidst loud applause, balancing himself very skilfully in his peculiar craft. The geese of course did not really draw him, but were themselves carried on by the current.'

Though surrounded by jovial spectators, J. G. Kohl calmly assumed an aura of contemplation:

'As I stood on the lofty bridge looking down on the scene, I began to understand something of the partiality of the Perth people for their Inches. On the North Inch there is neither house, tree, bush, nor ditch, to interrupt the perfect smoothness of the surface, which resembles an immense billiard-table; its effect, surrounded as it is by hills and mountains, is very striking [. . .].'

Open-air activities are today as popular as ever on the North Inch of Perth; and I imagine for the most part, there is not a clown or goose to be seen.

'[. . .] it is when he sings of Scotland that he sings best. His "North Inch of Perth" is really fine, and worthy of the lyre of Scotland [. . .].'

The Irvine and Fullarton Times,
24th October, 1884

Though originally published in Francis' early collection, the above quote refers to the slightly amended version of this poem in *Sparks from Sheffield Smoke,* which I have selected. It reveals my ancestor's fondness for the North Inch, before the Battle of the Clans of 1396 becomes the central theme. In the words of J. G. Kohl: '[. . .] in the reign of King Robert III, a different kind of spectacle was presented on this North Inch.' The battle involving Clan Chattan – a confederation of Highland Clans, and Clan Kay (who are named in the poem) was witnessed (in the words of Francis) by 'The Royal Robbie' – who desired them to fight out their feud. The use of Scots terms in this verse are sufficient to warrant full translation in the opening lines, but as it becomes increasingly anglicised, only an accompanying glossary is required. I am most grateful for the assistance of Dr Dauvit Horsbroch, Scots Language Centre, A K Bell Library, Perth:

'LINES ADDRESSED TO THE NORTH INCH, PERTH

ALL hail to thee, thou bonny green,

ALL hail to you, you bonny green,

Ance mair on thee I cast my een,

Once more on you I cast my eyes,

An' weel I wat, my early freen!

Indeed I must say, my early friend!

I am right vaunty,

I am very elated,

To see thee in the simmer's sheen,

To see you in the summer's light,

Sae spruce an' canty.

So tidy and cheerful / pleasant.

Tho' tousand years hae o'er thee pass'd,
Though a thousand years have passed over you,
An' mony a storm an' bitter blast,
And many a storm an' bitter wind,
Tho' white-beard Winter's dune his warst,
done his worst,
An' wrastled sair;
And wrestled sore / hard;
Thou stands right nobly to the last,
You stand very nobly to the end,
Nae waur o'wear.
No worse for wear.

In spite o' crusty Faither Time,
Thy coat's as green as 'twas lang syne,
'twas long ago,
He for thy downfa' sair may pine,
Sore downfall
But faith I doot,
I doubt means I'm sure in this sense
Though auld Decay wi' him combine –

You'll tire them oot.

Thou minds I ween in days o' yore,
Ween: guess / imagine
How thou wast steep'd in Highland gore,
were steeped
When Chattan an' Clan Kay before
The Royal Robbie,*
Fought wi' the target an' claymore,
A murderous jobbie.
task.

How buirdly Hal, for Chattan's weal,
burly Hal
Wi' willin' hand an' trusty steel,
Made the proud Gaels like ninepins reel,
Upon thy sward;
In vain they tried each dreadfu' peel
dreadful match / equal
To jouk an' guard.
evade and defend.

Nae doubt, slee Inch, that thou could'st tell

slee: wise

O' mony a prank, if't pleas'd thysel';

How robbers prowl'd for purpose fell,

fell: fierce / cruel

By winding Tay;

How monks cam' forth at vesper bell,

cam': came

Like beasts o' prey.

How lovers, in the gloamin' hour,

gloamin' hour: twilight time

Stroll'd dreamy to some lonely bower,

When Cynthia ower Kinnoull wad glower,

over Kinnoull would stare intently

Like siller lamp;

siller: silver (also word for money)

Thou'st seem, too, spunkie† aften scour,

spunkie: willo-the-wisp OR sparks of light

aften scour: often rush about,

O'er marshes damp.

Thou hast beheld the midnight gleam

O' dagger plung'd by hand unseen,

An' heard the victim's piercing scream
An' stifled cry;
Thou hast beheld the bloody stream,
An' seen him die.

An' thou hast seen the glaring eye,
O' suicide prepare to die;
Thou'st seen him to the bank draw nigh,
An' tak' the leap
And take the leap
Which plung'd him in Eternity,
An' death's lang sleep.
lang: long

An' thou has witness'd, when the gale
Sung loud its sang – a mither pale,
sang: song, mither: mother
The while her bairnie loud did wail,
bairnie: little child
Through murky night,
Thou'st seen the guilty parent quail
Before Heaven's sight,

As in Tay's waters deep she threw
The new-born babe, an' then withdrew,
An' heaven scowl'd, an' louder blew
    The angry blast;
The river changed to darker hue,
    At what had pass'd.

Thou hast look'd on the drunkard's fate,
As hame he reel'd wi' staggerin' gait;
he danced home in a staggering way
O'erpower'd wi' drink he'd seek to wait,
    Overtaken by drink
    'Neath some auld tree,
    Beneath some old tree,
Till frozen stark an' stiff he'd wake
    stark: hard
    In Eternity.

An' trow, sweet Inch, thou minds the day
    trow: believe
When Royalty on thee wad stray,
    wad: would
An' nobles wi' their ladies gay

Wad romp at large,
wad: would
Or skim the surface o' the Tay
In princely barge.

But noo these guid auld days are gone,
guid auld days: good old days
The hand o'Time moves swift along ;
Hours fly – days, months, an' years pass on,
Ne'er to return,
Till man's brief space shall close anon
Beneath the urn.

Inch, thou hast seen the rise an' fa'
fa': fall
O' Kings an' Priests – o' great an' sma',
sma': small,
Ilk generation slip awa'
awa': away
To that abode,
Prepared sin' Adam's time for a', –
sin': since, a': all,
Beneath the clod.

Fareweel! fareweel! my early freen',
Farewell! Farewell, my early (old) friend,
Though far awa' I'll mind I ween,
I imagine I'll remember though far away,
O' thee, an' Tay's romantic stream,
Till memory
Be void an' blank, an' close mine een
een: eyes
In death for aye.
In death forever.

* Robert III   *Vide* Sir W. Scott's "Fair Maid of Perth" for a spirited description of the "Battle of the Inch."

† Ignis-Fatuus.'

Francis Buchanan

* * *

The Bell Rock Lighthouse off the coast of Angus, not far from Dundee and Fife, was built by the Scottish civil engineer, Robert Stevenson between 1807 and 1810. It appeals to scores of visitors (as it did during the nineteenth century), who depart on a voyage from Arbroath Harbour in order to encounter the sea-washed attraction. I am very fond of the following poem taken from my ancestor's Scottish collection, and find it rather ingenious. Line after line, imagination takes hold, leaving the reader hungry for more. Readers please note – Inchcape is a Scottish Gaelic term meaning beehive, like the shape of the reefs:

'LINES

On the Steamer Britannia's *intended Pleasure Trip* to the Bellrock, April, 1847.

What's the matter, such a clatter,

Pushing, running down the quay,

Men and boys, what a noise;

Sure folks are mad about Dundee.

They're going away, to spend the day,

And see the frowning Inchcape Rock,

To breathe the air, salubrious, rare,

And leave behind their dirty smoke.

Aboard they've got, a motley lot;

At length the steamer's under weight;

She dashes through the waters blue,

And with her prow heaves out the spray.

The ladies fair, wi' costly gear

Bedeck'd, seem goddesses to-day;

Each winning smile the time beguiles,
　As proudly we sweep down the Tay.

　Here may be seen, the noble mien,
　　And sentimental looking face;
　The roseate dye, and laughing eye,
　　The blush of modesty and grace.

　Ye glorious nine!* is't love divine,
　Has seized the fortress of my heart? –
　My bosom burns, my caput turns,
　And rankling deep I feel the smart

* The nine muses

　　Of, I suppose – ah! here it goes,
　　Unlucky fate, I feel its power;
　Haste waiter here, a glass of beer,
　　Or I shall die within an hour.

　I'm wretched bad, I wish I had
　Remained on *terra*; oh! my heart
Beats not with love, ye powers above;
　'Tis ocean's god has thrown his dart.

I'm better now; but what's the row?
What means that piercing, ominous scream?
Here some do swear – some tear their hair –
Some lie insensate; what a scene!

A misty pall enshrouds us all,
Impenetrable to the ray
Of solar light: dark mirky night
Usurps the power of glorious day.

We make a halt, like hounds at fault,
As undetermined where to go;
They gaze around, and snuff the ground,
Bewilder'd, running to and fro.

Pale, dastard fear now lords it here,
And laughing joy and pleasure's gone;
That vacant stare, and silent prayer,
Speak of the anguish of the throng.

Each lovely one clings close to man,
As if in the impending hour
He could them save from watery grave,

And shield them from the ocean's power.

But self prevails, each bosom quails,
And nobler feelings must give way;
Sauve qui peut * is all the go,
And seems the order of the day.

* Save himself who can

Puff goes the steam – nought's to be seen
Around through dense and pitchy air;
And as they peer, with looks of fear,
It serves but to augment despair.

With fancy's eye, the weak descry
(As drifts the steamer 'fore the wind,)
The Inchcape Rock – the stunning shock –
The wreck! – oh! horrors of the mind.
To crown their woes, the cold wind blows,
And billows lash with chilly spray,
Gaunt hunger gnaws, but longing maws
Must want – the larder's clean to-day.

No joint to roast, nor bread to toast –
Their cravings not a bite to stop!

Oh! direst fate! But 'tis too late
To grumble now – live on in hope.
Where are ye, where, ye worms of care?
Ah! mocking echo answers, where?
Why idly gaze on gloomy haze –
Why rave – why fume – why stamp and swear?

The hand of time proclaims it nine,
And still the mist broods o'er the deep,
So down below they're forced to go,
And in the *hold* for shelter creep.

A mix'd up mass, of every class –
Man, woman, child, promiscuously,
Like frighten'd sheep, together creep,
Awaiting morn impatiently.

Sound be your sleep – ah! do not weep –
Come dry your tears, ye lovely fair;
Though hard your bed, and low each head,
Yet strive, sweet sex, to banish care.

Above there, ho! speak soft, tread slow,

Let wearied, hungry people rest –
Their dreams may be of *sweet* Dundee,
Of home, and viands of the best.

* * *

Now from the deck, a distant speck,
Like glimmering lamp afar is seen:
It larger grows, each bosom glows,
And shouting they hail morning's sheen.

Through darkness riven, ethereal heaven
Is seen beyond the widening seam;
And like a shield, on azure field,
The god of day pours through his stream

Of golden light, and with affright,
The misty shroud rolls far away;
And wavelets bright, dance with delight,
Beneath the beauteous solar ray.

Becalmed we lay, without the Tay;
Close on our beam the rugged shore;

Another hour, we'd known its power,
And German's waves had 'whelm'd us o'er.

Afar at sea, majestically,
The Bellrock rises to the sight;
Source of our woe, farewell, – we go
With feelings of unfeigned delight.

Like arrow's flight, our vessel tight,
Speeds swift along the sparkling main;
The fresh'ning gale, now swells her sail,
And on Tay's bosom once again

We safely ride, with wind and tide
Wafting us on right merrily;
And by and by, we e'en descry,
Afar the steeples of Dundee.

Like insect's hum, or distant drum,
A sound arises from the *hold;*
And sallying out, a torn down group
Appear, – ye Deities behold!

They rub their eyes, and with surprise
They rub again, and gaze anew,
Instead of spray and mist, the ray
Of morn brings Broughty to their view.

Instanter we will happily
Walk *terra firma* safe and sound,
And then, oh bliss! – reverse of this –
Each one will feast like greedy hound.

But here once more, we're safe on shore;
The steeple chimes the hour of five;
All right at last, the danger's past,
The "voyageurs" at home arrive.'

                                          Francis Buchanan

What an eventful poem! It boasts detail, imagination, and tremendous atmospheric activity. We are boarding the Britannia and setting out for a day trip to Inchcape Rock! Indeed we are there, you and I. The author's desire to create an all-pervading atmosphere is clearly realised, as we find ourselves joining the excursion – to revel in (or be *subjected to*) unfolding events. Many unfortunate and unprepared day-trippers become laden with anxiety, and little by little (or *wave* by *wave*), begin to feel off colour and surrender to biliousness. As the title of the poem suggests, what was meant to be a pleasure trip, before long becomes something of a debacle. Francis freely exploits his vivid imagination in this poem. And perhaps now is the time to reveal that this fanciful tale is based upon actual events. Yes, that's right . . . it really happened!

As a resident of the glorious Perthshire landscape adjacent to the River Tay, with a previous yearning to become a sailor, Francis was undoubtedly well aware of the local seafaring activities. It would be reasonable to assume he learned of the Britannia's somewhat disastrous excursion through the grapevine; or perhaps read detailed accounts published in local newspapers. I believe the title of the poem tells us it was written in April, 1847. And I know with certainty that a voyage not unlike the one this poem speaks of, took place one year earlier – as corroborated by the *Dundee Courier* and *Dundee, Perth, and Cupar Advertiser*, dated 21st April, 1846. On realising their doggerel potential, my great-great-grandfather likely stored away at least one of the articles, along with his own recollections of the episode. And I am delighted that he did. For his intuitive measures resulted in brilliant, and somewhat frenzied verse, which takes on board (excuse the pun) the discomfort of those affected, whilst still managing to propose an element of humour – nothing short of how the newspapers' commentary was conveyed. As one might expect, similar endeavours unfortunately occurred in the region on a regular basis – subsequently making local news. Though it seems very likely my forebear's poem alludes to the events of April, 1846, there is a chance it does not. In fact overwhelming weather conditions, seafaring incidents, sickness, alarming scenes of anguish – and tragically, victims of drowning – were reported frequently.

I realise this particular voyage was by no means chronicled as a great disaster, and might be deemed by some as inconsequential . . . barely worth reporting. But this popular day trip *was* reported, and (quite possibly) my forebear *did* (characteristically) seize the opportunity to poetically enhance the story. Being fully aware of Francis' powers of observation and capacity for poetically transmitting his findings, I wasn't the least bit surprised to learn of the Steamer Britannia's true existence, and thanks go to Karen Clarke of ANGUSalive Archives for suggesting that might be the case, and the poem is based on real events. What follows is a combination of coverage of the *actual* 'intended' trip to the Bell Rock, from each of the newspapers cited:

'[. . .] upwards of four hundred individuals availed themselves of the opportunity of enjoying for some hours the invigorating sea breeze and seeing the Bell Rock. At the hour of starting, the atmosphere was heavy and foggy – the sky betokening rain; but the passengers were sanguine that these evil omens would pass away, and a healthy and pleasant trip would be obtained.'

Thus in order to dispel doubts of a joyous voyage, a few young men in the party began to offer words of comfort to their sweethearts. But as conditions worsened the initial cases of sea sickness resulted in amusement among unaffected voyagers – who rapidly fell silent on realising the affliction was contagious: 'A lover was folding a shawl around the bosom of his fair one with more than ordinary care, when a rude breath from the eastern wind rewarded his blushing temples with the last cup of congu which she had drunk.'

As the sea breeze increased, the Britannia sailed on gallantly, as she dashed spray from her paddles whilst '[. . .] rising joyously to the caresses of the gathering waves [. . .].' Increasing winds from all quarters of the deck saw a surge in the number of ailing day trippers, as '[. . .] the Bell Rock at last loomed through the mist [. . .].' Then, retracing her course, the steamer continued on as '[. . .] the fog thickened, and the light of the Bell Rock soon became lost in the gathering blackness of the evening.' The cabin, with its offer of accommodation was quickly filled, as 'A plank was let down horizontally into the hold, and men and blooming maidens, old wives, and children were let slide down its surface promiscuously, like so many bales of goods, till no further room could be obtained.' The situation worsened as the number of sick increased ten-fold, and incidents of preposterous description could not be modestly described. Mercifully, the impending dawn brought with it clearer skies, and 'Captain Greig landed his passengers at five o'clock on Friday morning [. . .] amidst a hearty vote of thanks for the manner in which he had conducted himself on the occasion.' Bearing echoes of Francis' verse, the steamer arrived safely at five o'clock in the morning and '[. . .] the passengers disembarked, glad again to be on *terra firma*.' The newspaper's use of the Latin phrase meaning 'firm land' possibly inspired Francis to include the very same phrase in his poem.

Felicia Hemans (1793-1835) was a prolific and successful poet, and much of her work concerns the hardships of women. She also composed a simple poem with a clear message about the Bell Rock, the first few lines of which introduce its subject:

'THE BELL AT SEA

(The dangerous islet called the Bell Rock on the coast of Forfarshire, used formerly to be marked only by a bell, which was so placed as to be swung by the motions of the waves, when the tide rose above the rock. A lighthouse has since been erected there.)

WHEN the tide's billowy swell

Had reached its height,

Then toll'd the rock's lone bell

Sternly by night.

Far over cliff and surge

Swept the deep sound,

Making each wild wind's dirge

Still more profound.

Yet that funereal tone

The sailor bless'd,

Steering through darkness on

With fearless breast.

> E'en so may we, that float
>
> On life's wide sea,
>
> Welcome each warning note,
>
> Stern though it be! 1
>
> Felicia Hemans

> 1 It will be scarcely necessary to remind the reader, that the stealing of this bell by a Pirate forms the subject of Southey's spirited ballad, "The Inchcape Rock".'

Indeed Robert Southey's well-known ballad written in around 1802, was inspired by reports that during the fourteenth century the warning bell was installed by the Abbot of Aberbrothok. It was removed by a pirate with intentions to loot the goods from sinking ships, but the pirate (Sir Ralph the Rover, in Southey's verse) later perished in the dangerous stretch of rocky reefs by the Bell Rock. The poem thereby bares a lesson to all.

* * *

Francis was conversant with the work of notable poets – of course one such poet being Robert Burns. Published in my forebear's early volume is a poem written to the memory of the celebrated Scottish bard. What follows is a selection of lines:

'To The Memory of Burns

Now let me wander forth at e'en,

And linger mid yon silent urns;

And let this be my sacred theme –

The memory of Burns.

Transported, let my fancy roam

Where loved and sung the immortal dead;

Ah! let me gaze upon his home –

A tear to genius shed.

Hail! humble cot, where first appear'd

The future prince of Scottish song;

Whose name is yet by all rever'd,

Though time has roll'd along.

What heart but feels a warmer glow,

When "auld acquaintance" greets his ears? –

Remembrance bids his tears to flow,

A tribute to past years.'

Francis Buchanan

'Whistling Willie' of Perth

On 22nd March, 1883 the *Dundee Courier* announced the death of a much loved character, known in my great-great-grandfather's homeland of Perth. His name was William Wilson, but he was fondly known as 'Whistling Willie'. A tanner by profession, Mr Wilson had reached his 79th year, and 'His title of "Whistling Willie" was derived from his peculiarity of whistling through his teeth the popular airs of the day [and] he could be heard at a very considerable distance.' There was a long history of glove making in Perth, and as a member of the Glover Incorporation, Willie paraded the streets wearing a blue coat with brass buttons, white trousers, and vest prior to its annual dinner. The aforesaid newspaper reveals that '[. . .] about a dozen years before his death he seemed to have lost the gift of whistling, which in his better days, without exaggeration, delighted all classes of the community.'

A few months later (8th June, 1883 to be precise) Whistling Willie was featured in an article in the *Dundee Courier* entitled 'ECCENRTRIC CHARACTERS IN PERTH AND PERTHSHIRE'. The detailed piece about Willie ends with '[. . .] we cannot more appropriately conclude than by repeating one of the verses inscribed [. . .] by of our old friend and esteemed local poet Frank Buchanan (author of "The Crusader, with other Poems and Lyrics"), who has pitched his tent in Sheffield, and now tunes his Doric pipe on the banks of the Don, but whom we have not had the pleasure of meeting on the banks of the Tay for the last four-and-thirty years –

> Cheerfu' he whistled through Life's busy plain,
> Lilting and marching along;
> His lack o'men's guile to him was a gain:
> Doubtless we'll look for his equal in vain,
> Noo that his whistle is broken in twain,
> An' Death's let his wind aff the fang.'

Francis (indeed 'Frank') paid tribute to Whistling Willie by concisely portraying the popular fellow in verse. And how pleasing to see that my forebear – indeed the 'esteemed local poet' – was remembered in his homeland.

21

THE DUFTYS *of Sheffield*

There is little doubt in my mind as to the precise whereabouts of my great-great-grandfather at three o'clock in the afternoon of Thursday 8th March, 1888. He almost certainly was in attendance at Sheffield's General Cemetery for the interment of his dear friend, and fellow poet Joseph Dufty. In Sheffield Mr Dufty would be missed . . . and regrettably, nothing more was to emanate from his pen. The poem you are about to read was composed a few years earlier, and was Francis' way of dedicating *Sparks from Sheffield Smoke* to his comrade:

'TO

JOSEPH DUFTY, ESQ.,

AUTHOR OF

"A Blighted Life," "The Village Inn," and other Poems,

THIS SMALL VOLUME IS INSCRIBED, AS A TRIBUTE OF ESTEEM,

BY HIS OBLIGED FRIEND,

THE AUTHOR.

I with myself held grave debate
To whom my book to dedicate:
And as I scratch'd mine addled pate,
Servility
Reminded me of high estate
And pedigree;
But warm Reciprocation came
And hinted of thine honest name –
Thy soul sincere, and budding fame –
Thy manly merit.
Thou gav'st my *Sparks* a steadier flame –
Thine to inherit.
To thee, who hast the Muse's bays,
Who dost the soul dejected raise,
I here inscribe my humble lays
In modest rhyme;
And may our friendship be always
Till end of time.

Sheffield, 187, *Fowler Street,*
    August, 1882.' Francis Buchanan

It seems Francis considered Joseph Dufty's friendship to be a source of inspiration, and his tribute to him (a worthy ode in itself) introduces the reader to two of his poems: 'A Blighted Life', and 'The Village Inn'. Dufty's collection, *A Blighted Life, and Other Poems* was published in 1871, and I was eager to delve into his poetry and uncover what was behind his 'budding fame'. Thus I embarked on a journey and encountered love, faith, commitment, dedication, creativity, courage and triumph. I speak not only of Joseph, but individual members of his family, whom Sheffield should surely be proud of.

The 'Notice of Books' in the *Sheffield Daily Telegraph* of 28th February, 1871 announces Joseph Dufty's volume of poetry by summarising the poem designated as the book's title: '[. . .] A Blighted Life' is the woeful, historical tale of a fellow [. . .] over whose whole life one great shadow hung, his unhallowed love for the wife of another. The canker kept concealed from the world gradually saps away his vital powers, and he dies.' This is indeed what happens. The tale is narrated by an acquaintance, and portrayed in a lengthy poem of six parts.

Part I begins with

> 'I SAW him first in manhood's prime
> Ere yet his form with age was bent,
> Or ere his locks were thinned by time;
> The radiance of his eye unspent:
> He was a man in mind and frame
> That Nature might feel proud to claim.

> We wandered where the woods and flowers
> Were smiling to the summer sun:
> He knew their good and baneful powers,
> And named and classed them one by one;
> And every leaf that met his look
> To him was as an open book.'

Part II is entitled 'THE GREAT SHADOW', and what follows are the first few lines:

> 'Again we met: his eye had lost
> Its glow of intellectual fire;
> His pallid brow was high emboss'd,
> And mark'd with ridge and wrinkle dire;
> His locks were few, and scant, and gray,
> As though he walked life's downward way.'

His state of mind and general health declines. He dies, and there is a funeral. Part VI, the conclusion ponders the loss of life brought about by events, and ends with a warning to others:

> 'But why regret? No sigh of ours
> Can penetrate the chilly tomb,
> Or bid him wake – his manhood's hours
> Recurrent – from the sunless gloom:

> Peaceful and well he sleeps at last,
> His secret tears and heart-ache past.
>
> And thus, in pity for mankind,
> And for my woe-wrecked friend, 'tis time
> Above his place of rest to bind
> The hopeful cross – a warning sign,
> That others may avoid the snare,
> Where he and Petrarch found despair!'

Dufty's alternative title to 'A Blighted Life' is indeed 'A Songless Petrarch' and an indication of the significance of the fourteenth-century Italian scholar and poet Francesco Petrarch, whose love for a woman married to another man was all consuming. Thus a person who mirrors his actions might be referred to as a 'Petrarhcan lover'. The previously mentioned newspaper evaluates another lengthy poem from Dufty's collection – 'The Village Inn', which '[. . .] is an amusing picture of the company assembled one evening at the "Wheat Shock." We are introduced to the various village dignitaries, whose characters are well and distinctively brought out. Not the least amusing personage in the tale is Kate Cattermole, the village shrew, who appears unexpected and unwelcome among the jovial company in search of her husband, who,

> "hid behind the door,
> Would fain have sunk down through the floor." '

Curious to learn more, I referred to the poem without delay. This is how it begins:

> 'WHEN labours close, there's many a wight
>
> That loves to take a glass at night,
>
> Where he with friends may laugh and joke,
>
> Talk politics, hear news, and smoke [. . .].'

A wheat shock (or stook) was a stack of wheat stalks tied in bundles, piled vertically, and left to dry out in the fields. The atmosphere *inside* the drinking establishment named with this particular farming method in mind, is the very antithesis of what is occurring *outside*:

> 'The Village inn, of uncouth form
>
> Defied the blust'ring, freezing storm,
>
> And showed through many a window bright
>
> A ruddy glow of cheerful light.
>
> 'Twas cold without; but ah! within
>
> How bright and jovial was the scene!'

The poem brings the warm and merry atmosphere to life, as the reader becomes acquainted with some of those present. Then an unwelcome visitor is driven through the door by the equally unwelcome 'freezing storm':

'But ere had died the loud uproar,

Wide open flew the outer door;

The wind, that long had beat in vain

Against each door and window pane,

Rush'd in amongst the gleeful rout,

And put both fun and candle out:

In dashed the snow, and, worst of all

(Close o'er her head her old plaid shawl),

The village shrew – Kate Cattermole!

A shrew indeed! sharp-featured, tall,

And thin as a stout beanstalk, dried

– A very thorn in Johnny's side.

Loud screeched the wind, but louder still

Resounded Kate's harsh voice and shrill.

Poor Johnny, hid behind the door,

Would fain have sunk down through the floor [. . .].'

The newspaper's book review also proclaims the poet's love of the open-air, with all its natural charm and '[. . .] some of his best pieces are descriptive of the beauties of the woods and flowers and the changing seasons.' Like Francis, Joseph Dufty celebrated nature, and he too was featured in various anthologies of poets, and their poetry. The son of John Dufty and Mary Goodlad, Joseph was born in Sheffield on July 4th, 1842. His father was a Confectioner – a livelihood that Joseph would assume, before turning to homeopathy. During the 1870s he spent several months as an assistant physician to Dr. Edward Harris Ruddock in Berkshire, became a homeopathic chemist, and established a Pharmacy and Dispensary on West Street in Sheffield. As a physician Dr. Ruddock converted to homeopathy, and was a recognised editor and author concerning homeopathic principles.

Dufty also tried his hand at creative art, and as a member of the Sheffield Society of Artists, displayed some of his paintings at exhibitions. Indeed this is what I uncovered listed under the said society in the *Sheffield Independent* of 23rd July, 1878: 'Mr. J. Dufty exhibits a pretty view of "The Terrace, Haddon Hall". The sketch is admirably drawn, and the effect is picturesque [. . .].' Joseph had been married to Eliza Gibbins since 1863. Both were members of the New Jerusalem Church Society, which was originally formed in London during the late eighteenth century, and based upon the theological writings of Emanuel Swedenborg (1688-1772).

When Joseph Dufty died on 5th March, 1888 he had been a member of the society in Sheffield for twenty-five years, and occasionally attended Conference as its representative. My interest and research led me to Maeve Hawkins, a current member of the New Jerusalem Church (occasionally referred to as the New Church). Her father James Vernon Ayre was a Minister for many years, and during the 1960s was appointed by the New Church in Paisley, Scotland. Maeve holds very fond memories of that time. She is familiar with much of the Church's archival information, and very kindly unveiled details concerning the history of the New Jerusalem Church in Sheffield, and a tribute to Joseph Dufty that was published in its periodical. The church was formed in Sheffield during the early nineteenth century, when a group of people would meet every Sunday to worship at one of their homes. The group grew and meetings were held at various venues throughout the city, before a building was eventually erected on Whitham Road in 1912, which would survive until 1940.

The tribute to Mr Dufty includes a poem written by him, which was discovered after his departure. It reveals how anxious he was for those he would leave behind . . . a widow and eight children:

'O Thou who rulest even death!
I bow to Thy decree;
For in the hand of perfect love
It will be well with me.

Or soon, or late, Thou knowest best,
I have no word to say;
If in the twilight of the eve,
Or in the earlier day.

Some little time I would have stayed,
For those I leave behind;

The widow and the fatherless

Are to Thy care resigned.'

Joseph Dufty

One of those children was Joseph Gibbins Dufty, born in 1868. He was very committed to the New Jerusalem Church and attended its college in London for over three years. Following his acceptance into the church he was ordained during the early 1890s in Wigan, where his first pastoral appointment would be. *The Wigan Observer and District Advertiser* dated 14th October, 1892 confirms some of this detail by declaring that 'On Sunday evening Mr. J. G. Dufty, late of the New Church College, London, was formally recognised as the minister of the above place of worship [. . .].' Almost two years later the same newspaper – published on the 25th August, 1894 – announced the ordination of Joseph Gibbins Dufty, which took place in Wigan. The ordaining minister was Rev. Richard Storry, who informed the congregation that he had a good reason for travelling a considerable distance to take part in the ordination. For 'It was approaching fifty tears since he made the acquaintance of the parents of his young friend Mr. Dufty, at a time when that young friend had not been thought of. (Laughter.) That was the beginning of a friendship which had existed between himself and the family ever since [. . .].' The parents of Mr. Dufty were of course Joseph the poet, and his wife Eliza, who had a '[. . .] deep interest in the attainment of knowledge, and the manifestation of that knowledge to others [. . .].' It becomes clear that Rev. Storry knew the couple before their marriage, and they were '[. . .] always reading, thinking, seeking intelligent company, endeavouring to make progress in knowledge, and interested in anything that tended to the intellectual improvement of themselves and others.' How delightful to learn of such detail relating to Joseph Dufty.

Joseph Gibbins Dufty married in Sheffield around the time he was accepted into the New Church, and his wife Lucy, who prior to her marriage was a schoolteacher, strongly supported her husband in his role as Minister. Over several years the couple relocated and settled wherever life took them. There were other areas – indeed other churches – which included Derby, Dalton in Huddersfield, Camberwell, London and Paisley in Scotland. Reverend J. G. Dufty was repeatedly well received, popular and highly respected. There were two daughters from the marriage, Dorothy Olive Dufty, who sadly died at the age of twenty-four, and Lucie Marguerite Dufty.

Their mother Lucy had loved teaching and later in life, during the 1920s and 1930s, she wrote a number of children's books under the pen name Lucie B. Dufty (Lucie Brittain Dufty), which were regarded as delightful, charming and unlike other books of the time. Her daughter Lucie Marguerite was a talented artist, and the books were beautifully illustrated by her. Titles such as *Oh! Dash! A Dog's Autobiography, Rainbows and Railings, Both Sides of The Railings, Fairies and Pollie-Kids* and *Good-bye Pollie-Kids!* were very popular, and a number of original versions are available for purchase today. Lucie Marguerite illustrated other books, and some of her work was published alongside that of the well-known illustrator Rene Cloke.

Joseph Gibbins Dufty was also an author and generally wrote about the New Jerusalem Church and its principles. He also produced a series of books in three parts entitled *Lessons on Nature Topics from the Word for Young People*, published in Manchester by the New Church Sunday School Union. And during the 1930s the family sailed to the United States of America, and attended the General Convention of the New Jerusalem Church as British representatives. At that time Reverend Joseph G. Dufty and his family resided in Meikleriggs, Paisley and those were their happiest years. The family did however leave behind their friends and church members during the 1940s, when Reverend Dufty retired and settled in Wansted, London. Lucie Marguerite Dufty returned to Paisley in 1949 when she married Albert Clayton, who was also an artist and known to her for many years. In recent years his memoirs of life on the front line during the First World War were discovered within his family, by chance. They were edited and published to produce an honest, moving, and informative account entitled *Long Before Daybreak.* I am delighted to reveal that Lucie Marguerite (known as Greta), and Albert Clayton were known to Maeve Hawkins. And I am equally delighted to have . . . in the words of John Holland (see 'Wharncliffe'), talked with the lady who talked with the lady who talked with the gentleman (indeed minister), who had talked with Joseph Dufty . . . the dear friend of my forefather. And Joseph had of course, talked with *him*.

My opening lines to this chapter are true and accurate it seems. Indeed you and I embarked on a remarkable journey, as we learned that three generations of one family have undoubtedly left a lasting legacy.

EPILOGUE

As my story draws to an end, I readily embrace what appears to be the perfect conclusion – delivered rather unexpectedly, by the *Irvine and Fullarton Times* of Ayrshire, on 24th October, 1884. You may recall that a section of this article (largely concerned with Sheffield poets, and to include my great-great-grandfather) appears in the chapter entitled Francis. What follows is a continuation of this informative piece of writing, though tinged with disquiet:

'[Francis Buchanan] is now in years, in ill health, has a broken wrist, and what is worse – a broken spirit [. . .]. The poet we understand, is both needful and deserving of encouragement, so that a timeous recognition of his worth would come to him in the autumn or winter of life with a revivifying breath of vernal spring.'

The brief critique of Francis' Sheffield volume of poems resonates to some degree, with my own analysis and sincere fondness. Though mindful of my forebear's accident, the likelihood of determining precise details seems categorically unachievable. But thanks to an unsuspecting nineteenth-century commentator with the *Irvine Times*, I fully comprehend the quandary Francis was faced with. For just how performs a draper with a broken wrist? Unable to work and needful of an income, or some kind of support, he and his wife Susannah made the decision to join their daughter Catherine and her husband in Tennessee. I was saddened to learn of my forebear's 'broken spirit' and must perhaps attribute it to events clarified, all the while speculating on the significance of three of his offspring relocating to distant lands. Whether due to matters of the heart, or incapacity . . . what befalls the devoted poet whose pen falls motionless? Despite having no knowledge of whether or not his troublesome wrist was attached to the hand employed to record lines of poetry . . . the evidence suggests that Francis did in fact resume his longstanding desire to create it.

* * *

Our nineteenth-century long-reigning Monarch, Queen Victoria died on 22nd January, 1901. Francis Buchanan died the following day:

'OBITUARY

News has been received by his relatives in Sheffield of the death at Nashville, Tennessee, USA, of Mr Francis Buchanan the author of "Sparks from Sheffield Smoke" and other works. Mr Buchanan died on January 23 last.'

Sheffield Daily Telegraph   9th February, 1901

Alas, the 'minor poet' was silenced forever. In 1902 he and his widow Susannah were brought together once again, and lie peacefully beside each other in a Nashville cemetery.

I have undoubtedly delivered 'recognition of his worth', albeit more than a century later. And if this revised edition of Francis' Sheffield publication 'sparks' a 'revivifying breath of vernal spring' in memory of him . . . this particular devotee, and ancestral successor will be gratified beyond words.

S. K. Buchanan, 2023

Supplied by Picture Sheffield / Sheffield Libraries and Information. no. s08784 Herbert Moss, 'Upsey Daisy', Sheffield Character, selling laces on Lady's Bridge.
(Note - Francis' poem refers to 'Upsy Daisy').

18-20 Bank Street, Sheffield where Francis' chosen publisher, Leader and Sons was based in 1882.
Author's photograph.

Russell Street, Nashville, Tennessee during the 1890s, when Francis Buchanan and his wife Susannah resided there. It would be their final home.
Kind permission of Nashville Public Library - Special Collection.

SELECTED BIBLIOGRAPHY

ANDREWS, William *Modern Yorkshire Poets* (1885) Hull: A. Brown and Sons, London: Simpkin, Marshall and Company

BUCHANAN, Francis *Sparks from Sheffield Smoke: A Series of Local and other Poems* (1882) Sheffield: Leader & Sons

BUCHANAN, Francis *The Crusader, with Other Poems and Lyrics* (1848) Perth: Thomas Richardson

CLEARY, Bryan *Haddon Hall Bakewell Derbyshire The Home of Lord Edward Manners* (Guidebook) (2017) Haddon Hall & Jarrold Publishing (Photographed by Nick McCann)

DARBYSHIRE, E *Ballads, Poems, and Recitations* (1885) Sheffield: J. Wrigley, Printer, 12, Hartshead

DRYERRE, Henry *Love Idylls, Ballads, and other Poems* (1884) Blairgowrie: The Author, 10 High Street, Edinburgh: John Menzies & Co.

DUFTY, Joseph *A Blighted Life and Other Poems* (1871) London: Simpkin, Marshall & Co., Sheffield: Pawson & Brailsford

EDWARDS, David Herschell *One Hundred Modern Scottish Poets With biographical and critical notices* Eleventh Series (1888) Brechin: D .H. Edwards

ELLIOTT, Ebenezer *The Splendid Village: Corn Law Rhymes; and other Poems* Vol.1 (1834) LONDON: Benjamin Steill

FORD, Robert *The Harp of Perthshire: A Collection of Songs, Ballads, and other Poetical Pieces Chiefly by Local Authors with notes explanatory, critical, and biographical* (1893) Paisley and London: Alexander Gardner

FORSHAW, Charles Frederick (ed.) *Yorkshire Poets Past and Present, being biographies and poems of various Yorkshire authors* Vol.1 (1888) Bradford: T. Brown, S.Northgate, London: W. Nicholson and Son, Warwick Square

HALL, John *Alias "J.H.J." Thoughts and Sketches in Verse* (1877) Sheffield: Pawson and Brailsford

HEMANS, Felicia *Poems of Felicia Hemans A New Edition* (1849) Printed in London and Edinburgh by Blackwood and Sons

HOLLAND, John *Flowers from Sheffield Park A Selection of Poetical Pieces Originally Published in The Sheffield Iris* (1827) London: Hamilton, Adams, and Co., Sheffield: John Blackwell

HOLLAND, John *The Picture of Sheffield or An Historical and Descriptive View of the Town of Sheffield, In the County of York* (1824) Sheffield: George Ridge, 3, King-Street

HOLLAND, John *The Tour of the Don, Extempore Sketches made during a pedestrian ramble along the banks of the River, and its principal tributaries* (1837) London: R. Groombridge, Panyer-Alley, Sheffield: G Ridge, Mercury Office

HOLLAND, John and EVERETT, James *Memoirs of the Life and Writings of James Montgomery Including selections from his correspondence, remains in prose and verse, and conversations on various subjects* Vol. IV (1855) London: Longman, Brown, Green, and Longmans

HUDSON, William *The Life of John Holland of Sheffield Park From numerous letters and other documents furnished by his nephew and executor, John Holland Brammall* (1874) London: Longmans, Green and Co.

HUNTER, Joseph *Hallamshire The History and Topography of the Parish of Sheffield in the County of York: with historical and descriptive notices of the Parishes of Ecclesfield, Hansworth, Treeton, and Whiston, and the Chapelry of*

Bradfield (1819) London: Lackington, Hughes, Harding, Mavor, and Jones

HUTTON, Mary (ed. J. Holland) *Sheffield Manor, and other Poems* (1831) Sheffield: J. Blackwell, Iris Office

KOHL, Johann Georg *England, Wales, and Scotland (*1844) London: Chapman and Hall, 186, Strand

LEADER, Robert Eadon (ed.) *Reminiscences of Old Sheffield: Its Streets and its People* Second Edition (1876) SHEFFIELD: Leader and Sons, Independent Office

LEWIS, Samuel *A Topographical Dictionary of Scotland, Comprising the several counties, islands, cities, burgh and market towns, parishes, and principal villages* Vol. II (1851) London: S. Lewis and Co., 13, Finsbury Place

ROBERTS, Mary *The Royal Exile; or, Poetical Epistles of Mary, Queen of Scots, during her captivity in England; with other original poems By a Young Lady. Also by her Father, The Life of Queen Mary* In Two Volumes, Vol. II (1822) London, Longman, Hurst, Rees, Orme & Brown, and Taylor & Hessey

STERNDALE, Mary *The Life of a Boy* Vol. I (1821) London: Printed for G. and W. B. Whittaker, Ave-Maria Lane

TAYLOR, John *The Illustrated Guide to Sheffield and the Surrounding District Accounts of the Early History and Progress of the town, its public and religious bodies, edifices, and institutions, descriptions of its manufactures, and of the suburban scenery and places of interest in the surrounding district* (1879) Sheffield: Pawson and Brailsford

THAXTER, Celia *The Poems of Celia Thaxter* (1899) Boston and New York, USA: Houghton, Mifflin and Company, Cambridge, Mass. USA: The Riverside Press

VICKERS, J Edward *A Popular History of Sheffield* (1978) East Ardsley, Wakefield: E P Publishing Limited

WALTON, Mary *SHEFFIELD Its Story and its Achievements* Fourth Edition (1968) East Ardsley, Wakefield: S. R. Publishers Limited and The Corporation of Sheffield   First Published in 1948

WILLMOTT, Robert Aris (ed.) *Poems of James Montgomery* (1860) London: Routledge, Warne, & Routledge, Farringdon Street, New York, USA: 56 Walker Street

Various newspaper articles referred to or quoted from, and historical census records were located at the archive collection of the online genealogy service Findmypast. (www.findmypast.co.uk)

ACKNOWLEDGEMENTS

There simply would not be a book if my paternal great-great-grandfather had not been a poet. He could not have known that his fascinating choice of subjects would one day be explored by one of his descendants . . . who indisputably adores his poetry. And I am grateful to him for providing the perfect prologue for my book. Did I say *my* book? Dear Francis . . . this is of course, *our* book.

I am most grateful for the interest, encouragement, and assistance from numerous professionals, groups and organisations, as follows:

Chris Keeling, Arc Publishing and Print, Sheffield, The British Library, Sheffield Archives and Local Studies, Special Collections and Archives, Western Bank Library, University of Sheffield, All Saints Ecclesall, Sheffield, Penny Rea – Friends of Wincobank Hill and Friends of Zion Graveyard, Sheffield, Martin Gorman and Ron Clayton – Friends of Sheffield Castle, Peter Bull – Friends of Parkwood Springs, Sheffield, David Templeman – Friends of Sheffield Manor Lodge, Sheffield General Cemetery Trust, South Yorkshire Industrial History Society, Father Patrick Walsh, St Michael's Catholic Cemetery, Rivelin, Sheffield, Richard Beaumont, Think Tank Creative Design, Doncaster, Bradford Local Studies Library, Bereavement Services, Kirklees Council, Sheffield Newspapers/JPI Media, Colin Proudfoot, Senior Library Assistant, Local and Family History, A K Bell Library, Perth, Scotland, Rev. Graham Crawford, Kinnoull Parish Church, Perth, Dr Dauvit Horsbroch, Scots Language Centre, A K Bell Library, Perth, Karen Clarke, Archive and Local History Research Advisor, ANGUSalive, Angus Archives, By Forfar, Scotland, Deirdre Sweeney, Local History Centre, Dundee Central Library, Dundee University Archives, National Records of Scotland, Edinburgh, City of Edinburgh Council, Parks, Greenspace and Cemeteries, Katy Sternberger CA, DAS, Research Librarian and Archivist, Portsmouth

Athenæum, Portsmouth, New Hampshire, USA, Nashville Public Libraries Special Collection, Nashville, Tennessee, USA.

Sincere thanks also to family members and friends for their interest, support, assistance, and patience: My husband Anton, who listened to endless poetry and historical tales, my mother Patricia Buchanan (who also listened), my brother Nick Buchanan, Kim Goodlad, Alastair Buchan, Jan Buchanan, Diane Evans, Kristine Morgan, Catherine Buchanan, Jill de la Rey, Maureen Witchell, Emma-Jane Witchell, James Witchell-Jones, Kirsty Cosgrove, Anne Thompson, Hayley Thomas, Jean Faulkner, Tiffany Dickinson, Doreen Bussey, Clive Bussey, Helen Parkin, Anji Frankish, Maeve Hawkins, Caroline Hook, Gill Richardson, Les Lomas, Pat Lomas, Margaret Naylor, David Ludlam, Gill Bolton, Barbara Warsop,

Karen April Mills

1968 - 2022

a Beautiful Soul is Never Forgotten

INDEX

Poets, Writers, Notable People

Abney, Elizabeth, 206

Andrews, William, 60

Ball, Dinah, 51

Birch, Armer (Silver) Oliver, 91

Burns, Robert, 205, 323

Chrimes, Richard, 203

Clare, John, 77

Clayton, Albert, 338

Darbyshire, Edward, 159

Denham, Sir John, 155

Dryerre, Henry, 291

Dufty, Joseph, 327

Dufty, Joseph Gibbins, 336

Dufty, Lucie Marguerite, 337

Dufty, Lucie B., 337

Dyer, John, 155, 166

Edwards, David Herschell, 288

Elliott, Ebenezer, 204, 236

Everett, James, 223, 293

Fittis, Robert Scott, 24

Ford, Robert, 288

Forshaw, Charles Frederick, 22

Gent, William Thompson, 48, 187

Gray, Euphemia Chalmers (a.k.a. Effie), 31

Groome, Francis Hindes, 32

Guest, John, 203

Hall, John, 61, 187, 191, 254

Hall, Charles Edmund, 192

Hemans, Felicia, 321

Holland, John, 60, 192, 203, 215, 223, 230, 232, 234, 261, 293

Holroyd, Abraham, 61

Hood, Thomas, 79

Hudson, William, 217

Hunter, Joseph, 168, 223, 231

Hutton, Mary, 217

Jenner, Dr. Edward, 73

Johnson, Samuel, 234

Johnson, Stephen, 193

Kohl, Johann Georg, 301

Leader, John Daniel, 109

Leader, Robert Eadon, 49, 109

Lewis, Samuel, 24

Major, Edward, 111

Manners, Lord and Lady Edward, 251

Manners, Sir John, 251

Millais, John Everett, 31

Montagu, Lady Mary Wortley, 234

Montgomery, James, 54, 206, 220, 230, 237, 292

Mundella, A. J., 21, 168

Newsam, William Cartwright, 60

Nicoll, Robert, 300

Nixon, John, 44

Orczy, Baroness Emmuska, 66

Queen of Scotland, Mary, 113, 137, 140, 214, 222

Rawson, Mary Anne, 50

Rayner, Samuel, 251

Reilly, Catherine, 23

Roberts, Mary, 221

Roberts, Samuel, 220

Robinson, Sir Tony, 111

Ruddock, Dr. Edward Harris, 334

Ruskin, John, 31, 262

Scott, Sir Walter, 250, 310

Smythson, Robert, 247

Southey, Robert, 323

Sterndale, Mary, 232

Sterndale, William Handley, 232

Stevenson, Robert, 310

Stuart-Wortley, Charles Beilby, 168

Swedenborg, Emanuel, 334

Taylor, John 166

Templeman, David, 225

Tennyson, Alfred Lord, 76, 276

Thaxter, Celia, 68

Vernon, Dorothy, 251

Vickers, J Edward, 24, 177

Walker, Henty, 206

Walker, Joshua, 205

Walton, Mary, 43, 167

Watson, Henry Edmund, 168

Watson, Rosamund Marriott, 79

Willmott, Rev. Robert Aris, 237

The River Tay, from the Western Part of Kinnoull Cliff, by David Octavius Hill (1802-1870).
National Galleries of Scotland. Edinburgh Photographic Society Collection, gifted 1987.
It beautifully captures the scene that inspired Francis Buchanan to write poetry.